THE POWDER KEG

An Intelligence Officer's Guide to Military Forces in The Middle East 1996-2000

Major General Edward B. Atkeson
U.S. Army (Ret.)

NOVA Publications
Falls Church, Virginia

NOVA Publications

ISBN 0-9638692-5-6

Manufactured in the United States of America

NOVA Publications
7342 Lee Highway, #201
Falls Church, VA 22046

DEDICATION

This work is dedicated to Prime Minister Yitzhak Rabin; soldier, statesman, peacemaker, who gave his life in an heroic effort to change the insidious dynamics in the Middle East driving Israelis and Arabs to war with one another in decade after decade. His brutal assassination at the hands of a deranged countryman is an enormous loss to the security of Israel, its neighboring countries, and the world at large.

The only adequate tribute which can be made by men is a rededication of all of their efforts toward the defusing of the dangerous region, referred to herein as *The Powder Keg*.

THE POWDER KEG

TABLE OF CONTENTS

LIST OF TABLES AND FIGURES   vii

FOREWORD   ix

MAP OF THE MIDDLE EAST   xii

Chapter I   **Regional Overview,**
                 Critical Factors and Trends   1
   Overview   1
   Critical Factors   11
   Trends   15

Chapter II   **The Major States**   22
   Israel   22
   Egypt   39
   Syria   45
   Saudi Arabia   53
   Iran   61
   Iraq   75

Chapter III   The Minor States   84
  Jordan   84
  Lebanon   91
  The Small States of the Gulf Cooperation Council   94
  Yemen   106

Chapter IV   Force Calculations   111
  Sources and Methods   112
  Source Data and Observations   114

Chapter V   Comparative Analysis   138
  Flash Points   138
  Israel vs Iran   140
  Israel vs Iraq   141
  Israel vs Syria   144
  Israel vs Egypt   148
  Israel vs Jordan   152
  Israel vs an Arab Coalition   153
  Iran vs Iraq   155
  Iran vs Saudi Arabia and the GCC   156
  Iraq vs Syria   158
  Iraq vs Saudi Arabia and the GCC   160
  Syria vs Jordan   161
  Saudi Arabia vs Jordan   162
  Saudi Arabia vs Yemen   163
  Internal Conflicts   164

Chapter VI   Conclusions   166
    Israel   166
    Iraq   169
    Syria   171
    Egypt   172
    Iran   173
    Saudi Arabia   174
    Jordan   176
    The Smaller States   177
    The Bottom Line   178

Chapter VII   Implications for U.S. Policy   180
    Arms Control   180
    Security Assistance   184
    Technology Transfer   188
    U.S. Force Presence   190

Notes   195
Chapter I   195
Chapter II   197
Chapter III   212
Chapter IV   218
Chapter V   219
Chapter VI   220
Chapter VII   220

Index   222
List of Interviewees and Members of Discussion Groups   235
About the Author   240
Annex   Deep Strike Surface-to-Surface
               Missile Systems in the Middle East   241

THE POWDER KEG

TABLES AND FIGURES

TABLES

Number	Title	Page
1	The Militarization of Middle Eastern Citizenry	8
2	The Militarization of Middle Eastern Wealth	9
3	Combined Indices of Militarization in the Middle East	10
4	Trained Reserves and Mobilizable Forces in the Middle East	11
5	Anticipated Israeli Arms Acquisitions	37
6	Military Materiel Currently Sought by Egypt	45
7	Recent Syrian Arms Orders and Acquisitions	52
8	Anticipated Saudi Arms Acquisitions	60
9	Anticipated Iranian Arms Acquisitions	74
10	Captured Kuwaiti Military Equipment in the Hands of Iraqi Forces	80
11	Austerity Measures Instituted by the Jordanian Armed Forces	89
12	Jordanian High Option Active Force Structure	90
13	Anticipated Arms Acquisitions of the Small GCC States	105
14	Israeli Ground Forces	115
15	Israeli Air and Naval Forces	116

Number	Title	Page
16	Syrian Ground Forces	117
17	Syrian Air, Air Defense and Naval Forces	118
18	Egyptian Ground Forces	119
19	Egyptian Air, Air Defense and Naval Forces	120
20	Saudi Arabian Ground Forces	121
21	Saudi Arabian Air, Air Defense and Naval Forces	122
22	Iranian Ground Forces	123
23	Iranian Air and Naval Forces	124
24	Iraqi Gound Forces	125
25	Iraqi Air and Naval Forces	126
26	Ground Forces of Smaller Arab States	127
27	Air and Naval Forces of Smaller Arab States	128

FIGURES

1	Israel's Nuclear Program	38
2	Iran's Nuclear Program	73
3	Air-Ground Designated Force Potential for Major States of the Middle East	129
4	Air-Ground Designated Force Potential for Non-Gulf Minor States of the Middle East	134
5	Air-Ground Designated Force Potentials for Persian Gulf Minor States of the Middle East	135
6	Potential Middle East Flash Points 1996-2000	140

FOREWORD

The Middle East is a region of complex political problems, of which the Arab-Israeli conflict, while of great importance, is but one. The region may be the most heavily militarized and armed in the world, with potential conflict issues outstanding among most of the states situated there. This study of relative military power is based upon extensive interviews with Middle Eastern political and military leaders, defense intellectuals and U.S. Embassy personnel during four trips to the region and to study centers in the United States and the United Kingdom. Where not otherwise identified, the judgments are those of the author.

Israel stands apart from its neighbors as a regional superpower. It has nuclear weapons, access to U.S. research and development efforts, and a well-developed military-industrial complex capable of adapting new technology to its military needs, sometimes before equivalent weapons or reconnaissance systems are available to U.S. forces. With such advantages, Israel is in an altogether different class from the other states of the region.

Syria, presently the most powerful of Israel's opponents, has adopted a military strategy emphasizing long war over great depth. In case of war with Israel, Syria would likely attempt to prolong the conflict in order to exhaust the smaller state. It might seek cooperation with Iraq or Iran to gain additional strategic depth. However, it is not clear how the defense of Damascus might be handled.

Egypt has a lingering fear of fundamentalist Islamic encirclement and internal disorder, as well as concern for Israeli military supremacy. It is particularly concerned that Sudan might interfere with the Nile River waters and that some

Egyptian fundamentalists might create domestic disturbances. If a better strategic balance or security assurance cannot be reached with Israel through the Arab-Israeli peace process, Egypt could be driven to seek a unilateral solution to its principal security problem. Barring assurances from the United States on the matter, an Egyptian search for some form of mass destruction weapons cannot be ruled out.

Jordan has suffered from its association with Iraq during the Gulf War. Its leaders believe that it was badly misunderstood by its other neighbors and by the West during that period. Amman has gone to great lengths to demonstrate its acceptance of Israel and its determination to be numbered among the moderate states of the region. It looks now, particularly to the United States, for reassurance of its acceptance as a worthy strategic partner in the future.

Saudi Arabia changed its traditional strategy in the wake of the Gulf War to place much heavier emphasis on building an inherent capability for deterring attack from Iraq. Its objective is probably a defensive capability essentially equal to that posed in October 1990 by coalition forces, although a number of analysts seem skeptical of its ability to reach such an ambitious objective. Saudi Arabia is also wary of Iran and Yemen. While it may no longer consider Jordan a threat, some distrust may remain.

Iraq is bloodied but unbowed. It appears satisfied to maintain a smaller force structure than in the last decade, but may not have given up its historic territorial objectives.

Iran continues its emphasis on rearmament, including weapons of mass destruction. It probably seeks eventual mastery of the Persian Gulf, or at least a capability for denial of the basin to hostile powers. It apparently also seeks to carry on a religiously based opposition to Israel, and may harbor ambitions for eventual destruction of the Jewish state.

The objective of this work is to assess as objectively as possible the dynamics of shifting military power in the Middle East over the final years of the 20th century. In this regard, the volume is a sequel to a similar study published by the Strategic Studies Institute of the U.S. Army War College in December 1992. That work, which achieved a measure of success among analysts, employed a model which is again applied here to provide an important additional dimension of force effectiveness measurement. Any deficiencies in the process or the text is the responsibility of the author.

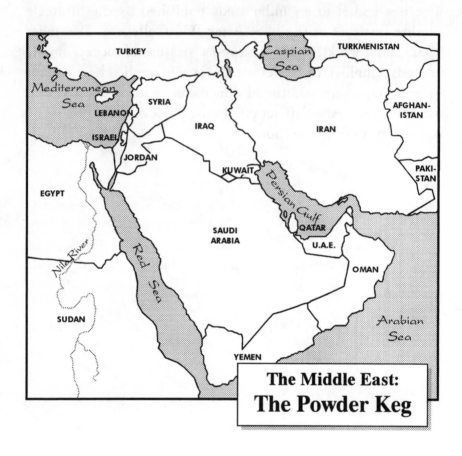

TURKEY

Mediterranean
Sea

Caspian
Sea

TURKMENISTAN

SYRIA

LEBANON

ISRAEL

JORDAN

EGYPT

Nile River

Red Sea

IRAQ

KUWAIT

SAUDI
ARABIA

AFGHAN-
ISTAN

IRAN

PAKI-
STAN

Persian Gulf

QATAR

U.A.E.

OMAN

Arabian
Sea

SUDAN

YEMEN

**The Middle East:
The Powder Keg**

THE POWDER KEG

CHAPTER I
Regional Overview,
Critical Factors and Trends

T he United States has had vital interests in the Middle East
at least from World War II when the Persian Gulf was a
major route of supply to Soviet allies. Considering the intrin-
sic volatility of the region, the U.S. must keep abreast of
changes in the security environment and be prepared to defend
its interests on short notice. The interests were loosely defined
in the President's 1994 National Security Strategy:

> The United States has enduring interests in the
> Middle East, especially pursuing a comprehen-
> sive break through to Middle East peace, assuring
> the security of Israel and our Arab friends, and
> maintaining the free flow of oil at reasonable
> prices. Our strategy is harnessed to the unique
> characteristics of the region and our vital inter-
> ests there, as we work to extend the range of
> peace and stability, while implementing a strate-
> gy of dual containment of Iraq and Iran as long
> as those states pose a threat to U.S. interests, to
> other states in the region, and to their own citi-
> zens.[1]

The National Strategy provided no clear statement of threats to U.S. interests, but, without indicating any particular order of cogency or reference to regions, it did lay out a list of tasks for which U.S. forces might be deployed worldwide:[2]

- Dealing with major regional contingencies
- Providing a credible overseas presence
- Countering weapons of mass destruction
- Contributing to multilateral peace operations
- Supporting counter-terrorism efforts and other national security objectives

The list is clearly applicable to the Middle East. During — and since — the 1991 Gulf War, U.S. forces have engaged in a constantly evolving series of operational actions and activities in the region in consonance with the tasks.

In January 1994 the Joint Chief's of Staff (JCS) issued a somewhat more focused statement of perceived military threats. Most cogent in their view was the spread of weapons of mass destruction and their means of delivery. The chiefs also identified the Middle East as one of the regions of prime concern in this regard.[3]

The region is one of ancient tensions and strife dating from biblical times. Even today, opinion leaders in the region often buttress arguments with citations from writings thousands of years old. For centuries the region formed the traditional land bridge for trade between Africa and Asia. Since the digging of the Suez Canal, it has been a focal point for travelers en route from Europe to the Orient. More recently, in the 20th Century, it has gained prominence for its rich petroleum deposits, and since mid-century, as the venue of Arab-Israeli conflict over Palestine. So high did the stakes become during the era of communist ascendancy in eastern Europe, and so closely were major power interests involved, that it appeared for a while that the Arab-Israeli battles might provide the catalyst for a third world war. Military expenditures in the region in the 1980s approached a trillion dollars.[4]

For much of history, the West has viewed the region in its geographic segments, partially according to colonial spheres of interest, but also as a matter of strategic convenience. The customary division has been among three sub-regions, from east to west: the Persian Gulf (Iraq, Iran, Saudi Arabia, the Gulf Sheikdoms and Oman); the area of the Levant and of primary Arab-Israeli confrontation (Israel and its immediate Arab neighbors); and the Maghreb (North Africa west of Egypt).[5] In many respects such convenience continues. The U.S. Unified Command Plan assigns responsibilities to U.S. European Command (USEUCOM) and U.S. Central Command (USCENTCOM) in accordance with these divisions.

It should be recognized, however, that in recent years military assessments limited in scope to the traditional sub-regions have become vulnerable to an increasing number of artificialities. The proliferation of long-range missiles and the rise of transnational Islamic fundamentalist groups, to cite two trends (noted later), mandate a broader strategic perspective than has been the norm in the past. Moreover, the involvement of Syria, Egypt and Israel in the Persian Gulf conflict of 1991 evidence a greater awareness among the countries of the region of new geopolitical factors and trends which have served to increase interdependencies in at least two of the sub-regions.

As will be noted later in this book, there is a strong possibility of the emergence of Iran as the strongest center of military power in the Persian Gulf. The country is uncompromisingly hostile to Israel. With Israel and Iran located in different sub-regions, conflict between the two would unquestionably breach traditional boundaries. And, as it demonstrated in the

Gulf War, Iraq can always play the part of a "swing" power between the Gulf region and the Levant, with potential commitments in both areas.

Further, it should be borne in mind that in the wake of the 1991 conflict, the Saudis expressed considerable concern over the possible emergence of a surrounding conspiracy of hostile neighbors: Iraqis, Jordanians, Palestinians and Yemenis. While the concern has subsided, it may not completely fade as quickly as we would like. There is a strong possibility that the Saudis are thinking in broader terms than just the Gulf basin in their security planning.

For many of these reasons, this analysis deals with the two most closely related sub-regions: the Persian Gulf and the territories at the eastern end of the Mediterranean Sea, treating them as a whole.

It should also be recognized that the United States, itself, with its broad range of interests, has become an active player in the region. The demise of the Soviet Union has left the U.S. as the sole surviving superpower; as such, it's political, strategic and economic concerns enter the calculations of all of the states of the region with greater weight than ever before. For better or worse, the United States is viewed in many quarters as the ultimate arbiter of all conflicts. In conformance with the national strategy, America defends the weak, deters or punishes aggressors, succors the persecuted, counsels allies, and discourages ambitious leaders bent upon acquisition of long-range missiles and weapons of mass destruction. U.S. interests are both region-wide and global, and its actions for better or worse, are perceived as a coordinated whole.

This is not to imply that the United States routinely pursues its interests in a unilateral mode. Quite the contrary, as we shall see later in the discussion, the U.S. normally seeks to exercise leadership within the context of the United Nations when the interests of one or more other states appear to have congruence with our own.   The American coordination of actions by a wide array of countries seeking to foil Iraqi aggression in the Persian Gulf conflict in 1990-'91 is a case in point.

While beyond the geographic scope of this study, we should take note of a related dimension.   The Islamic republics of the former Soviet Union have yet to respond clearly to ethnic and religious tugs from their sister states to the south, but the possibility of closer association exists.   In early May 1992, in Dushanbe, Tajikistan, for instance, having ousted the former government, militants called for the establishment of an Islamic state.[6]   Hence, we should bear in mind that as technology offers — and threatens — to extend potential battlefields, the breakup of the Soviet empire may eventually serve to increase the number of players in Middle Eastern affairs.

At a high level of aggregation, a visitor to the region gains the impression that the Middle East is peopled by a vast majority of souls with a yearning for change in the macro-regime under which they live and which they believe to have been imposed upon them principally by foreign (Western) interests. The principal symptoms of this emotion are expressions of pan-Arabism, resentment of royal oil wealth, resentment of Zionism, and resentment of historic foreign-imposed borders and foreign influence.   The suggestion is so strong that large numbers of people — perhaps a majority — are looking for radical changes in favor of greater autonomy, better distribution of wealth, and greater control of the lands which they believe to be their national patrimony.

On the other side one may see a smaller group of more privileged peoples who share a wariness for threats they perceive from radicals, revolutionaries, and terrorists. Here one finds the royal houses of Kuwait and Saudi Arabia, and right wing elements of the Israeli political spectrum. In Saudi Arabia the view manifests itself in xenophobia. With the exception of the Haj (religious pilgrimage), tourism is unknown in the Saudi state. Official xenophobia is compounded by a distrust of Shiia Moslems, particularly the Iranians and Shiite Iraqis.

In Israel, a perception of continuing threat from hostile neighbors is mixed with an historical and religious sense of mission for seizing and holding territories considered to have been designated for the Jewish people by divine authority. Arab claims to the same territory are viewed by hard-line Israeli political and religious elements as of a second order and fostered by undeserving and implacable elements bent upon the destruction of the Zionist state.

From time to time, charismatic Arab leaders have come to prominence with strong appeals to the dissatisfied masses, and promises for fulfillment of their aspirations. President Gamal Nasser of Egypt was notable in this regard. President Hafiz Assad, in a narrower context, may be another. Certainly President Saddam Hussein has attempted to play such a messianic role. He cleverly invoked the popular Arab yearning for change in connection with his invasion of Kuwait, striking responsive chords with the leadership of the Palestinians, Jordanians and Yemenis. In addition, he mustered strong sympathy among the peoples of most Arab states.

Followers of the Ayatollah Ruhollah Kohmeini in Iran have offered a different type of mass appeal, one based upon a return to Islamic fundamentalist principles, to include the Shari'a, or sacred law. In many respects the objectives are similar to those pursued in Saudi Arabia, but with important differences. The Saudis maintain an absolute monarchy and strive for amicable relations with their principal trade partners in the West. The international fundamentalist movement is theocratically ori-

ented, anti-royalist, and anti-West. It is also offensively postured, while the monarchies are defensive and conservative.
The fundamentalist movement has spread in recent years to
Sudan, and might yet take hold in Algeria, in spite of the
strong military backlash. In 1989 fundamentalists won almost
half of the seats in Jordanian parliamentary elections.
Substantial Islamic movements are also to be found in Tunisia
and Egypt, and to some extent in Libya. Egyptian leaders
express considerable apprehension of encirclement by fundamentalist states, but are hesitant to comment on the disposi-
tion of their own citizenry.

Of importance in the Islamic fundamentalist movement,
from a U.S. security point of view, is its anti-Western, anti-
Israeli bent. The more radical branches (Islamic Jihad,
Hezbullah, Hamas, etc.) evidence terrorist tendencies. In the
opinion of some, Muslim fundamentalism is an "insidious form
of anti-Christian, anti-Western religion," which may, particularly with the impending spread of nuclear arms, "destabilize
the whole of this region."[7] The oil-rich monarchies, on the
other hand, exhibit a readiness to cooperate in many areas with
Western countries, but even they have their limits (e.g.: refusal
of U.S. base rights in Saudi Arabia).

At a lower level of aggregation it is apparent that almost
everyone in the region perceives a threat of some sort from his
neighbors. The Arab-Israeli dispute is only one of the more
prominent threats to peace. Mutual antagonisms, distrust, and
wariness among the states is far more the norm than the exception. Almost any scenario for conflict is credible, given the
poisonous atmosphere under which the states have so long
existed. This point is discussed in greater detail in Chapter V.

While terrorism and guerrilla warfare are endemic to the
region, the greatest threats to long term U.S. interests stem

from international military conflict. This does not necessarily mean the Arab-Israeli struggle. As important as that is, one should bear in mind that of nineteen interstate conflicts in the region since 1947, Israel has been a party to less than a third — and in the most recent case, the Gulf War, Israel was only marginally involved.[8] The focus of this analysis is upon the states of substantial military potential or strategic location, with a view toward assessing their relative strengths and weaknesses. The calculus of military power is complex. As will be noted throughout this study, military characteristics may be measured in a number of ways. The following tables (1 and 2) provide rough gauges of the degree of militarization of the principal states under examination, as well as basic data on population, armed forces, gross domestic product, and defense expenditures.[9]

TABLE 1

THE MILITARIZATION OF MIDDLE EASTERN CITIZENRY

Country	Population	Armed Forces	Soldier/Citizen Ratio
Israel	5,100,000	172,000	1:30
Syria	14,360,000	382,000	1:38
Jordan	3,960,100*	98,600	1:40
Iraq	19,877,000	382,000	1:52
Saudi Arabia (native)	12,555,000	104,000	1:120
Iran	65,581,000	513,000	1:128
Egypt	60,776,700	440,000	1:138
Yemen	11,042,000	66,000	1:167

* Not including 250,000 Palestinian refugees

TABLE 2

THE MILITARIZATION OF MIDDLE EASTERN PUBLIC WEALTH (U.S. $)

Country	GDP	Defense Budget	Def/GDP Ratio
Iraq	17.9 bil	2.6 bil	.15
Saudi Arabia	125.5 bil	13.9 bil	.11
Israel	69.6 bil	7.2 bil	.10
Jordan	5.2 bil	411 mil	.08
Yemen	7.7 bil	375 mil	.05
Iran	57.8 bil	2.3 bil	.04
Egypt	43.3 bil	1.8 bil	.04
Syria	26.7 bil	778 mil	.03

One should note that there is little correlation between the order in which countries appear on one list with their places on the other. However, we may establish a rough order of militarization by combining the factors considered, assuming equal weight for each. The result is depicted in Table 3. It should be understood, however, that the combined index is not a reflection of the military power of the country, but provides an approximation of the relative priority which the political leadership has placed upon the military in the distribution of national resources, both human and material.

TABLE 3

COMBINED INDICES OF MILITARIZATION
IN THE MIDDLE EAST

Country	Designated Index*
Israel	16
Iraq	15
Jordan, Saudi Arabia	13 (tie)
Syria	11
Iran	8
Yemen	7
Egypt	5

*Maximum possible score: 18; minimum: 4.[10]

Somewhat more important in gauging the relative military prowess of the states — if still far from definitive — is a comparison of mobilization potentials. This dimension provides a different order of listing. Most of the states treat the time required for mobilization as a military secret. Such information would be important in a thorough examination. Israeli leaders, as an exception, have frequently referred to a 24 hour capability for fielding a 600,000 man force. None of the others are deemed capable of such achievement, and even Israel may fall short in some respects. Moreover, Israel, in particular, may have difficulty maintaining its mobilized power, once activated, because of its small population base.

TABLE 4

TRAINED RESERVES AND MOBILIZABLE FORCES IN THE MIDDLE EAST

Country	Trained Reserves	Paramilitary	Total Mobilized*
Iran	350,000	1,000,000	1,863,000
Iraq	650,000	24,800	1,056,800
Egypt	254,000	302,000	996,000
Syria	400,000	8,000	790,000
Israel	430,000	6,000	608,000
Jordan	35,000	210,000	343,600
Yemen	85,000	75,000	226,000
Saudi Arabia	—	72,000	176,000

* Includes active, reserve and paramilitary forces.

CRITICAL FACTORS

In response to interviews, selected knowledgeable American and British analysts identified a number of critical factors and trends relevant to the balance of military power in the Middle East. While there was by no means unanimity of views, there was strong consensus on most points. The most important factors identified by the analysts in the U.S. and U.K. are listed below, together with summaries of their comments on the military significance of each. (See list of interviewees and members of discussion groups, p. 235)

1.   The demise of the USSR and evaporation of Soviet influence. Soviet influence was broadly perceived as a pernicious factor, exacerbating Western difficulties in the region. The Soviets supported the Arab confrontation states with strong economic, political and military backing. The Soviet Mediterranean Fleet served as a foil to the U.S. Sixth Fleet, and, on occasion, Soviet airborne forces posed a potential threat of intervention in the region. Many analysts have discerned a double message from the demise of the Soviet Union. To the confrontation states they believe it conveys a message that the Arabs can no longer rely upon significant outside support in any conflict with Israel or the West. To the Israelis, they suggest, it says that their state can no longer count upon being perceived as a Western bastion of strength in context with a great power competition. However, as disruptive as the messages may be to both sides, the analysts believe, the results could be quite positive. They venture the proposition that the chances for settlement of the Arab-Israeli dispute, free of Soviet influence, are better now than they have been in decades.

2.   The role of the United States as a player in the Middle East. It has become abundantly apparent that the U.S. is deeply enmeshed in Middle Eastern affairs, not as distant interested party, but as an active player interacting with the other states of the region. Friendly countries have become dependent upon U.S. leadership, U.S. technology, and ultimately the support of the U.S. Armed Forces for their survival. The U.S. role in pulling together the 30 member coalition for the expulsion of Iraq from Kuwait, its role in bringing succor to the Kurds under attack from Iraqi Revolutionary Guards, and its role in bringing Arabs and Israelis together in peace negotiations have solidified American practical citizenship in the region. No longer is the United States simply another oil-dependent "imperialist" outsider. It is a member of the residents' club. This point was reemphasized as recently as January of 1994 with the meeting of Presidents Clinton and Al Assad of Syria in Geneva. Even while the United States persisted with its official identification of Syria as a state supporting terrorism, the American chief executive elected to meet with his counterpart in the interest of facilitating the peace process between Israel and one of its principal antagonists.

   3.   *Cooperation by the major powers in the United Nations.* It was the virtual unanimity among permanent members of the U.N. Security Council in 1990 and 1991 which permitted the formation of the coalition which drove Iraqi troops out of Kuwait. It is the continuing cooperative attitude of the same powers which offers at least a prospect for limiting arms deliveries to the Middle East, particularly long-range missile systems and weapons of mass destruction. While it is not apparent that accords are near, the absence of such official cordiality would greatly complicate the establishment and enforcement of any arms control regime. There is some danger that tariff disputes between the U.S. and China or U.S. sales of military equipment to Taiwan could adversely impact future major power cooperation in the security area. Similarly, U.S. pressure on Beijing over civil rights issues could create a backlash that would erode Chinese support for Western initiatives in the Middle East.

   It is apparent that Russian President Boris Yeltsin has come under increasing pressure to diverge from U.N. trade controls on Iraq and Libya. Sergei Karaoglanov, chairman of the Russian Economic Association, estimated in 1992 that his country had lost between $10 and $30 billion as a result of prohibitions on arms sales to the two Middle Eastern states. Karaoglanov argued that Russia would have been better off to veto the sanctions against Libya and to refuse humanitarian aid from the West. Yeltsin approved other sales to the Middle East, and in late July of that same year approved the sale of "excess" equipment abroad for the purpose of funding Russian military welfare programs. The income from these sales was expected to reach $500 million in 1993, and to grow to $1.5 billion by 1995.[11] More recently, the Yeltsin government has fallen under heavy pressures from domestic nationalist groups to reduce its cooperative attitude toward the West and to return to more traditional Russian positions on many international issues. An impending delivery and installation of a nuclear power plant in Iran, which could contribute to the development of nuclear weapons, is a case in point. There is cause for concern that these pressures may undermine the basis for progress toward peace in the Middle East.

   4.   The Arab and Iranian search for mass destruction weapons is likely to continue as long as there is no general settlement of Arab-Israeli differences. Virtually all influential Arabs and Iranians view Israel as a regional superpower. It is the only indigenous state believed to possess nuclear weapons in operational quantities, and it enjoys a special relationship with the United States, through which it obtains high technology weaponry not generally available on world markets. The 1982 Israeli invasion of Lebanon is viewed in Arab capitals as an instance of rogue elements of the Israeli leadership exploiting the country's military power without full government knowledge or sanction. Israel's military superiority and the apparent ability of some political factions to apply it without legal consideration is intimidating to its neighbors. There are strong pressures on Arab governments and upon that of Iran to seek mass destruction weapons and delivery capabilities to balance the perceived "Israeli colossus."

TRENDS

1.   *Proliferation of long-range missiles.* While both Arab and Israeli armies have had long-range missiles since the 1973 war, neither has employed them in a militarily effective manner. The weapons have had greater psychological than militarily exploitable impact. In the final stages of the 1973 campaign, the Egyptians launched a Scud missile, but it fell harmlessly in the Sinai desert. The subsequent use of missiles by both Iran and Iraq during the "war of the cities" in the mid-1980s and, more importantly, by Iraq in the 1991 Gulf War, has increased the likelihood of their use in any future conflict.

2.   *Proliferation of weapons of mass destruction weapons (MDW).* As noted above, there are strong pressures on a number of Arab states to acquire nuclear, chemical or biological weapons, both as a political-military counterweight and a deterrent to Israeli aggression. In addition to Iraq, Syria and Libya are believed to be capable of manufacturing and delivering chemical weapons on Israeli targets. Iran has stated a determination to develop all three types of MDW, and Tehran may now have a capability for delivering such devices by aircraft. Israel is reported to have some 200-300 nuclear weapons. Its chemical and biological warfare capabilities are unknown. The use of chemical weapons during the Iran-Iraq War and the knowledge of MDW programs in neighboring countries is likely to encourage some states, which might not otherwise be so inclined, to develop or to purchase their own weapons for deterrence or retaliatory purposes.

3.   *Advancing conventional weapons technology (quality over quantity).* The utility of high technology weaponry was dramatically demonstrated in the 1991 Gulf War, especially during the air bombardment phase. Single missiles were employed to destroy enemy structures and equipment with highly lethal effects and minimal risk to the attacking plat-

forms. In addition, electronic jamming and electromagnetic pulse weapons were employed to sharply degrade the performance of defending radars and communications systems, rendering them useless in some cases. As the battle developed, night vision devices, laser range finders, manned and unmanned reconnaissance aircraft, and data-linked long-range strike systems were employed to confuse and destroy the opposition. The Iraqi Army of over a million troops appeared incapable of responding to the high technology onslaught. Future military planners are certain to attach much greater importance to the quality of weapons systems than to their numbers.

4.   *Waning belligerence of confrontation states.* The original group of Arab states bent upon the destruction of Israel in 1948 has virtually disappeared. Lebanon opted out of the alliance shortly after the initial engagements (although it has been brought back in, to some extent, as a ward of Damascus.) Egypt took the lonely path to peace thirty years later, and Jordan signed its peace accord with Israel in 1994. Syria would probably opt out if it could recover the Golan Heights. Most analysts expect that the oil-rich monarchies would consent to almost any peace formula acceptable to the Palestinians and Syrians. The most virulently anti-Israeli states, Iraq and Libya, are physically removed from the area of confrontation (albeit within range of some strike systems). The same might be said of Iran. Clearly, Israel no longer faces a threat of dismemberment by proximate enemies. The acuity of the threat to Israeli survival, until such time as mass destruction weapons and delivery systems might become common currency, is substantially reduced.

5.   *Increasing Israeli population.* A serious threat to the survival of Israel since the foundation of the state has been its small population base. Israeli population growth rates

(approximately 1.3 percent per year) have never approached comparable Arab rates (2.5 to 4 percent).[12] The opening up of Soviet emigration in the late 1980s greatly enhanced Israel's prospects for strengthening its population. Soviet immigration to Israel in 1990 reached 200,000 persons. It declined in 1991 for a number of reasons to some 167,000, but Israeli sources indicate that total immigration for the period 1989-1995 may have reached one million.[13] If fully exploited, the new immigrants might contribute some 50,000 to 75,000 able bodied men to the military manpower pool.

　　6.　　*Increasing Israeli settlement of occupied territories.* In January 1992 some 245,000 Israeli citizens resided in about 250 settlements in the occupied territories, including East Jerusalem.[14] This represented a 25 percent increase in settlements over the previous year. The rate of construction of new homes jumped to 6,500 in 1991 — up from 1,800 the year before.[15] The principal purpose of the settlements under the Likud government was to "create facts" making surrender of the territories increasingly difficult to accomplish. But there were also strong security implications. Retention of the territories provided Israeli defense planners with both a substantially more compact area to defend and a vertical terrain screen against ground-based electronic or optical surveillance from Arab territories. In the words of Mr. Benjamin Netanyahu, at the time deputy foreign minister under the Shamir cabinet, the West Bank provides Israel "strategic height."[16]

　　The Labor prime minister, Yitzak Rabin, drew a distinction between "security" and "political" settlements, promising "severe and substantial" cutbacks of the latter. The implication seemed to be that the Israeli civilian presence in the occupied territories might continue to grow, but at a reduced pace, pending a final accord dealing with all outstanding issues.[17]

Israel's agreement with the Palestine Liberation Organization (PLO) to grant administrative independence to Jericho and the Gaza area, and its subsequent withdrawal from most urban areas on the West Bank, has created doubts about the government's long term support of Jewish settlements. Similarly, Israeli Labor government discussions with Syria regarding troop withdrawals on (or from) the Golan Heights leaves doubts about the fate of some 13,000 Jewish settlers in that area. Whether these recent developments will reverse settlement trends remains to be seen.

Militant extremists among Jewish settlers in the occupied territories have come to be recognized as as great a threat to regional peace as their Palestinian counterparts have been in the past. Dr. Reuven Gal, director of the Israeli Institute for Military Affairs, has pointed out that "these fanatics could ignite the whole Middle East." There is a growing awareness that the warring factions can no longer be identified purely as Arabs or Jews, but more accurately now as moderates and extremists.[18] The assassination of Prime Minister Yitzak Rabin in November 1995 underscored this point.

7.   *Increasing legitimization of Israel.* From a low period in the 1970s, Israel has established or reestablished diplomatic relations with most of the non-Arab countries of the world. The exchange of ambassadors with China at the time of the Kuwaiti crisis in the Persian Gulf facilitated great power coordination of actions against Iraq. In addition, it has been conducive to a close Sino-Israeli relationship in the design, manufacture, and marketing of high technology weaponry. Israel's arms exports are essential to the survival of its arms industry. Israel currently exports almost seventy percent of its arms production to over sixty foreign countries.[19] Diplomatic relations are not essential to arms trade, but they facilitate the process.

8.   *The widening appeal of radical Islamic funda-mentalism.* Radical Islamic fundamentalism has been a polit-ical factor in the Middle East since early in the century. One of the more prominent groups, the Muslim Brotherhood, was founded in Egypt in 1928 and spread to most other Arab countries in Africa and the Levant. The rise of the Kohmeini regime in Iran brought a different strain of the movement to power in that country. Similar groups have seized power in Sudan and attempted take-over in Algeria and Tunisia. Strong fundamentalist groups are also to be found in Jordan and Egypt. Reportedly there are three training camps located outside Khartoum, Sudan, for what are alleged to be "fanatical, suici-dal zealots" intent upon de-stabilizing pro-Western Arab countries. The groups are strongly anti-West and rejectionist toward peace with Israel. While some leaders have been elect-ed to office, others operating clandestinely, seek to evade coun-termeasures until they gather sufficient strength to seize con-trol of a country.[20] The groups have not yet demonstrated a degree of coordination which would make them a strong mili-tary threat, but if they were to gain power in additional capi-tals, such a problem could arise.

9.   *Growing Iranian potential for active involvement in the Arab-Israeli conflict.* Iranian declaratory policy toward Israel has been highly adversarial. Until recently, however, Iranian actions against the Zionist state have been largely lim-ited to support for extremist Shiite groups in Lebanon (e.g. Hezbullah). In 1991 Iran acquired 25 Su-24 (Fencer) high per-formance, long-range attack aircraft from the Commonwealth of Independent States. The Fencer can deliver a 3,000 kilo-gram bomb load a distance of 1,300 km using external fuel tanks. In addition, with Chinese and North Korean assistance, Iran has developed a variant of the Chinese M-11 intermediate range surface-to-surface missile, dubbed "Tondar-68," with a

range of approximately 1,000 km, probably with at least a marginal capability for striking Jerusalem from Iran's extreme western border.[21] The principal significance of these developments may be the emergence of an additional enemy confronting Israel, in a sense replacing neighbors which either no longer desire, or no longer have a capability, to play a role in the Arab-Israeli struggle.

10.   *Continuing Syrian influence in Lebanon.* In October 1989 Lebanese parliamentarians drew up a Charter of National Reconciliation (the Taif agreement). Among other things, the document granted Syria troop deployment rights in the country. While no termination date was established, Syrian troops were supposed to withdraw to the Bekaa Valley by September 1992.[22] In the meanwhile, it was envisioned, they would provide military assistance to Lebanese forces. Another stipulation of the accord was the withdrawal of Israeli forces from South Lebanon, which has not happened. The practical effect of the arrangement has been to grant Syria rights as a protecting power. Syria maintains about 40,000 troops in Lebanon, about half of which are in the Bekaa.

The chief military significance of Syrian presence for both Syria and Israel is that in the event of war, the front between the belligerents is likely to be broader than the traditional one on the Golan Heights. For Israel the situation offers opportunities as well as risks. Due to the nature of the terrain in the Bekaa Valley, with narrow spaces between hills in the south, the valley is more defensible from the south than from the north. Consequently, the Bekaa offers an avenue of relative advantage to Israeli forces seeking objectives in the mountains northwest of Damascus. In the event of renewed hostilities between Israel and Syria the Israelis would not be limited to penetrating well prepared Syrian positions on the Damascus plain as in past conflicts. As we shall see in later discussion, the Israelis could choose to outflank the plain, via the Bekaa Valley.

11.   *Increasing Palestinian population in Jordan.* Prominent Israeli leaders opposed to the establishment of a Palestinian state have pointed to Jordan as the appropriate homeland of Palestinians not content with life under Israeli control.[23]   In fact, the Jordanian population has evolved as increasingly Palestinian.   The influx of expellees from Saudi Arabia and Kuwait since the Gulf War has added to the large proportion of the population with loyalties possibly oriented toward others than the Hashemite royal house. If the bulk of the remaining population of the occupied territories were to choose — or to be forced — to move to Jordan, the stage could be set for emergence of a radical Palestinian regime in Amman.

As discussed below, Jordan has been subjected to a period of severe economic depression. The impact on the military establishment has been of such magnitude as to virtually rule out the possibility of the country recovering as a military power of consequence before the end of the decade without substantial assistance from abroad.   However, the departure of the monarchy could result in the conversion of a relatively pacific state and a force for moderation into a hotbed of revanchist, anti-Zionist, anti-West terrorist groups bent upon wreaking vengeance upon Israel and others supporting it. Under such circumstances, there would be a strong probability of renewed Jordanian affiliation with Israel's enemies, such as Iraq or Syria, in the event of renewed Arab-Israeli hostilities.

THE POWDER KEG

CHAPTER II
The Major States

This chapter reviews the security perceptions of the major states in the Middle East and their strategies and programs for dealing with threats and security requirements. Wherever possible, the perceptions and strategies are drawn from statements by responsible leaders, while the programs are largely as reported in the public media and tabulated by Jane's Information Group Ltd. and the International Institute of Strategic Studies. The chapter also provides brief sketches of the military-industrial power of the various countries and points out particular strengths and weaknesses. The intent here is to provide a comprehensive, yet succinct, view of the threat perceptions and military policies and potential of the countries discussed. Where insufficient data is available the author has turned to secondary sources and exercised judgment to present as fair and balanced a view as possible.

ISRAEL
Most Israeli leaders recognize that the collapse of the Soviet Union and the defeat of Iraq have greatly reduced the magnitude of threats to the security of their country. They believe, however, that this is a temporary situation, and that matters could deteriorate in the latter part of the decade. They profess concern in the longer term for the large military forces of

neighboring countries which might be brought to bear against them in another outbreak of fighting. Many leaders perceive the number of potential enemies to be increasing, rather than decreasing, as technology and political changes bring additional, more distant Muslim states into the circle of potential adversaries. They believe that long-range missiles and the proliferation of mass destruction weapons (MDW) in the Middle East bode ill for Israeli security and that Israel must constantly strive to maintain a qualitative edge and quantitative sufficiency to be able to defeat any combination of possible opponents.

The Israeli leadership is not enthusiastic about arms control for containing these threats for a number of reasons. First, they are skeptical that progress is possible in the area until there is greater progress in peace negotiations. Second, considering the difficulty United Nations inspectors have had in locating Iraqi MDW, they do not believe that adequate verification is possible. Third, they are skeptical that arms control agreements are enforceable without extraordinary measures. Spokesmen argue that reliable arms controls depend upon intrusive measures which states harboring ill intent are unlikely to permit, or will find a way to subvert. Fourth, even if adequate controls were to be exercised by outside equipment suppliers, some of Israel's foes might be able to manufacture contraband items themselves. And finally, the Israeli leadership believes that the country can maintain an edge over its potential enemies in virtually all fields, and does not desire limitations on its options.[1]

On occasion Israel's fixation on maintaining its qualitative edge has placed it in a paradoxical situation vis-à-vis the United States. In 1993, for instance, the U.S. offered the Israeli Defense Ministry a number of AIM-120 Advanced Medium Range Air-to-Air Missiles (AMRAAM) for its air force. Israel refused at the time, preferring to spend its grant aid dollars on other items. Yet in 1995, after the U. S. had sold the same missiles to the United Arab Emirates, Israel demanded "compensation" in the form of reduced rates for the weapons or technical means for countering their use.[2]

With respect to regional competition in the nuclear field, the 1981 Israeli raid on the Iraqi nuclear installation at Osirak revealed the limits of Israel's tolerance. In June 1992 Maj. Gen. Herzl Bodinger, commander of the Israeli Air Force (IAF), indicated that his government's position in that respect had not changed. Referring to reports of the Iranian nuclear program, he said:

> We should first try to work against [nuclear
> proliferation] by political means. And if that
> doesn't work we may consider an attack.[3]

Others have argued for broader capabilities for coping with such threats at great distances, calling for the development of larger airborne and commando units. These they see as capable of striking deep into Iran or Iraq to deal with specialized targets on the ground. They also point to a need for increased airlift and for ever more sophisticated weaponry for fighting on far away fronts.[4]

With regard to frontier security, the Israelis talk in the following terms:[5]

1. Northern frontier (Lebanon): the threat of guerrilla ("terrorist") infiltration, ambush and short-range bombardment has increased since the Gulf War. The guerrillas are considered to have the approval of Damascus inasmuch as Syrian troops stationed in Lebanon make no apparent effort to stop them.

2. Syrian frontier: quiet, but Syrian forces are concentrated in the area in a high state of readiness for launching an attack

with minimal warning. They are acquiring many new weapons and have activated one reserve division, but they are not strong enough to take the Golan Heights by force.

3. Jordanian border: Jordanian authorities have long exercised reasonable control over their side of the line to prevent cross-border incidents. The 1994 peace accord effectively removed the sector as a matter of serious concern as long as the present government remains in office.

4. Southern (Egyptian) front: Security related incidents are rare.

5. The worst case for Israeli planners is the continuing threat of coordinated attack by several Arab countries. If war broke out between Israel and Syria, Israeli leaders believe that it is likely that Iraq would become involved. In addition, they believe that Egypt's attitude toward Israel could change very quickly.[6] In the words of the chief Israeli Defense Forces (IDF) planner, "We must assume that a future enemy will probably try to surprise us. ...[Egypt] is a potential threat, but right now we have peace and I hope they will not break it."[7]

There is no central or comprehensive statement of Israeli military strategy because major elements remain politically unmentionable. Israel's policy for avoiding discussion of nuclear weapons removes a key matter. Access to U.S. technology is treated somewhat more openly, but rarely with the attention it merits. As a result, a description of the strategy at the highest level of aggregation can only be inferred from a broad spectrum of sources, in and out of the government. With this important reservation, we may characterize the strategy as a triad, with major elements pertaining to nuclear deterrence and war planning, the maintenance of technological superiority over all potential opponents, and maximization of state power through high militarization of the society. (We have noted Israel's position as the most militarized state in the Middle East in Table No. 3 in the previous chapter.)

War planning is based upon a number of assumptions regarding the current security regime and the nature of the kind of war which might break out. These include:[8]

1. Israel can count on a window of opportunity lasting three to six years during which hostilities are highly unlikely. During that period it must prepare for another round of fighting.

2. The war, if it occurs, will be of brief duration, but intense ("short and sharp").

3. Israeli planners must expect to be on the defensive initially. The political leadership is unlikely to grant permission for preemptive strikes against developing threats for fear of provoking international criticism, especially in the United States.

4. Tactical reconnaissance assets are likely to be used against strategic targets. Missiles and unconventional warfare teams may be used by both sides to strike deep into hostile territory. There will be no completely secure rear areas for either side. In the words of Lt. Gen. Ehud Barak, former IDF chief of staff, "We plan for a conventional war, but missiles are our biggest problem, and we should not discount the possibility of an Arab country getting a nuclear capability by the end of the decade."[9]

5. Secret, high technology weapons are the key to "befuddlement" of the enemy. These are described as the "ability to unhinge an enemy offensive at the very outset, within the very first few hours of engagement, and thereby completely upset its original plan." Israel cannot afford a prolonged slugging match with Arab armies.

Traditional Israeli strategy has evolved with a number of fundamental characteristics.[10] These include:

1. Israeli security policy is strategically defensive, but its military operations are offensively oriented.

2. Israel cannot entrust its security to an alliance. It must have full control over forces defending its population.

3. Israel must have sufficient indigenous military power to deter attack by its enemies, or to defeat the enemies in every engagement if deterrence fails.

4. War must be conducted on enemy territory.

To these fundamentals, and with the assumptions above in mind, the current leadership has added some specifics pertinent to present circumstances.[11]

1. Israel will cooperate with the U.S. and Russia sponsoring the international peace negotiations.

2. The Israeli Air Force (IAF) will be maintained in a high state of readiness. It is the nation's first line of defense.

3. Israel will make continued heavy investment in defense programs. Particularly critical is the development of secret "befuddling" weaponry within the 3-6 year window of quiescence, whatever the cost. The maintenance of control of the occupied territories also requires large resource commitments. Prior to the withdrawal of Israeli forces from Jericho and Gaza, troop requirements ran in the range of 120-150 company-size formations.[12] These high priority programs continue, and are expensive, but they must be fulfilled, even at the risk of the degradation of Israeli standards of living.[13] A reasonable assumption regarding current troop requirements for occupation duty would be 80-100 companies considering the smaller population to be controlled.

Some indications of the thrust of Israeli thinking on defense strategy and programs have been revealed in public discussion. As defense minister in 1989, Yitzhak Rabin remarked:

Our main strategy is to prevent war through credible deterrence, and once war is enforced [sic] on us, to win it as quickly and decisively as possible. We believe that having the most offensive type of conventional forces — being a modern, efficient air force — is the best way to achieve both goals, and that's why it has first priority.

Stand-off is the name of the game in air, land and sea battles as far as we are concerned. We are striving to identify and locate a target in real-time from as far a distance as possible, as well as attack it from stand-off ranges.

...the gap between us and our potential enemies has actually widened, not reduced. The dogfight ratios our air force has achieved clearly prove this, increasing from 1:20 in the 1967 war to 0:90 in the 1982 Lebanon campaign. ...And that is probably why the Arabs went to push-button SSMs [surface-to-surface missiles], so that they can avoid the confrontation in the areas of quality and motivation.[14]

In line with Rabin's thinking, strong arguments have been made for development of weapons systems with great accuracy. These include anti-ballistic missile (ABM) systems and remotely piloted vehicles, both deemed critical to providing Israel the necessary qualitative edge. Other systems, acquired principally from American production or weapons stocks include attack helicopters and long-range multiple launch rocket systems (MLRS).[15]

Also critical for the small country is high quality intelligence. In addition to the regular operations of the legendary Mossad (Israel's national intelligence agency) and military tactical reconnaissance vehicles, the Israelis have invested heavily in space. Three "Ofek" (Horizon) platforms have been launched — the latest one in April 1995 — providing periodic optical observation of Israel's neighbors. A more ambitious half-billion dollar program, dubbed "Amos," was also launched in early 1995. "Amos" is designed for geosynchronous orbit to provide continuous coverage of the Middle East. While touted as a "commercial communications satellite," Amos is believed to carry communications, imaging, and infra-red (missile launch warning) packages. The combination of high and low orbiting vehicles should reduce Israeli dependence on the U.S. in this area.[16]

The Israelis recognize the limitations of the Patriot air defense system for engagement of missiles. Former Defense Minister Moshe Arens exhibited particular enthusiasm for development of the Arrow ABM system which would engage enemy missiles at ranges greater than Patriot's capabilities, reducing the risks of damage on the ground on Israeli territory from falling debris. The first fire control radar for the system was completed in December 1994.[17] The full system is scheduled to become operational by 1997 with an Arrow-2 missile. It is anticipated that Israel will deploy two four-launcher batteries of the Arrow-2, one near Tel Aviv, the other south of Haifa. Together, the fire units will protect about 85 percent of the country.[18]

The costs of Arrow development have been high, and the system has experienced a number of set-backs, but the United States has provided most of the money. In May 1995 the U.S. agreed to continue funding the project at a level of $40 million per year from 1997 to 2001.[19] But there is little reason to attach much importance to that figure. Lt. Gen. Malcom

O'Neil, director of the Pentagon's Ballistic Missile Defense Organization, remarked to Congress that "based upon data gathered in Israel, [the estimated deployment costs were] significantly below $10 billion" — suggesting that much higher requirements for U.S. funding may be forthcoming.[20]

If for any reason the program cannot be completed, a fallback may be available. The U.S. is separately developing a Theater High Altitude Area Defense (THAAD) system, which could be ready in a similar time frame. THAAD would intercept approaching missiles at still greater ranges and higher altitudes than Arrow, virtually eliminating ground damage in any instance of successful engagement.

Besides early-warning satellites and ABM, current Israeli acquisition programs include at least two large air defense radars, a squadron of AH-64 Apache attack helicopters, F-16, and possibly F/A-18 fighters.[21] Facilitating these acquisitions has been the authorization of an extraordinary grant of $700 million worth of equipment from stocks of the U.S. armed services. Ten F-15A/B fighter aircraft are included in the grant.[22] Other important items Israel is seeking are 42 Multiple Launch Rocket Systems (MLRS) and 2,640 TOW-2A/B anti-armor missiles. They also expect to acquire 305 tactical rocket pods, 28 M-577 armored command post vehicles, 31 High Mobility Multi-purpose Wheeled Vehicles (HMMWV) and night vision goggles.[23]

The Israelis attach particular importance to the Air Force. Unlike Israel's ground forces, the IAF is a highly professional service, with less reliance on reserves. Of some 815 combat aircraft (including armed helicopters), all but 250 are believed to be in active service. The total Israeli force potential of its air arm exceeds that of its closest competitor (Syria) by over 40 percent, and almost matches that of all of the other Arab forces in this analysis combined.[24] The versatility of the IAF should also be borne in mind. Over 80 percent of Israeli combat aircraft have dual capability (air superiority and ground attack), while almost all the aircraft of its potential opponents are optimized for a single mission.

Israel plans to purchase 21 long-range F-15I combat aircraft (a version of the high performance fighter especially tailored for Israeli needs) for approximately $2 billion. Paradoxically, the order may depend to some extent upon a parallel order by Saudi Arabia for a different version of the aircraft. Riyadh has been experiencing some funding problems for its large arms procurement programs, and if it is forced to reschedule its F-15 orders, the manufacturer, McDonnell Douglas Corporation, might be obliged to shift some of its costs to the Israeli order. This, in turn, might reduce the number of units the Israelis could buy.[25] However, there are indications that Israel may actually increase its buy. In June 1995 the commander of the Israeli Air Force, Major General Herzl Budinger, said he expected that all of the aircraft would be delivered by 1998, and that the number may be increased to 25, which is the normal size of an Israeli squadron.[26]

In addition to the F-15Is, Israel expects to receive 50 used F-16 aircraft from U.S. Air Force stocks. The F-16s are expected to gradually replace Israel's aging A-4 and Kfir fighters. The purchase of the F-15Is may necessitate some delays in the acquisition of other equipment, including Blackhawk helicopters.[27]

Israel is also acquiring two German built Dolphin submarines.[28] These boats, which will have a missile firing capability, could play a role in intelligence gathering and in protecting Israel's sea approaches from missile firing ships or hostile submarines. Reportedly, the Israelis have also recently developed a new anti-ship missile, up to 64 of which are to be vertically mounted on each of its new Saar-5 class missile boats. Nicknamed "Barak," the missile will have a range of 10 km.[29]

The identity of the Israeli "befuddling" weapon, or weapons, is a matter of some speculation. The highly classified U.S. STAR-1, loitering anti-radar missile, which recently completed its development phase, would seem to fit the definition. The STAR-1 includes a "Delilah" unmanned aerial vehicle which simulates the presence of an attack aircraft. The system flies a preprogrammed path to the battle area where it assumes an autonomous search orbit. Capable of detecting a broad spectrum of electronic emitters, it selects a high priority target, and homes in on the victim. Such a weapon, if used in mass, could destroy the ground-based elements of an extensive air defense system, or force it to shut down to avoid destruction.[30]

Another candidate could be the U.S.-developed "high-power microwave" weapon which converts the energy of a conventional explosion into a pulse of radio energy. If the pulse is sufficiently strong it can penetrate computerized weapons systems and disrupt or burn out electronic components. The microwave weapons were first used by the U.S. Navy on an experimental basis in the Gulf War. Conceivably, they could be made available to Israel under the right circumstances.[31]

Anticipated Israeli arms acquisitions through 1999 are summarized in Table 5 below. The list is illustrative of Israel's dependence on the United States high technology weaponry. In an interview in February 1993, General Giora Rom, the Israeli defense attache in Washington, confirmed the importance of Israeli access to American technology. He pointed out that the United States had provided for a downlink station in Tel Aviv during the Gulf War capable of receiving data directly from satellites concerning Iraqi Scud missile launches. The arrangement was expected to become permanent under a new post-war bilateral agreement on enhanced military cooperation.[32] The following month, President Clinton reaffirmed to Prime Minister Rabin, during the latter's visit to Washington, that the U.S. would continue to ensure Israel's technological edge over all potential opponents.[33]

Surprisingly, when asked what the United States can do to help Israel, informed Israelis sometimes reply, "Stop sending us so much money." However, they are quick to differentiate between military assistance and economic aid. The former, they argue, is still necessary to insure a military technological edge over potential enemies. The latter, on the other hand, tends to feed Israel's long-term dependency on the United States, and is counterproductive to the country's dignity and independence.[34] This point was made publicly in January 1994 by Mr. Yossie Beilin, deputy foreign minister, before a meeting of the Women's International Zionist Organization in Jerusalem. "If our economic situation is better than in many of your countries," he said, "how can we go on asking for your charity?" Mr. Beilin's remarks were quickly disowned by the prime minister, but the issue is likely to resurface in other arena.[35] In any event, Israel's pleas for continuing military assistance are likely to remain strong.

The Israelis have no overt strategy for guiding the acquisition or employment of nuclear weapons. Their sole declaratory policy in this regard is contained in the oft recited, and ambiguous, "Israel will not be the first country to introduce nuclear weapons into the Middle East." In 1987 the Israeli nuclear technician, Mordechai Vanunu, told a London newspaper that the nuclear plant in which he had worked at Dimona had processed enough plutonium to manufacture 200 bombs.[36] Various press revelations indicate the total inventory may consist of as many as 300 weapons of different types.[37]

Opinions differ regarding the purpose of such a large inventory. After the 1973 conflict, Israel is believed to have established at least three nuclear-capable artillery battalions, each consisting of twelve self-propelled 175mm guns.[38] Clearly the formation of nuclear-capable artillery units indicates some thinking in terms of tactical nuclear warfare. On the other hand, no observer has yet reported any indication of Israeli doctrinal or training developments along that line. Coordination of tactical fires with conventional maneuver units is complex, and would be risky to inaugurate without training and rehearsals.

Another possibility is suggested in the title of a popular book, *The Samson Option* (Seymour Hersh). Some Israeli leaders could be desirous of posing a threat of total annihilation of enemy countries if Israel were subjected to MDW attack. Prime Minister Yitzhak Rabin, for example, stated that Israel should be prepared to inflict one hundred times as much damage on any opponent as it might visit upon Israel.[39] Anoushiravan Ehteshami reports a mind-set among some Israelis which says, "If we are going to be destroyed we will take all our regional enemies with us."[40] One study indicates that such a task (with targets in Syria, Jordan, Iraq, Libya and Egypt) could be accomplished with either 138 weapons of 20 kilotons yield or 26 weapons of one megaton each.[41]

A third possibility is suggested by a number of U.S. Embassy officers: simple bureaucratic run-on. The Israelis have been making nuclear weapons for over twenty years.[42] They may be prone to making new ones without disposing of older designs.

On the other hand, the Israeli stockpile may have been developed with one eye on the possibility of Soviet intervention in the region. The development of the intermediate-range (1,500 km) Jericho II missile, capable of reaching the territory of the former Soviet Union, would lend credence to this possibility. If this is true, the Defense Ministry may have been thinking in terms of classical nuclear deterrence, or even warfighting. The reported location of the primary base for Jericho II missiles at the center of the country near Kefar Zekharya, west of Jerusalem, has been interpreted by some analysts as indicative of a last-resort strategy. "This clearly signals that Israel does not consider the nuclear option to be a first-strike weapon," wrote Harold Hough in the authoritative *Jane's Intelligence Review* in November 1994.[43] In any event, potential opponents cannot disregard the disturbing "Samson option," as well as lesser reactions, in their calculations of possible warfighting scenarios. For the distribution of major components of Israel's nuclear weapons program see Figure 1 below.

The Israeli arms industry is a large, highly sophisticated and capable complex with experience in manufacturing and servicing virtually all types of modern weaponry, to include tanks, missiles, jet aircraft and nuclear weapons. At its peak, in the mid-1980s, it employed over 62,000 persons. Between 1984 and 1988 production ranged from $ 2.25 billion and $ 2.4 billion worth of military goods. Critics of the industry argue that it grew without direction and became excessively competitive in later years as it outstripped the requirements of the IDF which it was intended to serve. In 1990, for example, in the field of image processing, eight domestic industries competed for missile contracts. Increasingly, excess capacity was devoted to export. By 1991 the number of workers had dwindled to 46,500, and the volume of exports were twice that of sales to the IDF.[44]

Proposals have surfaced from time to time for restructuring much of Israel's defense industry to improve its competitiveness. Frequently, privatization has involved large labor layoffs, so the government has had to move slowly in the public sector to avoid provoking the labor unions while it has been involved in sensitive peace negotiations with Arab leaders. Matters reached a critical point in March 1995, however, forcing a proposal for the merging of the country's leading aerospace manufacturers, Rafael, Israel Aircraft Industries and TAAS. If the proposal goes through, the surviving company would be known as Jewish Aerospace.[45]

High quality Israeli military products are now to be found in over 60 foreign countries. Paradoxically, the CSS-2 intermediate range missiles purchased by Saudi Arabia from China are believed to contain Israeli components in the guidance packages.[46] Some analysts speculate that, if true, that fact may afford the Israelis a way to neutralize the weapons if they were to be fired toward Israel rather than Iraq or Iran.

Since the signing of the Declaration of Principles with the Palestine Liberation Organization and the peace treaty with Jordan, Israeli views regarding the potential market for their weapons systems have been undergoing substantial change. Some officials view the Arab gulf states as potential future customers, particularly if Iraq and Iran continue to menace the area. Others are less optimistic, preferring to focus on Turkey and developing states further removed from the venues of traditional Arab-Israeli conflict. In particular, Israeli industrial officials would like to be in a position to provide spare parts and maintenance services to countries around the globe with forces equipped with Russian and other eastern armaments. They especially have MiG aircraft in mind.[47] In any event, it appears likely that the peace process may strengthen Israel's hand in the competition for arms markets worldwide.

TABLE 5

ANTICIPATED ISRAELI ARMS ACQUISITIONS[48]

142 - 162 Combat Aircraft
(Including)

15 F-15 A/B   50 F-16 A/B/C/D

5 F-15 D   42 (?)   F-18

21-25 F-15I (F-15E)   25 AH-64 Apache Attack Helicopters

? Blackhawk helicopters

305 Tactical Rocket Pods

100 Merkava III Tanks

42 Multiple Launch Rocket System Launchers

28 M577 Command Armored Vehicles

2,640 TOW-2A/B Anti-Armor Missiles

2 Dolphin Class Attack Submarines

? "Barak" Antiship Missiles

2 Batteries (8 Launchers) Arrow 2 ABM Missiles

? "Befuddlement" Weapons:

STAR-1 Loitering Anti-Radar

Missiles(?) or

High-Power Microwave Weapons(?)

FIGURE 1

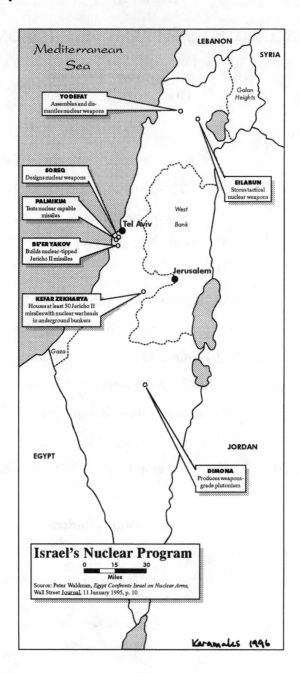

Israel's Nuclear Program

Source: Peter Waldman, *Egypt Confronts Israel on Nuclear Arms,* Wall Street Journal, 11 January 1995, p. 10

EGYPT

Egyptian leaders identify three principal threats to their national security:

1. a lack of regional strategic balance, stemming from the overwhelming preponderance of Israeli military power;

2. the threat of encirclement by Islamic fundamentalists; and

3. internal threats to domestic order.

Representatives of the political-military elite in Cairo express no sense of acute threat from Israel, but argue that the magnitude of the military imbalance between Israel and its neighbors is an unnatural and unhealthy state of affairs. They cite Israeli superiority in both the "post conventional" high technology and nuclear weapons fields. They believe the imbalance to be conducive of ill-considered actions on the part of the Jerusalem leadership, such as the 1982 invasion of Lebanon. Israeli superiority, they argue, tends to facilitate Israeli resort to force for dealing with many types of issues which could be settled by political means among nations entertaining greater respect for their neighbors. Indeed, they interpret the Arab-Israeli peace negotiations of the first half of the 1990s as exactly the sort of discussions which should have been undertaken long before, but were impossible because of reckless attitudes among some officials in Jerusalem, fostered by confidence in Israeli military prowess.[49] The renewal of Israeli offensive operations in Lebanon in the spring of 1996 — however cast as "retaliatory action" — is bound to reinforce Egyptian misgivings regarding Israeli faith in military solutions to political differences.

Egyptian leaders also express an uncertainty with respect to Israeli objectives. While they are happy to have recovered the Sinai, they question whether Israel is satisfied with the 1967 borders on other fronts, or if, perhaps, it seeks additional territory at Arab expense. They blame this problem on a lack of "political transparency" in Israeli policy.[50]

Cairo is further disturbed by the spread of Islamic fundamentalism to Sudan and Algeria. They are fearful, for example, that a hostile Sudanese government could interfere with the Nile River water supply. In June 1995 matters with Sudan came to a head in a clash of border troops in the disputed Halaib triangle on the Red Sea coast which may contain significant oil deposits. The importance of the incident was magnified, coming as it did in the wake of an earlier attempt by unknown terrorists to assassinate President Hosni Mubarak. If it is subsequently discovered that the Sudanese Government was behind the attempted assassination, or if further provocations occur, some Western diplomats believe that Egypt might launch bombing raids against military camps north of Khartoum where Muslim militants have been reported to be training.[51] If one or more fundamentalist factions were to come to power in additional countries in the region, strong reactions could be triggered in Cairo of unforeseeable dimensions and ramifications.[52]

While Egyptian spokesmen are not keen to discuss internal security problems in great detail, it is apparent that they recognize a vulnerability among the Egyptian people to the march of militant Islam. In 1992 Islamic militants began attacks on foreigners in Egypt, killing a British subject in October and injuring five Germans three weeks later. With the $3.3 billion tourist industry at stake, and a quarter of a million visitors in the country each day, the Government reacted sharply. But domestic killing goes on. There were over 750 fatalities over the next three years of violence. Virtually all fundamentalist groups are outlawed in the country, including the Muslim Brotherhood which denounces terrorism.[53]

In early 1994 there appeared to be an escalation of the campaign to undermine the Egyptian economy, and hence the regime. In February the militants issued a warning to foreigners living and working in Egypt to leave the country. An attack on a bus full of Romanian engineers at the Asyut Cement Company, 210 miles south of Cairo, punctuated the notice. Foreign embassies took the warning seriously, advising their nationals of the risks of travel or residence in the troubled areas.[54]

During the next year, however, the Egyptian Government gradually gained the upper hand over the radical groups operating under the title, *Al Jama'at Al Islamiya*. The government's tactics may have been heavy handed, but seemed effective.[55] A spectacular attack and massacre of 18 Greek tourists in Cairo on 18 April 1996 appeared to be a misguided attempt at vengeance against Israel for its attacks on civilians in Lebanon rather than a resurgence against the government. *Al Islamiya* claimed responsibility for the action, but admitted that it had misidentified the target group. Nevertheless, the government responded sharply, arresting some 1,500 suspects and taking legal action against more than a dozen police officers responsible for the protection of tourists.[56]

Cairo looks primarily to the U.S./Russian sponsored peace process for solution to most of its difficulties with Israel. Egyptian leaders were enthusiastic about the American concept of a "new world order," as expressed in 1991 by former President George Bush. They warmly embraced the notion that the age of naked force was over. They are supportive in principle of American arms control proposals, but express concern that the U.S. is addressing matters in the wrong order. They argue that the large number of Israeli nuclear weapons is the greatest threat to the security of the Middle East, hence it should be addressed first. Israeli evasiveness on nuclear matters, in their view, casts a shadow over the entire arms control question. Finally, in this regard, one Egyptian analyst has suggested somewhat enigmatically, that if the U.S. were unable to focus attention on this matter, Egypt would have to find its own solution to the problem.

Egypt possesses a large, obsolescent military establishment, numbering about 440,000 troops. 50 to 60 percent of the equipment is of Soviet design, none less than 20 years old. Egypt has no apparent ambition for expanding the forces, but seeks to modernize them through gradual transition to Western equipment. In the short run, the country will be looking for opportunities to make small improvements through limited acquisition of surplus materiel on the open market.

The United States provides Egypt an annual military subsidy of $1.3 billion, the great bulk of which is used for procurement of U.S. materiel. This sum constitutes about 75 percent of the Egyptian defense budget, and some 85-90 percent of the military procurement budget.[57] In 1993 about 40 percent of the Egyptian Air Force aircraft was of former Soviet or other Eastern manufacture. The Egyptians have set a goal of converting the entire force to Western design by 2005. A major initiative under the U.S.-Egyptian "Peace Vector" series of military sales programs has been to equip first line fighter squadrons with F-16 A/B/C and D aircraft. Some 126 units are being delivered. Egypt has asked for additional F-16s under the U.S. program for disposal of surplus equipment.[58]

The Egyptians also assign a high priority to the modernization of their tank fleet. In addition to the funding mentioned above, the U.S. has recently provided Egypt with 700 M60-A1 tanks with the understanding that they will be used to replace a like number of older Soviet vehicles. The Egyptians are in the process of up-grading the new tanks to the M60-A3 standard, which will afford the vehicles additional capabilities, such as tracking targets 10 times faster than the Soviet T-54s they replace.[59]   Cairo may purchase an additional lot of 340 M60-A3 vehicles from American stocks in Europe.[60]

The heart of the Egyptian arms industry is the Arab Organization for Industrialization (AOI), formed in 1976 by a consortium composed of Egypt, Saudi Arabia, Qatar and the United Arab Emirates. The complex has produced Tucano and Alpha jet aircraft, tactical rockets and missiles, many calibers of small arms and artillery ammunition, light armored vehicles, communications equipment, radar, helicopters, Jeep and Wagoneer trucks, and NBC protective equipment. Under a memorandum of agreement with the General Dynamics Corporation, the complex is co-producing some 550 120mm gun M1-A1 tanks, gradually assuming a larger share of the manufacturing task from the American firm. A sufficient number of M1-A1s is expected to be available to equip the Egyptian 2nd Armored Division by 1996.[61] As the current production run nears its scheduled completion in 1997, Egypt and the U.S. will have to decide whether a new contract should be drawn up for production of the more modern M1-A2 tank, and possibly M2 Bradley infantry fighting vehicles. Egypt would like to build the vehicles both for domestic use and for export.[62] AOI endeavors to market its products both inside and outside the Arab community, but thus far sales have been modest.

Another high priority matter on Cairo's agenda is the acquisition of improved anti-tank guided missiles. The Egyptian inventory of some 1400 old Soviet Sagger systems has only half the penetration power of U.S. TOW-2 missiles at a time when large numbers of modern tanks are being acquired by other powers in the region. Egypt has placed orders in the U.S. for 692 TOW launchers with at least 2,132 TOW-2A missiles.[63]

The Egyptian Navy has traditionally had a low priority among the national services, but may soon receive some remedial attention. Cairo reasons that it has a regional security responsibility, stemming from its role in the Gulf War, and recognizes that recent enhancements of Iranian naval power increase the vulnerability of Egyptian forces operating at a distance from the homeland. Egypt has received two Knox class frigates on lease from the U.S. to protect its coastline and the line of communications to any forces which may be deployed abroad. It may also receive one frigate from the U.S. as excess military property. The frigates are being upgraded with MK-46 anti-submarine warfare (ASW) torpedoes, Harpoon anti-ship missiles and Phalanx close-in weapons systems for protection against hostile missiles. As a complement to these vessels, it is also receiving 10 U.S. excess SH-2G naval helicopters suitable for either ASW or surface surveillance work.[64]

In addition, Egypt has undertaken the upgrading of four Chinese-built Romeo class submarines with Harpoon missiles, NT-37E torpedoes, new sonar, new communications systems, and new electronic surveillance and fire control systems. The upgrading was expected to be completed by 1995. Other prospective naval programs include acquisition of up to 30 fast attack missile boats and a number of coastal patrol aircraft.[65]

While Israeli nuclear capabilities are very disturbing to Egypt, and have been characterized as "unacceptable" to Cairo, few believe that Egypt is more than marginally involved in nuclear weapons development. Egypt has reportedly undertaken some research projects in the field, but it is not believed capable of producing a weapon before the year 2002, if then.[66]

War materiel currently sought by Egypt, primarily from foreign suppliers, is summarized in Table 6 below.

TABLE 6

MILITARY MATERIEL CURRENTLY SOUGHT BY EGYPT[67]

550 M1-A1 tanks
? M1-A2 tanks
340 M60-A3 tanks
600 YPR 765 armored infantry fighting vehicles
374 M113 armored personnel carriers

692 TOW missile launchers, 2,132 TOW-2A missiles
Phase III improvement for 12 HAWK SAM batteries

65 F-16 fighter aircraft
36 Apache attack helicopters

24 Lantrin (low altitude navigation and
targeting system) pods for F-16s

C-130 cargo aircraft
? Tanker aircraft

3 Knox class frigates
6-8 Oberon class submarines
30 missile boats

10 SH-2G anti-submarine/surveillance helicopters
? Naval patrol aircraft

SYRIA

Syrian leaders perceive their country to be a potential
"Germany of the Middle East." They point with pride to their
strong agricultural base, their diligent work force, their boom-

ing tourist industry and their self-sufficiency in oil. They feel that the country is mired down in a wasteful arms race with Israel because Israel continues to hold Syrian territory and poses an acute threat to Damascus. Large armed forces are necessary to protect the country from further Israeli aggression. Israeli tanks are stationed a scant 40 miles from the Syrian capital.[68]   Perhaps unwittingly, but nevertheless revealingly, Israeli Likud Party leader, Benjamin Netanyahu, reinforced this point. In 1994 he remarked, "Whoever does not understand that the reason missiles are not fired at us from Damascus is that we are within spitting distance of Damascus and Israeli tanks hold Syria by the throat."[69]   Other reports indicate that the Syrians have a mounting fear of encirclement as Israel concludes separate agreements with Turkey and Arab countries, possibly to include one with a post-Saddam Hussein Iraq.[70]

Syrians do not recognize the disparity of size between Israel and Syria as completely to their advantage. Israel's compactness, they argue, facilitates its rapid mobilization in an emergency. Syria, they believe, would require more than a week to mobilize because of its dispersed population, necessitating the maintenance of a substantially larger standing force.[71] If Israel would return the Golan, the leadership argues, Syria could turn its principal energies to commerce and industry and raise the standard of living of its people.[72]

According to the leadership, that would be very important in overcoming the other major threat to Syria's security — internal subversion by radical Islamic groups. The Syrians acknowledge that they need large armed forces to maintain internal security. Without tight internal controls, they believe, Syria could slip into the Islamic fundamentalist orbit which would hurl its social programs backward in time. The "great crimes" of which President Hafiz Al-Assad has been accused, they say, have largely been provoked by insurrection-ist elements which, if not suppressed, could topple the govern-ment.[73]

Syria realizes that it can no longer compete with Israel on a military plane, without allies and without the backing of a superpower. Instead, it looks to the peace negotiations for jus-tice. These, however, are not proving to be as strong a force as was anticipated. If the U.S. were a real superpower, spokesmen argue, it would pressure Israel to withdraw. By not doing so, the U.S. makes it look as though Israel is the real superpower and the U.S. simply a supporting actor.[74]

But some observers are skeptical of the depth of Assad's commitment to the peace process. Former Israeli Foreign Minister Ehud Barak believes that the Syrian president is wor-ried over the future status of his Alawite minority and Syria's position in the Arab world if he shows too much flexibility. These concerns, the former army chief of staff suggests, cause him to keep his personal distance from the negotiations.[75]

Barring a settlement with Israel, Syrian strategy is to wait for things to change, "even if it takes 100 years." Recovery of the Golan Heights is a matter of national honor, the leaders argue, and nothing can ever make them accept anything less than the entire area. They may suffer many reverses, but they are resolved to recover their territory.[76]

According to one report, President Assad has revised his strategy toward Israel. Rather than seeking "strategic parity," as the government claimed in the 1980s, the goal is now "strategic deterrence" to discourage Israeli attack. The strate-gy has three components: (1) the upgrading of the armed forces with advanced military equipment, (2) the development of a concept for "long and protracted conflict, unlike previous Arab-Israeli wars" in the event deterrence fails, and (3) an emphasis on "strategic depth" as a decisive factor in any large-scale conflict.[77]

Some informed American observers in Damascus have expressed the opinion that the likelihood of another war in the region in the next ten years is greater than 50 percent. If a rightist leader were to come to power in Israel and to consolidate Israeli control of the occupied territories, the probability would approach certainty. The chance that the Syrians can be cowed into surrender is very low. Further, the matter of nuclear warfare in the region must be taken seriously.[78] The nuclear issue aside, some credence was given to the American view in remarks by Israeli Prime Minister Yitzhak Rabin when, in June 1994, he commented that if there is no peace treaty with Syria, Israelis should "prepare for war 3, 5 years or 7 years from now, or 10 years from now."[79]

Others have a different perspective. While not addressing the likelihood of a new war, Mr. Peter W. Rodman, director of security programs at the Washington based Nixon Center for Peace and Freedom, suggested that Assad had his chance to make peace with Israel and squandered it. The Syrian leader must have known as early as 1992, Rodman argued, that the Rabin/Peres Israeli leadership was prepared to relinquish the Golan Heights, but he made only grudging and marginal moves in return, largely for domestic security reasons. The result was paralysis.[80]

While, indeed, the Syrian-Israeli armistice has been stable for almost three decades, Syria has been ambiguous about supporting hostile Arab groups operating against Israel in Lebanon. One of the most notable is the fundamentalist Hezbollah, or "Party of God." In May 1994, U.S. State Department officials announced that Syria had arrested several Hezbollah leaders after they led a demonstration in southern Lebanon. However, the guerrillas were later released, and the following month there were reports that President Hafez Assad was considering shipping former Soviet SA-14 and SA-16 shoulder-fired anti-aircraft missiles to the Hezbollah to help them defend themselves against Israeli air attacks. The group has been equipped with the older, and far less effective, Soviet SA-7 "Strela" missiles for some time. The shipment has not been confirmed, and may be deliberately reserved by the Syrians as a deterrent to further Israeli air attacks. If the weapons are delivered, however, it would represent a significant escalation of the balance of power in Lebanon, and would likely stimulate some form of Israeli retribution.[81]

Reports of funds received by Syria from Kuwait and Saudi Arabia in 1991 for its part in the war with Iraq range from $700 million to $2.5 billion. It has been the intention of the Syrian Government to spend the money largely on arms acquisitions. In June 1994 the Russian chief of staff, General Mikhail Kolesnikov, visited Damascus in connection with a program for resumption of the arms trade between the two countries. He arrived in the wake of Russia's forgiveness of most of Syria's $10 billion debt from earlier purchases from the Soviet Union. The new agreement concluded in June was estimated to have a value of about $500 million. No details were released, other than that payments were henceforth expected to be made in cash, and a broad promise was made by Russian Deputy Foreign Minister Boris Kolokov that no "offensive" weapons would be included.[82] While the Russians had previously demanded cash payments for the full $10 billion before any new contracts could be signed, they apparently realized that if the Syrians were unsuccessful in getting any new Russian materiel, they were likely to turn to other suppliers, notably China, North Korea, or other former Soviet republics.

However, it is not clear that all of Syria's former sources

will be able to be as responsive or forthcoming as in the past. There have been conflicting reports regarding a consignment of some 250 T-72 tanks ordered from the former state of Czechoslovakia in 1988. The vehicles were to be built with state funding in Slovakia's ZTF Martin tank plant, one of the largest in the Warsaw Pact. But when Czechoslovakia broke apart in 1993, Slovakia was reported to be in dire financial straits and unable to complete the contract. Nominally, ZTF Martin was left with 200 tanks sitting idle without a prospective buyer.[83] Other reports, emanating from Lebanon, however, indicate that the Slovak foreign minister, Edward Kukan, met with President Assad and signed a new agreement providing for delivery of the tanks.[84]

In any event, moderately sized arms deals are likely to continue in Syria, as elsewhere in the Middle East, as long as there is no comprehensive peace accord for the region. As much as Russia and the Western powers may protest their desires to dampen such sales, economic factors often override all others. In August 1993, for instance, a Russian company was instrumental in flying truck chassis for Scud missile launchers from North Korea to Damascus even after vociferous American complaints to Moscow.[85] Anticipated Syrian arms acquisitions by 2000 are indicated in Table 7 below.

In the longer term, Syrian initiatives to develop its domestic missile industry could be more important than the purchases from abroad. Reportedly, Syria and Iran have undertaken a joint effort to construct a plant in Syria, with Iranian funding, for the production of Scud-C missiles. North Korea will provide technical support.[86] The project could substantially enhance Syria's capability for massed missile offensives.

It is possible that Syria is also preparing to manufacture a missile with a more rapid response capability than the liquid-fueled Scud. One possibility is a version of the Soviet SS-21 (Scarab). While more limited in range, the SS-21 is more accurate than the Scud and less vulnerable to detection during its preparation for firing. China may have delivered as much as 90 tons of solid fuel missile propellant to Syria for this purpose.[87]

Syria's major element of military strength is its large active land force. Deployed largely on the Damascus plain facing Israel, the army would require few relocations to mount a massive armored and missile attack on the Israeli held Golan Heights. Some analysts believe that the Israelis might not receive more than twenty minutes to two hours warning.[88] Syrian artillery is trained and equipped to deliver massed fires, and has recently been strengthened through the acquisition of modern Soviet self-propelled howitzers.[89] The air forces are heavily weighted for air defense, but, together with air defense missile forces, they could provide strong cover for such an operation. With coordinated massive missile and air attacks on Israeli airfields, reserve equipment parks, and command and control centers, the Syrians might calculate that such an offensive could score some initial successes.

Syria is a signatory of the Nuclear Nonproliferation Treaty and thus far has shown no more than marginal proclivity for breaching the agreement. While some believe that Damascus is seeking nuclear weapons, no analyst has suggested that Syria has progressed beyond the research stage.[90] Syria's chemical warfare capability, including nerve agents, however, is well developed. As early as 1985 U.S. officials were quoted as saying, "...the Syrians have the most advanced chemical weapons capability in the middle East."[91]

In July and August 1994 President Hafez Assad abruptly dismissed at least 16 senior military officers, including two generals, in what was interpreted by Western observers as an attempt to weaken the hand of officers who might not be in sympathy with his intentions to seek peace with Israel. It was also seen as likely linked to the question of presidential succession, which had been complicated by the death of Assad's eldest son in January 1994. Whatever the causes, the purge is not associated with any expectations of either a liberalization of the regime or a decrease in presidential powers.[92] Syria remains a tight dictatorship, firmly in control of one of the most feared and respected Arab leaders in the region.

TABLE 7

RECENT SYRIAN ARMS ORDERS AND ACQUISITIONS[93]

48 MiG-29 (Fulcrum) fighter aircraft
(possibly plus an additional 48)
22 Su-24 (Fencer) fighter/bombers
(possibly plus an additional 22)
20 Su-27 fighters

700 T-72 tanks
250 SP artillery pieces

SA-10 "Grumble" air defense missiles (all altitudes)
SA-11 "Gadfly" (low-to medium altitude)
SA-13 "Gopher" (low altitude)
SA-16 no NATO nickname (low altitude)
Surface-to-air command and control radars
174 Scud-C missiles
20 Scud launchers

SAUDI ARABIA

Saudi Arabia suffers under self-imposed isolation from much of the rest of the world. It permits no visitors to the country other than Islamic pilgrims fulfilling their religious obligations and industrial workers under contract with the government. Not only does it fear the influence of foreign culture, but it perceives itself as virtually surrounded by hostile states. Jordanian and Yemeni support of Iraq during the Gulf War were seen as acts of treachery in Riyadh. Saudi suspicions run high that had Iraq ventured further to invade Saudi territory, both Jordan and Yemen would have joined in the attack to settle old scores dating back to the Ottoman period.

Minor border clashes with Yemeni troops continue. There is no agreement between Riyadh and San'a on the location of the boundary, and the issue is complicated by expectations of discovery of significant oil deposits in the area.[94] Early in 1994, during the Yemen civil war, Riyadh is reported to have smuggled armored personnel carriers to southern forces and to have paid for southern MiG-29 purchases from Bulgaria in hopes of restoring the independence of the Aden government. After the reunion of the two Yemen states, the Yemenis were able in December to score a significant local victory over the Saudis on a mountain which they claim to be situated on their territory. Both sides maintain heavy concentrations of forces in the area. Clearly, the Saudis would have preferred to have two small, weaker states on their southwestern border than a unified Yemen.[95]

To the east, Iran is viewed as a powerful potential foe. The Saudis supported Iraq in the Iran-Iraq War (earning no credit from either side), and they experienced the sting of Iranian-supported riots at the Sacred Mosque in Mecca during the 1979 Haj season. Moreover, they are aware that Iran has trans-Gulf claims which could impinge sharply on Saudi security.

Analysts associated with the prestigious Jane's Information Group Ltd. of London estimate that in coming years Saudi Arabia is more likely to be involved in confrontation with Iran than Iraq. Further, if the two more powerful states were to square off against each other again, the analysts believe that the Saudis would be likely once more to support Baghdad.[96]

The Saudis believe that their traditional practice of "rialpolitik" (the paying off of potential enemies with rials — the national currency) failed them in their most extreme test. Strapped for cash in the wake of the Gulf War anyway, they resolved to shift their strategy to seek deterrence of foreign attack primarily through heavy investment in arms, rather than bribes. Their objective is the development of a credible deterrent force on the model of the coalition armies which faced Iraq on October 20, 1990. This was the level of military capability deemed appropriate for the defense of the kingdom. Thereafter, coalition planning focused on the assembly of larger forces capable of expelling the Iraqis from Kuwait.[97]

While there is little expectation that the Saudis will match the Desert Shield model, their plans are ambitious. They would like to triple the size of their forces, building to a total strength of 200,000 men (regular and national guard) by the year 2000. The ground forces would expand to 90,000 men with as many as 7 divisions. Large orders have been placed abroad for armaments (see Table 8).

In addition, they have contracted for construction of new airfields and installation of a high technology $837 million "Peace Shield" air defense system, tying together various national components (radar sites, sector control centers, surface-to-air missiles, airborne warning and control aircraft, and civil air). Altogether the system involves 310 sites. The pinnacle of the network is an underground command operating center in Riyadh. From there lines of control fan out to five bunkered sector command and operations centers at the main operating bases of the Royal Saudi Air Forces at Khamis Mushayt, Taif, Tabuk, Al Kharj, and Dhahran. Interoperability with U.S. Air Forces is provided through the use of standard DEC VAX computers.[98]

Some analysts have expressed skepticism that the Saudi population base is large enough to sustain armed forces of 200,000. A CIA estimate placed the number of native born, physically fit males between the ages of 15 and 49 in the year 2000 at 1.08 million, a little over five times the number required.[99] Official Saudi statistics indicate that the total number of males between 18 and 32 in 1992 was 1.65 million.[100] If the official census is roughly correct, a force of 200,000 would give the country a soldier to citizen ratio (counting only native born Saudis) of less than 1:61, a figure substantially lower than either Israel or Syria, but well within the norms of the region (see Table 1, Chapter I). Militarization of the populace on this scale would probably require conscription, and could pose a disruptive factor in Saudi society. Nevertheless, the goal appears feasible, if distasteful. The Saudi Government, itself, expresses confidence that it can be done by increasing recruitment quotas among the Bedouin tribes and by tapping the increasing pool of urban youths.[101] Most likely, policy, or economics, rather than population will prove to be the limiting factor.

Saudi Arabia has traditionally relied upon Western contractors for supply and maintenance of its war materiel. However, a major component of the new Saudi program for expansion of its defense forces will entail investment in more elaborate facilities for logistical support. The government now seeks to develop an indigenous capability for depot rebuild of aircraft and vehicles. The effort will be highly expensive, involving personnel training, parts stockage, tools and physical plant. Conceivably, the project could eventually develop into a limited manufacturing capability, but no such plans have been reported. As will be noted later, Saudi Arabia has already invested heavily in the Egyptian-based Arab Organization for Industrialization (AOI), which produces many types of armaments. The principal benefits of the domestic effort would appear to be to increase assurance of responsive support to the larger armed forces after 2000 and to provide some diversification of the country's industrial potential.[102]

The emerging naval threat posed by Iran in the Persian Gulf is prodding the Saudis to pay greater attention to maritime security. Table 8 indicates a current program for increasing the number of deep water combatants by about 35 percent. Two of the frigates for which the Saudis have placed orders are French La Fayette class anti-aircraft ships. The $3.5 billion order includes base facility construction and training for 750 Saudi crewmen. The first of the 3,500 ton vessels is due to be delivered in 1999, while the other will follow by three years. The principal armament will be Crotale anti-aircraft missiles, Exocet anti-ship missiles and 20mm and 100mm guns.[103]

The Saudis have also shown interest in acquiring as many as three Canadian Halifax class anti-submarine warfare (ASW) frigates. Iran's purchase of Kilo class attack submarines has undoubtedly spurred the interest. If the proposal advances, the keel of the first of the 4,750 ton vessels could be laid in 1997 when the New Brunswick yard completes its current Canadian Government order.[104]

Another significant possible acquisition for the Saudi Navy for countering the Kilos is an ASW version of the British Merlin EH-101 helicopter. The aircraft has sufficient range to provide cover for most of the Persian Gulf from Saudi land bases.[105]

Not likely to affect the balance in this decade, but indicative of the depth of Saudi concern for the growing Iranian naval power, is Riyadh's interest in acquiring several U.S. Aegis class warships in the early 2000s. Aegis equipped cruisers and destroyers have multiple capabilities, including anti-surface ship and anti-submarine warfare, but most especially for detection and destruction of incoming anti-ship missiles. The systems are also effective against aircraft and some ballistic missiles, such as the Scud. Contracts for the vessels may be signed in 1998, with initial deliveries in 2002 or 2003. Costs might range from $900 million to $1 billion per ship.[106]

The depression of oil revenues beginning in 1993 caused the Saudi Government to reconsider its national expenditures for 1994. In January of that year the king slashed the budget by 20 percent and declared an intent to stretch out $20-$30 billion in arms payments to the U.S.. Under an agreement reached later that month Saudi Arabia would have limited the planned acquisition of F-15S aircraft to about twelve per year until the total of 72 was reached, rather than twenty-four per year in the original plan.[107] At the same time, the Saudis indicated that they were interested in a buy of 315 M1A2 main battle tanks by the year 2000, rather than 465 as had been previously mentioned.[108]

Upon more careful consideration of the matter, however, the Saudis realized that a delay of the F-15S fighter deliveries would actually exacerbate their funding problems as costs would escalate. Accordingly, in January 1995 they decided to proceed with the original delivery schedule, but to stretch out the programs for support equipment and training services. The result will likely be that the Saudi aircraft inventory will increase sharply up to 1998, but that the corresponding operational readiness will lag until sometime after 2000. A similar arrangement may be made for deliveries of additional M1A2 tanks. Saudi expenditures for U.S. military equipment climbed from $4.5 billion in 1994 to $5.5 billion in 1995.[109] An additional $4 billion is expected in 1996. However, no further military sales are anticipated to be made to the kingdom until the outstanding debt of approximately $14 billion is substantially reduced.[110]

It is not clear whether, or to what extent, Saudi Arabia may eventually support a significant U.S. force presence in the region. The Pentagon would like to preposition essential support equipment for five or six tactical fighter wings (some 400 aircraft) in the region, most of it in Saudi Arabia. In addition, it would like to preposition sufficient equipment for a complete armored division in the Gulf area. The U.S. has agreements with Kuwait and Qatar for a brigade set in each country, but has not achieved an understanding with Riyadh for similar space for the third brigade. In the wake of the June 1996 terrorist bombing of a U.S. housing area at Dhahran, of course, security will be a prominent consideration.

The U.S. Navy already deploys a carrier battle group to the region for 183 days per year, and may increase the duration to 270 days. The U.S. Air Force has been directed to deploy a team of fighters and support aircraft to the region when there is no carrier group nearby. If Saudi Arabia were to agree, the U.S. force presence could increase substantially. But the legitimacy of the Saudi Government rests largely on its guardianship of the Muslim holy shrines in Mecca and Medina. Some 2.5 million Muslims, including 1 million from abroad visit the holy sites during the Haj each year. A visible Western presence would do nothing to strengthen the stature of the regime — and could do much harm — in the eyes of the royal family's principal domestic constituency, the Bedouins and other conservative Islamic groups.[111]

A senior U.S. defense official assessing U.S.-Saudi cooperation may have been somewhat premature when he commented, "We now have the ability to give anybody pause [in attacking Kuwait or Saudi Arabia]."[112] The opening of the kingdom to real cooperative defense preparedness — and with it to Western influence and culture — is not likely to come easily. There may have to be some compromise and sub-optimization of prepositioning and training exercises to minimize political embarrassment to Riyadh. Undoubtedly, Defense Secretary William Perry was reminded of this in March 1995, when he presented recent U.S. intelligence regarding the rebuilding of Iraqi forces to Saudi leaders, only to receive vague promises of increased readiness of indigenous forces in return.[113]

The Saudi position should not have come as a great surprise. Cultural issues aside, the Saudis had been hinting at a softening toward Iraq as early as December 1994. Foreign Minister prince Saud Faisal told reporters at that time that he foresaw an end to Iraq's isolation by the time of the next Islamic summit in 1997. "It is clear," he said, "that the situation which arose as a result of the Iraqi invasion of Kuwait must end quickly...[so that] the suffering of the Iraqi people ends."[114]

If the country is to attain an adequate and reliable defense regime against either Iraq or Iran, it must achieve a balance of indigenous capabilities, reliance on U.S. reinforcement, and costs. An important matter yet to be addressed is the cost of U.S. deployments to the region in time of tension between the Arab monarchies and their neighbors. Such deployments in October 1994 cost about $600 million. Kuwait shouldered about 40 percent of the burden while Saudi Arabia paid $330 million, in spite of its tight financial position.[115]   While

Riyadh aspires to an indigenous deterrent and defense capability, it recognizes that such is not likely to be achieved before the end of the decade, if then. But even when (and if) such capability is reached, the need for U.S. forces is likely to remain to bring any conflict to a successful conclusion in a minimum period of time. The dependence of the modern world upon the steady flow of oil is too important to be left to chance.

TABLE 8

ANTICIPATED SAUDI ARMS ACQUISITIONS[116]

Mid 1995 Level Probable	On Order	Total by 2000	Goal
68 Tornado Jets	48	116	?
98 F-15C/D Jets	20	128	132
Few F-15S Jets	72	72	?
0 HAWK 1/200 Jets	60	60	?
12 AH-64 Atk Hel	12	24	48
10 Blk Hwk Hel	88	100	?
5 E-3A AWACS Aircraft	2	7	9
8 Patriot Batteries	13 Batteries	22 Batteries	26 Batteries
Some M1A2 Tanks	315	465	700-765
200 M2 Bradley IFV	300	500	?
1,700 Lt Armd Veh	1110	2810	?
8 Frigates	3	11	14-18
4 Cntr Mine Ships	1	5	11

IRAN

In many respects Iran is in a stronger strategic position than at any time since the fall of the Shah's regime in 1979. First, the collapse of the Soviet Union removed a major threat from the north and interposed weak, mostly Islamic states between Russia and Iran. Second, the 1991 Gulf War reduced the military threat from Iraq to manageable proportions — about half its previous stature. Third, Iran is well endowed with petroleum resources and has pressed ahead with exploitation of its natural wealth to develop both political and military leverage vis-à-vis it neighbors. Few expect the U.S. embargo on Iranian trade to have much effect on the country's economy. The lack of natural allies or political friends close by has nudged Iran along a path of self-help.[117]

On the other hand, the Iranian Government has had difficulty establishing its political bearings since the death of the Ayatollah Ruhollah Khomeini, founder of the Islamic state. However much moderate elements may wish to steer the nation toward a more relaxed relationship with the world community, no element has proven strong enough to break away from the self-limiting radical rhetoric. Following a series of riots in seven cities and an abortive plot to assassinate President Ali Akbar Hashemi Rafsanjani in early 1994, radical Islamic clerics moved to tighten their grip on the country at the expense of moderate elements. Mr. Rafsanjani, considered by some to represent the moderates' interest, was termed "increasingly irrelevant" by one Western expert, and his economic plan "all but shattered."[118] The voice of Tehran has continued to be largely the voice of volatile extremism.

In April 1995, during Rafsanjani's absence, Iran's radical commander-in-chief, Ayatollah Ali Khamenei, appointed a protege civilian to the post of military chief of staff, over the heads of the country's leading generals. Hassan Firouzabadi, with no previous known military rank, was appointed a major general with nine years seniority — four more than the leading contenders for the position. Firouzabadi's experience had been with the Basij Islamic volunteer force, raised during the 1980-88 war with Iraq. Significantly, it was the Basij that subdued riots in Qazvin in 1994 after the army garrison refused to fire on demonstrators. The civilian casualties were heavy, with 40 reported killed and ten times that figure injured.[119]

In spite of changes since the Gulf War, Iran has reason to fear the resurgent power of Iraq. Iran is in the grip of a substantial arms build-up, but as Kamal Kharrazi, the country's ambassador to the U.N., has pointed out, much of it may be justified as prudential measures against a reoccurrence of the beating the country took at the hand of Saddam Hussein in the 1980s.[120] Iran has largely complied with the U.N.-mandated isolation of Iraq; notably it has retained for its own use some 115 combat aircraft flown to the country during the Gulf War to escape destruction by the coalition. Russia is supplying replacement parts, ammunition and personnel training for many of these planes.[121]

Nevertheless, the government chooses to isolate itself from the peace process in the region. In December 1990, President Ali Rafsanjani called for the establishment of a pan-Islamic army for the annihilation of Israel.[122] A year later Dr. Robert Gates, then U.S. Director of Central Intelligence (DCI), identified Iran as a state "hostile to U.S. interests," and said that "Tehran is rebuilding its military strength not only to redress the military imbalance with Iraq, but also to increase its ability to influence and intimidate its gulf neighbors. ...Its clerical leadership has not abandoned the goal of one day leading the Islamic world and reversing the global dominance of Western culture and technology."[123] Dr. Gates' successor,

Mr. R. James Woolsey, speaking before the U.S. Senate in early 1994 sounded a similar chord. Iran, he said, continues its "ambitious multibillion-dollar military modernization program" and seeks to buy nuclear material and ballistic missiles.[124] The point was struck again in early 1995 by Lt. Gen. James Clapper, director of the Defense Intelligence Agency, when he suggested that Iran was seeking to become "the preeminent regional power" in the Gulf.[125]

Albeit tardily (7 months after the United Nations' arms register reporting deadline), Iran reported purchases of substantial quantities of equipment in 1993. These included 100 tanks, a warship, and 89 armored combat vehicles from Russia, and 25 combat aircraft and 106 130mm artillery pieces from China.[126] In early February 1994 the chief of the Iranian air staff, Brigadier General Mansoor Sattari, went on to boast that the Air Force had been rebuilt and expanded since its losses in the war with Iraq. He said that the arm had "reached self-sufficiency in all fields, including pilot training, missiles, radar, air defense, maintenance and repair, manufacture of parts, and basic repair of facilities."[127] Tehran underscored its resurging strength in June 1995 by mounting the largest military maneuvers since the 1980-88 war with Iraq. Reportedly, 450,000 troops took part. Live fire exercises took place over 400 square kilometers in the Neivana area south-west of Tehran. Brig. Gen. Harmoun Mohamadi, commander of a brigade of the Guards 16th Qods Division, said that the exercises were "a warning to the USA and the enemies of Islam."[128]

Iran experienced a rapid turn-around in its economic fortunes following the Gulf War. The nation's growth rate averaged over 9 percent in 1991 and 1992, thanks largely to large increases in oil production. In 1992 it became the world's second largest petroleum exporter, after Saudi Arabia, with earnings estimated at $13.5 billion.[129] But at the same time, foreign debt was increasing — to approximately $30 billion by the end of 1993[130] — influenced to some extent by falling oil prices, but also quite likely by its expenditures for foreign arms. By 1994, the growth rate had sunk to about 1 percent, but the government had also managed to reduce its debt by a third.[131]

Iran also appears interested in extending its influence among the former Islamic republics of the USSR. In May 1992, Iranian leaders convened a meeting of representatives of a number of the former Soviet republics to discuss construction of a 3,000-mile rail link extending from Bandar Abbas, on the Iranian gulf coast, northeastward to Alma Ata, in Kazakhstan. The route would transit Turkmenistan, Uzbekistan, and Kyrgyzstan. Observers noted that while all of the parties exhibited interest, their perspectives may be different. The republics are believed to be interested primarily in aid and trade, while Iranian motives may have more to do with becoming a pivotal power in a new bloc of Muslim nations capable of counter-balancing the Arab League.[132] The initial Turkmenistan-Iran link may be completed soon.[133]

In late 1994, Iran completed another accord with Turkmenistan to build a gas pipeline from the producing state, through Iran and Turkey, to the West. In the eyes of one senior Western diplomat, the agreement "could turn out to be the most significant geopolitical development in Central Asia since [Turkmenistan's] independence." Some observers believe that through such ties Iran is attempting to build a network of influence in the vital Central Asian region.[134]

Further, Iranian military personnel have been reported active in providing aid to Islamic forces in the former Soviet Union. An Iranian military mission, including four general officers, was reported engaged in training five Azeri battalions northeast of Baku in early 1994.[135]

Iranian personnel have also been active in Bosnia. A detachment of 350-400 Revolutionary Guardsmen arrived in the former Yugoslavia in May 1994 with a mission of organizing terrorist groups modeled on the Palestinian Hezbollah (Party of God) in Lebanon. According to intelligence reports, the group will also strive to establish networks of pro-Iranian cells in Bosnia to work toward breaking U.S.-imposed restrictions of trade on Iran.[136]

At sea, Iran seeks to gain control of the Strait of Hormuz. It has received 2 Kilo class attack submarines from Russia, and delivery of a third is imminent.[137] Tehran may have an objective of as many as 5 submarines for its navy.[138] Reportedly, the submarines will be based primarily at Chan Bahar, outside the Persian Gulf, where the deeper water may afford greater security. Iran already has some 9 to 18 CSS-N-2 Silkworm anti-ship missiles deployed on three coastal sites which, together with mines, could prove hazardous to shipping entering the Gulf.

In early 1994 it was reported that Iran was negotiating with China for the purchase of EM52 rocket-propelled mines, which can be laid at depths up to 110 meters. The greater depth of emplacement decreases the weapons' vulnerability to detection. When triggered by a passing ship, the mine activates, speeding the warhead in the direction of the target. As Vice Admiral Douglas Katz, commander of U.S. Naval Forces Central Command, remarked, "The biggest threat to the [Persian] Gulf [is] mines. They are the fastest way to clog up the Strait of Hormuz, which would have a major impact on the world [oil supplies]."[139]

U.S. Navy officials have also expressed concern over reports of an Iranian purchase of eight SS-N-22 "Sunburn" supersonic cruise missile from Ukraine. The weapon flies four times as fast as the better known French Exocet which

achieved notoriety in the Falklands War. The speed of the
Sunburn missile is so great that even without a warhead the
kinetic energy transmitted can break a ship in half. Like the
Silkworms, the Sunburns are believed to be emplaced near
Hormuz.[140] The Iranians are also believed to have some 60-
100 Chinese C-801 anti-ship missiles, with a range of 70 km.,
which can be fired from coastal sites, ships or aircraft.[141] Some
of them might be found in such locales as Sirri Island, inside
the Gulf, near the oil terminal. The Iranians are reported to
have already based U.S.-supplied HAWK air defense missiles in
the vicinity.[142] They are also believed to have a total of 9
long-range surface-to-air (SAM) sites on the mainland and
islands in the Gulf. These are equipped with SA-5 and SA-6
missiles, as well as HAWKs.[143]

A number of these developments may be related to Iran's
1992 expulsion of Arab residents of Abu Musa Island, a key
joint UAE and Iranian territory just west of Hormuz, and the
conduct of extensive amphibious exercises in the area. The
week-long exercise "Victory-3," employing fighter-bombers,
destroyers, missile-launching frigates, and assault and antisub-
marine helicopters, in May 1992, depicted operations to prevent an opponent from entering the Gulf.[144] In 1993 the
Iranians held some 36 naval exercises of various sorts.[145] More
recently, in March 1995, Iran began exercising its submarines
in and around the Strait of Hormuz and the Gulf of Oman in
conjunction with aircraft and surface combat vessels. The
exercises were described as "tactical operations, sea war games,
communications techniques and enemy evaluation actions."
Western analysts interpreted the exercises as further preparation of Iranian capabilities for closing the strait. The submarines were reported to have test-fired advanced wake-hom-
ing and wire-guided torpedoes.[146] The former U.S. chief of
naval operations, Admiral Jeremy M. Boorda, remarked that,

"I am surprised how well they are doing in operating that sub."[147]   In May 1995 President Rafsanjani called to Iran's neighbors to join Iran in "stand[ing] up against the sinister [U.S.] plan of permanent military presence of foreign forces in the region."[148] The events bode ill for nations seeking to maintain unfettered passage through the strait in the future.

In early 1996 the Iranians demonstrated a capability for launching another shipboard missile, the Chinese-built C-802. According to Vice Admiral Scott Redd, the commander of U.S. naval forces in the region, the firing demonstration signified a "new dimension" to security considerations in the gulf.[149]   In February U.S. intelligence photographed five new Chinese *Hudong* fast attack patrol boats enroute to Iran. It is expected that the boats will be fitted with the 70-75 mile range C-802 missiles, as were five other *Kaman* class boats previously delivered. Iran is believed to have about 40 of the missiles.[150]

No less disturbing has been an agreement between Iran and Sudan for the use of naval facilities at Port Sudan on the Red Sea by Iranian fleet units. The agreement is alleged to be part of a joint effort to confront what the parties believe to be a "vicious Western assault" on Muslim fundamentalist regimes.[151]

Iran has also opened channels to New Delhi for strengthening its armed forces. President Rafsanjani led a group visiting India in April 1995, at which time he received assurances of Indian assistance in maintaining its Kilo class attack submarines. At the same time the Iranians asked their hosts to provide advanced models of T-72 main battle tanks and to upgrade their older T-55 tanks, to include replacement of the 100mm main guns with Indian-made 105mm high velocity weapons. New Delhi, which has developed a large, high- quality arms industry capable of producing many advanced Russian-designed weapons systems, has assured Tehran that it will provide all support necessary for maintenance of the estimated

$5 billion Iranian inventory of Russian-designed equipment.[152]

Estimates of Iranian defense spending vary widely. The DCI has stated that procurement of foreign weapons totaled $10 billion for the period 1990 to 1994. While some reports from Iranian emigre sources indicate that total defense spending reached as high as $19 billion in 1991 and that the figure for 1992 would be $14.5 billion, it seems unlikely that the figure exceeded $5-6 billion at any time. Expenditures in 1994 and 1995 are believed to have been about $2.5 billion.[153] Some analysts have suggested that Iranian expenditures for arms slipped badly in the mid-1990s, perhaps as low as $500-$800 million in 1995. Coupled with operational and other costs, these figures would indicate total military expenditures at mid-decade (exclusive of nuclear and other mass destruction weapons programs) at a little more than $1 billion — less than half of that estimated by the prestigious London-based International Institute for Strategic Studies.[154] The low figures seem improbable. Known purchases from Russia alone match them. In February 1996 the Ministry of Foreign Trade in Moscow confirmed that Russian sales of military goods to Iran in recent years had averaged $500 million per year and that projections for the next two years totaled $1 billion. Total Iranian arms purchases from all sources may double or triple the Russian figures, not including domestic production. Sales over the next decade were placed at $4 billion.[155] Table 9 lists current reported arms procurement programs.

The supersonic "Backfire" bombers included on the list are particularly significant. They are part of a possible $11 billion sale of former Soviet equipment to Tehran. If the deal has or does materialize, the aircraft could provide Iran with a capability for striking ships in the Indian Ocean or any country within a 2,400 mile radius (unrefueled). Typical weapons loads for the Tu-22M are two AS-4 "Kitchen" air-to-surface missiles or 12-18 1,100 lb. gravity bombs. A low altitude attack approach to Israel would take no more than an hour at Mach .9 from bases in western Iran. High level flight might take less than half the time.[156]

Whether or not the Backfire sale is concluded, Iran's ability to strike at ever increasing ranges is a matter of great concern. In August 1995 Tehran announced development of in-flight refueling for its MiG-29 aircraft, describing the new capability as one of "multi-purpose offensive and strategic missions." There was no mention of applications for other fighters, but the long-range Su-24 "Fencers" would seem a logical choice.[157]

The North Korean-developed "Nodong 1" missile (a Scud derivative) is reported to have a range of 1,000-1,300 km, which could place Tel Aviv at risk from launching sites in western Iran.[158] The cogency of this type of threat was underscored in June 1995 when the CIA indicated that Iran had received important missile components and associated computerized machine tools from China which could substantially increase the accuracy of Tehran's long-range missiles.[159] The principal significance of this development from a regional perspective is to possibly convert the missiles from simple mechanisms for population terror to practical military weapons for destruction of selected targets.

Besides current foreign procurement, Iranian expansion of their arms production base is continuing apace. In 1991 it encompassed 240 state-owned plants, 12,000 privately owned workshops, and some 45,000 workers. The number of persons employed is expected to expand to 60,000 by the end of the decade. Iran is self-sufficient in ammunition of all calibers, and is known to manufacture remotely piloted aircraft and spare parts for helicopters, tanks, artillery, and surface-to-air missiles. Tehran claims to seek self-sufficiency in the production of main battle tanks, ballistic missiles, and some types of aircraft by the year 2000. Indeed, in April 1994 Tehran announced completion of its first domestically produced main battle tank, dubbed "*Zulfiqar*," from the legendary sword of the historical Muslim hero Ali. The vehicle reportedly took two and a half years to build, although some Western analysts believe that it may be little more than a reengineered Russian T-72.[160] Later reports indicated that both the new tank and an indigenously built armored personnel carrier were being delivered to troops.[161]

Iran also appears to have developed an upgrade package for tanks captured from Iraq during the 1980-1988 Gulf War. The rebuilt T-54s (and, presumably, T-55s) were reported to have greater motive power, firepower and target acquisition capability. In addition, the accuracy of the main gun and the armor are being enhanced. According to Maj. Gen. Mohsen Rezaie, commander of the 120,000 man Islamic Revolutionary Guard Corps, all components used in the upgraded vehicles — dubbed "*Safir*" (Messenger) 74 — are being manufactured in Iran.[162]

Iranian innovation should not be underestimated. In February 1995 it was reported that, short of air-to-air missiles, the Iranians had taken to mounting HAWK surface-to-air missiles on its F-14 Tomcat jet fighters for use in engaging other aircraft.[163] And in October 1995 Ayatollah Ali Khameni, the commander-in-chief of Iranian forces, boasted that Iran was producing advanced electronic warfare equipment.[164] In the meanwhile, China has offered to provide Iran with assembly plants for production of F-6 and F-7 jet fighters and surface-to-surface missiles.[165]

Some idea of Iranian aspirations in the armaments field was revealed at the Dubai international arms exhibition in January

1992. Of 26 national participants, Iran had the largest display. Systems offered for sale included long-range missiles, pilotless aircraft and armed speed boats. Also offered were contracts for the maintenance of older models of U.S. jet fighter aircraft.[166] The Iranian R&D effort includes development of a 1,000 km range version of the Chinese M-11 intermediate range missile, named "*Tondar* 68." Also, the Iranians have been working with North Korea to develop a two-stage weapon, dubbed "*Nodong-2*," capable of carrying a 1,750 lb. warhead (conventional, chemical, or nuclear) probably to even a greater range. Either the Tondar 68 or the Nodong-2 might be able to place Jerusalem at risk from a firing site on the extreme western edge of Iranian territory.[167]

Iran probably has active programs for the development of weapons of mass destruction in all major fields. President Rafsanjani stated in 1988, "We must fully equip ourselves with defensive and offensive chemical, biological and radioactive weapons."[168] Iran demonstrated a chemical warfare capability during the war with Iraq, and in March 1995 Secretary William Perry announced that the country had stocked 155mm artillery chemical munitions on the disputed islands in the Gulf.[169] Reportedly, Iran has "large stockpiles of lethal and non-lethal chemical agents and has significant facilities for production of mustard gas, phosgene gas, blood agents and even possibly nerve agents." Its forces are believed to train for chemical warfare and to have ample delivery systems. Tehran's biological warfare capability is also believed to be "quite substantial," but few details are available.[170]

Iran is currently conducting nuclear research at Qazvin and Isfahan, and is constructing a fuel enrichment facilities at Darkhovin and Karaj. In 1992 it concluded a contract with France for delivery of enriched uranium ordered prior to the Islamic revolution.[171] But more disturbing was the announcement in February 1995 that Russia might deliver as many as four nuclear reactors to Iran, worth about $1 billion. The first would be of water-pressurized design with a capacity of 1,000 megawatts, to be located at Bushehr on the Gulf. Expressions of concern from Washington over possible Iranian diversion of nuclear material for weapons applications caused Moscow to withdraw gas centrifuges, storage silos and related separation equipment from the deal, but the major items are not likely to be affected.[172]

Also in 1995 it was reported that Beijing had dispatched a group of nuclear experts to Iran in connection with delivery and installation of a calutron system at Karaj, 100 miles northwest of Tehran. The equipment is designed for enriching uranium to weapons grade material. Allegedly, the London Sunday Telegraph obtained copies of a secret report to President Rafsanjani detailing work being accomplished by the Chinese to assist Iran in its bomb project. The report also gave credit to Russian scientists in assisting in the building of a nuclear arsenal.[173] Shortly thereafter, there was a series of contradictory announcements regarding the sale of two 300 megawatt pressurized water reactors to Iran by China. But not only was the status of the reactor sale unclear; the matter raised questions about the calutron deal as well.[174] (See Figure 2 for a map of principal installations related to Iran's nuclear program.)

In early 1992 an Italian judge announced discovery of international smuggling operations transferring weapons grade uranium and plutonium, and even complete nuclear weapons, out of former Soviet republics. Allegedly, the materials were going to high bidders in the Middle East. Other reports indicated that three nuclear weapons, ranging in yield from 2 to 5 kilotons, were missing from a depot at Semipalatinsk, Kazakhstan. At least two of the weapons were

FIGURE 2

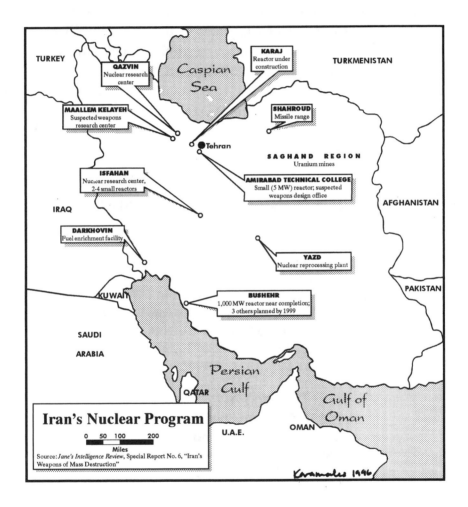

Iran's Nuclear Program

believed to have reached Iran in 1991. They were presumed to be nuclear artillery shells, which would not be too difficult to move. Suspicions existed that high Kazakh officials were involved in the transfer. The CIA reportedly investigated the matter, but was unable to substantiate the allegations.[175]

Whatever the truth of that matter, the U.S. intelligence Community has issued a range of estimates regarding Iran's ability to produce a weapon of its own manufacture before 2000. While Tehran is believed to be spending $1.5 billion per year on its nuclear program, most analysts expect that it will take the Iranians at least five years to produce a domestically built weapon.[176]

TABLE 9
ANTICIPATED IRANIAN ARMS ACQUISITIONS[177]

72 F-7 fighter aircraft
68 MiG-29 fighter aircraft
25 Su-24 fighter aircraft
? Su-27 fighter aircraft
24 MiG-27 fighter aircraft
24 MiG-31 fighter aircraft
12 Tu-22M "Backfire" bombers
2 Il-76 "Mainstay" AWACS aircraft

400-500 T-72 tanks
170 Scud Missiles (B and C)
150 N Korean "Nodong 1" missiles
Air Defense Missiles including:
SA-5 "Gammon"
SA-11 "Gadfly"
SA-13 "Gopher"

Up to 5 Kilo Class Submarines

IRAQ

Most Western analyses of Iraqi motivations deal with Baghdad's aspirations rather than its fears. However, a sizable sector of the Iraqi populace views Saddam Hussein as a man desirous of raising Arab national consciousness and of leading the people to a destiny — their birthright — beyond the influence of Western "neo-imperialism." His confrontations with U.N. officials visiting Baghdad in the wake of the Gulf War have been explained as gestures to remind the Arab people that he is still in command and unbowed, if somewhat bloodied for his efforts.[178]

It is not clear to what extent the Iraqi leadership has been dissuaded from its aspiration of recovering the "lost province" of Kuwait. Baghdad has recognized the existence of the Kuwaiti state, but that seems a thin reed upon which to rely for responsible Iraqi behavior, given its record. On the other hand, it is reasonable to assume that there are some genuine concerns in Baghdad over the country's security situation. First might be the threat of domination by the West or by Arab groups serving Western interests. Certainly Iraq is concerned with the U.N. mandated restrictions on its foreign trade and on its access to Kurdish territory in the northern part of the country. Second might be a fear of becoming a dependency of the same parties. Third, Baghdad must entertain latent concerns over the hostile Syrian neighbor to the west, and a possibly revanchist Iran to the east. To these worries we might add the threat of revisitation of the air offensive inflicted on the country in 1991 by coalition forces. Iraqi leaders have been careful to avoid unnecessarily precipitating another such attack. After lengthy stalling, they largely met U.N. minimal demands for cooperation in locating and destroying nuclear research and manufacturing facilities and missile weapons. They also restrained their forces from attacks on Kurdish minority groups, and more especially, from invading Kuwait anew in October 1994.

The former assistant secretary of defense for international security affairs, Joseph Nye, expressed the view that it was probably Saddam Hussein's plan in October to create an incident inside Kuwait between stateless Bedouin tribesmen and the Kuwaiti security forces. Once a "cause" had been established, he said, Iraqi troops would have been sent in to reestablish order. The Iraqi plan, Nye supposed, did not take into account the likelihood of a rapid U.S. response. "I think Saddam expected a lot of dithering and waiting around," he said. "We were able, in a matter of days, to present him with quite a credible response.[179]

This capability was tested again in August 1995 when U.S. forces were ordered back to Kuwait and to Jordan to deter possible Iraqi aggression. Two of Saddam Hussein's sons-in- law had defected to Amman with stories of the dictator's plans to again invade Kuwait and Saudi Arabia. U.S. intelligence had noted some significant movements of Iraqi troops toward the southern part of the country, adding credence to the stories.[180] It appears that Iraqi ambitions for military expansion have not been curtailed. However, American readiness to counter military moves southward may cause Baghdad to at least delay further action until it can free itself of U.N. imposed sanctions and again acquire the weaponry and technology it requires. Ambitious strategy clearly cannot be fulfilled on a shoestring.

In the opinion of the Mr. Robert Gates, speaking as DCI, Iraq probably still has a couple hundred Scud missiles hidden in the country. In addition, there are reports that Iraq has taken advantage of its relationship with Jordan to sequester certain key materiel in that country and possibly to transship some to Sudan. These may include Scud missiles and nuclear

materials.[181] Failing that, Gates estimated that it would take
Iraq several years to restart its nuclear weapons program after
the removal of international controls. Iraq's ability to pose
either a chemical or bateriological threat might occur much
sooner.[182] In February 1994 Israeli Kenesset Member Ephraim
Sneh lent credence to the chemical estimate when he reported
to the Israeli legislature that a shipment of some 35 tons of
ammonium perchlorate, used in the manufacture of chemical
weapons, had been seized in Jidda, Saudi Arabia. The material was aboard a German vessel bound for Beirut. Allegedly, the
shipment was to be transported overland to Iraq.[183]

However, some analysts believe that Iraq could have a rudimentary nuclear device in much less time than Dr. Gates suggested. Michael Eisenstadt, of the Washington Institute for
Near East Policy, has pointed out that Iraq has already been
implicated in efforts to obtain fissile material from the former
Soviet Union. The threat of Iraqi success in this endeavor, of
course, will increase sharply if and when the sanctions are
removed. Iraq has not disbanded the team of nuclear scientists
previously working on its clandestine program. As a consequence, some officials believe that the time required for Iraq to
produce a truck-transportable nuclear device might be as little
as three to six months after all U.N. controls are lifted.[184]

Iraq emerged from the 1991 war with substantial quantities
of military equipment intact. It still has more combat aircraft
and tanks than Iran, and probably almost as much artillery; and
significant reconstruction has taken place at artillery and
ammunition plants.[185] The U.S. Air Force has reported that
Iraq has sharply increased the number of air fields in the country, as well as command and control facilities and SAM and
Scud missile sites. The reconstruction of the principal Defense
Ministry building was reported in 1994. More recently, the

missile research and development facility at Al Kindi has been reported not only rebuilt, but substantially expanded.[186]

Of particular importance may be reports of Iraqi acquisition of blueprints of the latest uranium enrichment centrifuge, code named TC-11. Officials at The International Atomic Energy Agency believe the blueprints have been hidden for use in a revived nuclear weapons program once international trade sanctions are lifted.[187]

The Iraqi military establishment is outclassed in the region only by those of Israel, Syria and Egypt. Further, Iraq probably has sufficient manufacturing capability and expertise to maintain its forces for some time, but inevitably the forces will degrade as they are denied critical replacement parts. Some analysts believe that the real strength of Iraqi forces is substantially less than their current force structure would indicate. One estimate places the effective combat power of the forces, for example, at about one third of that indicated by official strength figures. The explanation lies in the degrading impact of equipment spare parts and total lack of modernization since 1991.[188]

Barring a radical change of government, and unless closely monitored restrictions are maintained upon Iraq indefinitely, one should expect that the time will come when Iraq will move rapidly to recover much of its former military prowess. In the opinion of General Joseph Hoar, speaking as commander-in-chief, U.S. Central Command, it would take Iraq some eight or nine years from the time that the restrictions were removed to match its former might.[189] This would place the date sometime in the year 2005 or 2006 if the Saudi foreign minister, Prince Saud Faisal, is correct. The prince is reported to have voiced the expectation that Iraq's isolation would end by the time of the next Islamic summit in 1997.[190]

Madeleine K. Albright, U.S. delegate to the United Nations, has suggested that some important dimensions of the Iraqi threat might be reconstituted much more quickly. If Iraq could obtain large quantities of money from the sale of oil, she argued, and if there were no international inspectors on the ground, Baghdad would be able to resume full-scale chemical weapons production within two years and ballistic missile production within one year. There is wide belief that Iraq has retained a number of Scud missiles — perhaps in excess of 100 — and some 10-12 launch vehicles. It has also managed to continue to acquire sophisticated missile components, specialty metals and machine tools for missile fabrication from abroad in violation of the U.N.-imposed trade ban. Analysts estimate that much of Iraq's equipment could be made ready for employment in a matter of hours — days at the most — once it was ordered returned to service.[191]

The cogency of this situation was underscored by U.N. representative Rolf Ekeus in August 1995 when he revealed that Iraq has managed to conceal enormous stores of biological agents in weaponized form from Western eyes. He reported that Iraqi officials had admitted to him producing 130,000 gallons of botulun, a deadly toxin, and over 13,000 gallons of anthrax bacteria.[192]

Six months later Mr. Ekeus suggested to the U.N. Security Council in a closed-door session that there was a possibility that Saddam Hussein was seeking to modify his Al-Hussein missile to reach selected European capitals. Members of the special commission for investigation of the Iraqi missile program reportedly found new gyroscopes which might be used in missiles with ranges up to 1,200 miles. In the opinion of some inspectors, the Iraqis could be seeking ranges up to 2,000 miles. U.S. intelligence officials are skeptical of the reports, but concede the possibility of rudimentary efforts in the field.[193]

Some of the conventional military equipment captured by the Iraqis in Kuwait in 1990 has already been issued to troop units. Photographs indicate that Russian-made FROG-7 rocket launchers and hundreds of BMP-2 armored vehicles seized in Kuwait, for example, were assigned to the elite al-Nida Republican Guard unit when it was deployed near the Kuwaiti border in October 1994.[194]

The total booty believed to be in Iraqi hands amounts to some 9,000 pieces of military equipment, plus other non- military items, including 27 busses, 100 Mercedes trucks and 60 forklifts. Among the most notable military pieces are shown on Table 10 below.

TABLE 10

CAPTURED KUWAITI MILITARY EQUIPMENT IN THE HANDS OF IRAQI FORCES[195]

15 FROG Missile Launchers
120 FROG Missiles

206-215 BMP-2 Armored Infantry Fighting Vehicles
55-58 M113 Armored Personnel Carriers
(possibly with mounted anti-tank launchers)
18 155mm M-109A2 Self Propelled Artillery Pieces

3000-4000 TOW Anti-Tank Missiles
3 Portable Air Defense Systems
"Thousands" of Military Trucks

Whatever the condition of Iraqi forces, their ultimate reconstitution could prove to be more qualitative than quantitative. The former Iraqi defense minister, Maj Gen Ali Hassan Al-Najid, has denied any intention to rebuild the armed forces to their previous levels. He told Baghdad's Al-Thawra newspaper in January 1992:

> [The government decided to build] a small, but powerful, well-maintained and effective army. We have turned a page in determining the size of the army. ...Iraq needs a strong, though small, army to fulfill two roles. One at the Arab level and to be used in response to an Arab resolution, and one at national level to protect Iraq's borders, especially following the abuses which occurred after the Gulf conflict.[196]

It would seem from these remarks that Baghdad has learned from the Gulf War experience the value of quality in force development in comparison with quantity. Quantity may still be of value in internal security operations, but high technology quality is clearly in the ascendancy on the conventional battlefield. If General Al-Najid was reporting government views accurately, we may expect a very different distribution of military investment in Baghdad when (and if) import restrictions are lifted.

In the final analysis, the principal determinant of Iraqi policy and behavior will be the survival of the regime itself. Increasingly, analysts are detecting internal weaknesses and contradictions which encourage speculation regarding Saddam Hussein's ability to hold the country to his rigid historic blueprint. While there is little effective opposition, reports of successive attempted coups, purges, and executions of high ranking officials reflect the tenuous nature of the regime.

To mention only recent events, we should note the sacking

of the prime minister in May 1994. Saddam Hussein apparently wanted to redistribute cabinet posts to members of his own family and other members of his Takriti tribe. This was followed a month later by the arrest and execution of three top-ranking officers and purge of a dozen others for reportedly no greater crime than replying negatively when asked whether Hussein's son, Uday, should be appointed defense minister.[197]

In October, three senior intelligence officers, including one general, were executed on charges of corruption. At about the same time a number of medical officers in Baghdad, Basra and Kirkouk were executed for refusing to cut the ears of army deserters.[198] The international organization, Human Rights Watch, reported in June 1995 that some 1,700 youths had had their ears amputated and foreheads branded for desertion since the promulgation of a set of fundamentalist Islamic laws a year before.[199]

March 1995 was the month of a wave of rumors regarding a possible attempted coup and attempted assassination of the defense minister. At the time, Baghdad was hard pressed to deal with dissident groups in the both the Kurdish north and the Shiite south. The pressures may have contributed to the rumors of impending disaster.[200] In April Saddam sacked his chief of staff.[201] Two months later further stories of rebellion emerged, dealing with rioting in the town of Ramadi, 40 miles west of Baghdad.[202]

While the sources of some of the information are suspect, the reports are indicative of the atmosphere of instability surrounding the government. As one analyst has written, "The economic and security situation inside Iraq is deteriorating daily. ...The armed clashes that erupted in the south in February and in the north during March may indicate a sense of desperation on Saddam's part."[203] Certainly, the defection of members of Saddam's immediate family in August must have seriously wounded the leadership and undermined its credibility.

But Saddam is a survivor. The point is not necessarily that he is about to be forcibly removed from power, but that almost anything is possible and that change could occur quickly and in a unpredictable direction at any time in Iraq.

THE POWDER KEG

CHAPTER III
The Minor States

The minor states addressed in this assessment include Jordan, Lebanon, Kuwait, Bahrain, Qatar, the United Arab Emirates (UAE), Oman and Yemen. The first two are notable for their historic exposure to Western culture and their roles in the Arab-Israeli conflict. The next five, all members (with Saudi Arabia) of the Gulf Cooperation Council (GCC), enjoy relatively high per capita incomes — most exceeding the average of the major states. Lebanon and Yemen, ruined by years of internal strife, and Jordan, depressed as the result of its "misunderstood" policies in the 1991 Gulf War, can be considered impoverished.

This chapter makes the same sort of strategic appraisal of these states as the previous chapter did of their more powerful neighbors. The royal houses of the Persian Gulf are treated as a group in the GCC.

JORDAN
While neither the largest, the wealthiest nor the most powerful of the minor states of the Middle East, Jordan has borne the burdens of a land with high strategic value because of its location next to Israel. So important was it in Tel Aviv's eyes during Israel's formulative period that any indication that Jordan was mobilizing, even its modest forces, or any hint that anoth-

er Arab state might use it as a passage for shifting forces on Israel's flank, was a *casus belli*.[1]

Jordan's security situation deteriorated in the wake of the Gulf War because of its support for Iraq. In addition to a hostile Israel and a suspicious Syria on two of its borders, it was obliged to consider another potential adversary, Saudi Arabia, which appeared both suspicious and hostile. In the words of a high ranking Jordanian military official, threats to Jordan's security in late 1991 originated from "360 degrees of the compass."[2]

The Jordanian leadership insisted that its position during the Gulf War was badly misunderstood abroad. Jordan, senior officers argued, was not in sympathy with the Iraqi occupation of Kuwait, but had hoped, as a friend of both parties, that it could broker a settlement of the dispute which would avoid war and achieve the greatest good for the people of the region. Jordan has a large Palestinian population, the officers said, and therefore has a special domestic constituency to speak for. The government has always taken pride in representing the people, as well as ruling them, hence, the voice of Amman was heard to echo some of the more seductive notes of messianic appeal struck by Saddam Hussein.[3]

But it was not only Amman's rhetoric which irritated the members of the anti-Iraqi coalition. No less disturbing were reports of Jordanian military cooperation with Iraq. While U.S. government officials were less than specific in accusations of transshipments of American military aid materiel through Jordan to Iraq, the issue tended to sour relationships.[4]

The Saudi and Kuwaiti regimes, of course, were particularly displeased with Amman's attitude. While the Saudi Government never officially threatened retaliation against Jordan, King Hussein essentially confirmed perceptions of threat from the east when he refused to answer media queries

regarding Saudi efforts to destabilize his government.   In
March 1992, he sought to undo some of the damage done by
announcing that his country would cooperate in the economic
sanctions program mandated against Iraq by the U.N. Security
Council. The program imposed severe burdens on Jordan inasmuch as it was Iraq's most important trading partner before the
Gulf War. However, the recovery of the good graces of the
both the Gulf monarchies and the United States had become
important elements of Jordan's national strategy.

King Hussein surprised the international community in
1994 by concluding a treaty of peace with Israel. It was a surprise because few observers had anticipated that the king
would risk antagonizing the Assad government in Syria.
However, the move also had a number of important benefits. It
fulfilled the king's objective of pleasing the U.S. Government,
and raised the possibility that economic aid from that quarter
might be reinstituted. Secondly, it bestowed upon Israel an
interest in the maintenance of stability and security in the
Hashemite Kingdom. Before that, the Israeli Likud Party,
while in power, had considered Jordan as "the Palestinian
state," into which many of the inhabitants of the occupied territories could be displaced in order to facilitate the development of additional Jewish settlements on the occupied West
Bank.[5]

The prime (and defense) minister of Jordan in 1994, Abdel
Salam Majali, identified Israel as the primary threat to the
country, but he made it clear that he was not speaking in conventional military terms. Israel, he said, "has pushed all these
[Palestinian] and displaced people on us. Syria, Iraq or Saudi
Arabia never did that." Majali painted the Israeli threat
almost exclusively in terms of the erosive impact of its policies
on Jordanian stability.[6]   After the conclusion of the peace
treaty, the king, together with Crown Prince Hassan, met with

Likud leaders to emphasize that Israel could no longer expect to pressure Palestinians to abandon their homes and move across the Jordan River if it expected or desired the monarchy in Amman to survive.[7]

Much to the king's disappointment, there was little response from the United States to Jordanian appeals for economic or foreign military assistance (FMA). U.S. FMA and training funds, which had been trickling in between $9 million to $17 million per year from 1993 to 1995, was increased to $30 in 1996, but that represented a small fraction of the kingdom's needs. Some of the money was earmarked for border surveillance equipment; most of the rest was for spare parts for TOW missiles, M60-A3 tanks, and F-5 and C-130 aircraft. As Field Marshal Fathi Abu Taleb, chairman of Royal Jordanian Joint Chiefs of Staff, pointed out before his retirement, the amount could do little to ensure the maintenance of the bulk of Jordan's U.S. origin equipment. The cost of maintaining the full inventory runs at about $170 million per year.[8] Hard pressed for internally derived funds, the government sliced the military budget to $411 million in 1994, the lowest level in modern memory.[9]

King Hussein had been led to expect that the peace treaty would open the gates to large stocks of excess U.S. military equipment and to substantial sums of money for military and economic assistance. Reportedly, President Reagan had promised as much as $1 billion annually in economic and military support, but the matter had been kept secret to avoid Israeli counteraction in the U.S. Congress.[10] In late 1994 the Pentagon developed aid packages ranging from $250 million to $2.5 billion for Jordan, further whetting Amman's appetite. King Hussein spoke of troop and mission requirements for 36 to 72 F-16 fighter aircraft and more than 200 M1A2 main battle tanks.[11] The best that could be accomplished by early 1996 was a promise of 16 used F-16A/B fighters and 50 M60A3 tanks.[12]

While the issue remains open, there has been no rush within the U.S. Government to respond to the appeal. Other than some reassuring words, such as Vice President Al Gore's, "We will continue the defense needs dialogue with Jordan, and we will help Jordan meet its needs...," there was little evidence of interest in Washington.[13]

Because of the cogency of its economic predicament, Jordan has been unable to purchase new equipment for its forces for 15 years. The Jordanian leadership had hoped to be able to persuade government officials in the United States that Jordan's forces could be useful, not only for insuring the country's internal security, but also in cases of crisis in the area of the Persian Gulf. Jordanian military leaders had been looking beyond the peace treaty to possible new roles for their forces. Thought was being given to the creation of a rapid deployment corps capable of operations at distances beyond the borders of the kingdom. A number of American analysts agreed that Jordan could make a valuable contribution to regional security, but most emphasized the need for maintaining good forces at home where the stability of the country will likely be important to the new regional regime for peace. Many believe that the stability of the large Palestinian population, both in Jordan and on the West Bank, may be best guaranteed by a steady hand in Amman.[14]

General Abd Al-Hafez Marei, chief of the Jordanian General Staff, expressed the hope that the United States would look to Jordanian forces for future contributions to regional peace the same way it does to those of Egypt and Israel. Rather than posing a threat to Israel, he said, new Jordanian military power would be a regional asset. He went on to say that the forces should be equipped with new mobile air defense missiles; modern jet fighters, such as the F-16 and

F/A-18; both troop lift and attack helicopters; and new ground vehicles, communications systems, and night vision devices. In addition, he pointed out, there remains a critical need for large quantities of spare parts to bring the existing equipment of the forces up to serviceable standards.[15]

Other elements of Jordanian strategy for surviving its period of economic hardship include reorganization and further reductions of the armed forces well below the 98,000 level, the postponement of modernization plans, and the sale of excess equipment. Table 11 summarizes the principal points in this effort.

TABLE 11

AUSTERITY MEASURES INSTITUTED IN THE JORDANIAN ARMED FORCES[16]

1. Reduction of forces to below 98,000 men and conversion to an all-volunteer force.

2. Reorganization of the principal ground forces combat structure from two armored and two mechanized divisions to one armored and one mechanized division and a light strategic reserve division suitable for border patrol and other duties.

3. Postponement of a scheduled upgrade of Phase II HAWK SAM to Phase III.

4. Selling or scrapping all tanks older than the U.S. M60-A3 (1/3-1/2 of the tank fleet).

5. Selling a number of F-5 fighter aircraft.

6. Cancellation of an order for 12 Mirage 2000 fighters and of British Tornado aircraft.

7. Curtailment of training programs by one third.

Some of the savings realized from these measures are expected to contribute to an upgrading of the remaining equipment, particularly the U.S. F-5 and French F-1 aircraft in service.[17]

On the other hand, Jordan's appeal for assistance from the United States and other suppliers and its argument for the reestablishment of its forces as an instrument of stability in a chronically unstable region of the world could find support in the waning years of the century. The abiding Iraqi military threat to the region and Jordan's recent estrangement from Baghdad could fuel such a move. If that were to occur, the kingdom could have a respectable force at its disposal — or at least under development — by the year 2000. Table 12 presents a possible profile of a Jordanian "high option."

TABLE 12

JORDANIAN HIGH OPTION
ACTIVE FORCE STRUCTURE 2000[18]

Ground Forces
85,000 troops,

Organization:
1 Armored Division
2 Mech Divisions
1 Royal Guards Division
1 Border Guard Division
1 Light Mobile Strategic Reserve Division

(Continued Next Page)

**Jordanian High Option Active Force Structure 2000
(Continued)**

Principal Ground Weapons:
Tanks: 700 (M1A1/A2, M60A3)
AIFV: 1000 (M2 Bradley, BMP-2)
Artillery: 400 (2/3 SP)
ATGW: 300 (TOW-2)
SAM: 10 Batteries (Improved HAWK, Patriot)

Air Forces
10,000 personnel
80 Combat Aircraft, 48 Armed Helicopters

Organization:
5 Combat Squadrons (F-16, F-5 upgrade)
4 Atk Helo Squadrons (AH-64A)

This is highly dependent upon the U.S. internal political climate, however, as well as upon Jordanian assessment of continued military threats in the region and its foreign policy. Nevertheless, it is not unreasonable to expect that there will be some movement toward the development of Jordanian forces along the lines outlined here by the end of the decade.

LEBANON
The militias of Lebanon, which stalked and scarred the country so badly in the 1970s and '80s with inter-communal wars, have largely been abandoned, with their equipment turned over to the national army. The army, with some 50,000 soldiers and 330 tanks, nominally constitutes the principal gov-

ernment instrument for the security of the state. However, it plays little role in shaping the destiny of the land. In this respect, even within its own borders, it is outclassed by forces belonging to, or controlled by, Syria, Iran and Israel. Typical of Iran's role was an attempt to smuggle three truck loads of arms through Turkey to Lebanon in early 1996. The lot included mortars, rocket launchers and large quantities of ammunition.[19]

Between 1993 and 1995 the U.S. made significant deliveries of war materiel in an effort to bolster the country's indigenous defense capabilities. These included more than 800 M113 armored personnel carriers, 16 UH-1 helicopters, hundreds of utility trucks and spare parts for the Lebanese M-48 tank fleet. An additional shipment of 16 UH-1s was expected to be delivered in the first half of 1996. Nevertheless, for practical purposes, Lebanon remains a ward of Damascus. Syrian troops are deployed over two-thirds of the country. The Taif agreement of 1989, which called for a Syrian withdrawal to the Bekaa Valley two years later, is virtually a dead letter. Damascus' military contingent in Lebanon numbers about 40,000 troops, including four armored and mechanized brigades, with supporting artillery and special forces units.[20]

Also deployed in the southern part of the country are some 3,000 Iranian-supported Hezbullah guerrillas and an equal number of the Israeli-supported "South Lebanon Army" (SLA), backed by about 1,000 Israeli soldiers.[21] These forces are engaged in sporadic warfare, to the dismay of both the government and the inhabitants. Occasionally Israel has mounted large scale offensives north of the area, allegedly in reprisal for guerrilla attacks on the SLA, on border settlements in Israel, or other Israeli facilities at home or abroad. For a while there seemed to be a general understanding that attacks on densely inhabited areas in Lebanon were to be avoided, but in 1996 such restraints were abandoned, possibly in connection with Israeli domestic political pressures.[22]

While Syria's territorial ambitions in Lebanon may be somewhat ambiguous, Israel makes no permanent claims. Prime Minister Rabin provided assurances that if the Hezbullah were to disband, the Israelis would withdraw. He insisted, however, that the Lebanese Army would have to absorb the SLA into its ranks, with the SLA continuing to carry responsibility for the security of the border area. But the Hezbollah shows no signs of disbanding. In fact, some observers detect increasing signs of effectiveness among the guerrillas — with better training and better equipment. Reportedly, the new organization's effectiveness has obliged the Israelis to abandon some frontier posts and to replace SLA guards with Israeli soldiers at others. And it may have had an effect on something else.

In April 1995 the Israeli Navy began patrolling the Lebanese coast, firing at Lebanese fishing boats venturing more than a half mile from shore. While no official explanation was given, sources in Lebanon speculate that the intent was to signal Syria that Israel was not about to be ousted from Lebanon by Hezbollah guerrillas. The reasoning went that the Israelis saw the Lebanese Government as serving the interests of Damascus and wished "to cause [it] some inconvenience and loss of revenue" to emphasize their displeasure.[23] An even more aggressive naval patrol program was initiated in April 1996 as part of the general Israeli anti-Hezbollah campaign, to include shelling of the shoreline.

Just as it is difficult to determine the effective role of the Lebanese Army, it is difficult to describe the government's national objectives and strategy. Many assume that the government may be simply biding its time, husbanding its resources, and waiting for the foreigners to go away. There was a day when Beirut was the "Switzerland of the Middle East," and it would not be unreasonable to anticipate that similar days could yet lie ahead for the city — a city with its great American University, its entrepreneurial spirit, and its agreeable climate.

The great shoe waiting to drop, of course, is the Israeli-Syrian peace accord. If that were to occur before the end of the century, all things great and small would be possible — both favorable and unfavorable. The presumed departure of Syrian and Israeli troops might give the Lebanese Army a fresh mission and raison d'être. On the other hand, depending upon Iran's inclination at the time, it could ignite a fresh round of struggle between Israel and the Hezbollah. Because of the many uncertainties in this area, and, to an extent, upon the limited scale of military consequence, it does not appear either particularly practical or worthwhile to hazard an estimate of the likely changes in the balance of power with respect to Lebanon by 2000.

THE SMALL STATES OF THE GULF COOPERATION COUNCIL

Saudi Arabia, discussed in the previous chapter, is clearly the largest and most powerful of the six-nation Gulf Cooperation Council (GCC).[24] But while small, some of its partners are developing military forces worthy of note. We shall examine them here.

Formed in 1981 from the shock wave of the Iran-Iraq War, the GCC has provided a minimal forum for coordination of defense matters. Proposals for substantial efforts, such as that forwarded by Sultan Qaboos of Oman, suggesting that the group form a 100,000 man defense force, have come to little. The organization has been troubled by territorial and other disputes among the members, and questions have arisen regarding the ability of the members to provide sufficient personnel capable of operation and maintenance of high technology equipment. Moreover, the Saudis have harbored doubts regarding command and control of a truly international force and are not enthusiastic about the stationing of foreign troops on their territory. Instead, they would prefer to strengthen the Saudi led GCC "Peninsula Shield" force of less than 10,000 men.[25] In January 1994 the GCC issued a joint communique at the completion of a heads-of-state summit meeting expressing a desire to substantially strengthen the common defense. Particular measures announced included the expansion of the "Peninsula Shield" force to 25,000 troops, and the expenditure of some $5 billion for the purchase of three or four AWACS aircraft. The aircraft would supplement the operations of five such machines currently operated by the Royal Saudi Air Force.[26]

Whatever may come of the specific proposals, the likelihood of much closer cooperation among the partners in the near time frame is not high. There are too many outstanding disputes within the group. Qatar, in particular, has been dissatisfied for some time with the organization's inability to settle important issues among the members. In December 1995 the Qatari emir, Sheikh Hamad bin Khalifa al Thani, walked out of a GCC meeting when a Saudi, rather than a Qatari, was elected to be the alliance's next secretary-general. The Doha government followed up the action the following March by refusing to participate in military exercises sponsored by the GCC.[27]

At the same time, a number of the council members have undertaken significant armament programs themselves and pursued programs leading to closer bilateral security relations with the U.S.. Kuwait has essentially rebuilt its forces from scratch. Kuwaiti leaders sense that they will continue to be vulnerable to attack from Iraq and that their country is too small to offer a successful defense by itself. Nevertheless, they believe that with high technology weapons training and specialized equipment they might be able to offer a strong deterrent to aggression. Consequently, they have made a number of major equipment acquisition decisions and analyzed various approaches for maximizing their potential force effectiveness.[28] Notably, in November 1993 Kuwait signed a 10-year security pact with Russia, similar to others with the U.S., the U.K. and France, including provisions for the stockpiling of Russian war materiel in the country. In late December of that year the two countries held a brief joint naval exercise.[29]

Kuwait's objective has been to develop national forces capable of fending off an Iraqi attack for several days until U.S. and other friendly powers can come to its aid. The army would number 21,000 men — approximately double its strength in 1995. The acquisition costs would run about $12 billion. The original target date set for fulfillment of the program was 2003. The concept envisioned the acquisition of military materiel from all five countries holding permanent seats on the U.N. Security Council under the assumption that such an arrangement would strengthen the likelihood of a positive response by the world body in case of renewed aggression.[30]

A number of factors have intervened to throw the plan off track. First was the depression of the price of oil, Kuwait's life blood. Second was the renewed threat of Iraqi aggression in October 1994. Kuwait pledged to pay for half of the cost of allied reinforcement, a pledge which may exceed $1 billion. Third was the revelation by Kuwait's legislative Fact Finding Committee that the government incurred some very large waste in its arms acquisition practices before the 1990-1991 war. A principal finding of the investigation was that funds which planners were counting on for the principal program were spent for inconsequentials much earlier in the decade. The sheikdom must either slim down its program or postpone the target date — perhaps both.[31]

As indicated in Table 13, below, the United Arab Emirates (UAE) and Oman have also committed large sums to the acquisition of late-model arms. Not reflected here is a UAE attempt to purchase space reconnaissance satellites in late 1992. Israeli objections may have influenced U.S. rejection of the approach.[32]

The UAE, with their $64 billion economy and $24,000 per capita income, form the wealthiest of the small coastal royal states sharing the Arabian peninsula.[33] The country is composed of seven semi-autonomous sheikdoms, Abu Dhabi, Dubai, Sharja, Umm al Quwain, Ras al Khaimah, and Fujairah. All but Fujairah face the Persian Gulf, while Fujairah overlooks the Gulf of Oman and separates the Omani capital, Muscat, from its territory on the strategic Strait of Hormuz. Sheltered from Iraqi aggression, the UAE has been subjected to Iranian and Saudi pressures which have prompted increasingly heavy investments in arms. Iran has seized three islands of disputed sovereignty in the Persian Gulf, Abu Musa and the Greater and Lesser Tunbs, while Saudi Arabia has encroached on land claimed by Abu Dahbi, forming its land bridge to Qatar. It is just such contentious issues as this latter one among GCC states that have prevented the development of effective coordination in dealing with Iran and Iraq.

The UAE perceive a multi-dimensional threat from Iran. After seizing the islands, which it had previously shared jointly with the UAE, Iran announced in September 1994 that it "would keep the islands forever."[34] Such belligerency, coupled with fortification of selected islands in the Gulf, poses threats of air, sea and missile attacks on the Arab mainland. Further, considering Iran's burgeoning navy, it has raised the specter of amphibious assault. The UAE has responded with accelerated programs for arms acquisition and force development.

UAE leaders are particularly interested in acquiring top-of-the-line air superiority aircraft. They have sought proposals for unique advanced versions of both F-15 and F-16 fighters, preferably more capable than those provided to either Israel or Saudi Arabia. The U.S. Defense Department has denied that it would authorize sale of weapons systems superior to those provided Israel, but it may approve sales technically the equivalent of new Saudi acquisitions.[35]

In addition to these aircraft, UAE representatives have flight tested many others on the international market, including French Mirage 2000C; Russian MiG-29, Su-25TK, -27, -30 and -35; and the U.S. F/A-18. UAE officials indicate that they have an immediate need for 15 additional fighters in the air force, and another 30 at a later date, working toward a planned total of 80 late-generation high performance aircraft. In addition, they seek additional helicopters. The U.S. is providing 10 AH-64A Apaches to improve the country's capability for rapid reaction to threats to its off-shore oil drilling platforms.[36]

To counter Iranian Scud missiles, the UAE are considering purchasing either U.S. Patriot or Russian A-300V (SA-10/12) anti-missile systems. A U.S. purchase would indicate an interest in standardizing air and missile defense acquisitions and operations with other GCC members, particularly Kuwait and Saudi Arabia. It might also strengthen existing UAE air defenses by providing Patriot radar which could be used to cue HAWK missile systems already deployed. The Russian proposal, however, would be much cheaper. Moscow has offered to provide its system at virtually no cost, in return for cancellation of an outstanding $500 million debt, for which it has no other means of paying.[37] The installation of the Russian equipment could also convey the UAE's message to Riyadh of continued displeasure over the troublesome border issue.

The UAE is also active in the search for a counterforce to balance Iran's growing naval power. The UAE is seeking immediately from 2 to 4 helicopter-carrying ASW frigates, with a like number at a later date. The U.S. has offered leases on Perry class ships, while the U.K. has made a similar offer of Royal Navy F-23 class vessels. The ships are expected to be fitted with advanced low frequency sonar and sophisticated command and fire control systems of German design. They will probably also mount both hull-fitted, Type 481 echo sounders and towed array devices. On deck, they will mount U.S. Standard missiles for area defense.[38] Two S-class frigates will come from the Netherlands, with deliveries in 1997 and 1998. Both are expected to be equipped with "Goalkeeper" short-range missile defense systems.[39]

Particularly interesting is the UAE's venture into domestic shipbuilding and repair. In January 1995 the government signed an accord with the U.S. Newport News Shipbuilding Corporation for construction of a yard capable of handling ships up to 10,000 tons, to be located in Abu Dhabi, next to the Mussafah Channel.[40] The facility could gain considerable strategic and economic importance if Iran continues to stimulate current trends in naval armaments in the Gulf.

For its ground forces, the UAE expects to broaden and accelerate its acquisition of main battle tanks. Its current program envisions the addition of 80-90 French Leclerc tanks each year until it reaches a total of 436 (including 46 armored recovery vehicles) in the year 2000.[41] Apparently separately, the Dubai Army is also considering acquiring 70 to 150 tanks. Some observers believe that this may increase the number of Leclercs for the UAE, but others disagree. There is strong interest in Dubai in acquiring Russian T-72s or T-80Us for compatibility with the existing fleet of BMP-3 infantry fighting vehicles.[42] Not to be outdone, Abu Dhabi is also strengthening its ground elements. Most notable is the acquisition of modified M109A3 artillery pieces to provide long-range (32 km.) fire support.[43]

Special note should be taken of Bahrain, both as a strategic asset and as one with special vulnerability. Bahrain provides important support facilities to the naval component of USCENTCOM, and its rescue units were the first on the scene in 1987 when the USS Stark was struck by an Iraqi missile. During the Gulf War, Bahrain was host to some 17,500 U.S. servicemen and 200 combat and support aircraft.

At the same time, Bahrain has special security problems. Most perplexing is the response of dissident youths to calls from religious leaders in exile to protest government policies with implications for radical and violent change of the government. In 1981 50 to 60 persons, mainly Shiite Muslims were arrested in connection with such a plot. A new season of violence was opened in December 1994 when similar groups staged two weeks of rioting, attacking stores, banks and police cars with fire bombs. Government officials pointed to instigators in Iran and the Hezbollah fundamentalist movement, but opposition leaders blamed human rights violations and the lack of democracy in the country.[46]

Demonstrations and riots continued spasmodically for the next four months, with 700-900 Shiites being placed under arrest. The 1,500 U.S. military personnel and their families resident on the island sought to maintain a low profile during the disturbances.[47] No less troublesome is a dispute with Qatar over control of the Hawar Islands lying between the two countries, but considerably closer to Qatar than to Bahrain. The matter has been submitted to the World Court in the Hague for resolution.

More dangerous for Bahrain are vulnerabilities to Iraqi and Iranian attack. The island was struck twice by Scud missiles (albeit inconsequentially) during the Gulf War. Further, Bahrain lies 20 miles off shore in the Persian Gulf, like a bite-sized chunk of land, which might appear tempting to a preda-tor seeking control of maritime traffic in the area. Significantly, Iranian leaders have not renounced an outstand-ing claim by the former Shah over the territory. Unlike the other GCC members, Bahrain is only a marginal, and slowly declining oil producer. As the national income slipped, so did defense expenditures. For a time, it was heavily dependent upon Saudi Arabia for maintaining its forces. Bahrain's real-ization of its vulnerabilities may have prompted its move in June 1992 to open diplomatic contacts with Iraq, perhaps to off-set some of its dependence on others.[48]

Ultimately, Bahrain looks to the United States for its secu-rity. Both Manama (Bahrain) and Riyadh (Saudi Arabia) real-ize that Bahrain represents a Shiia enclave next to the Sunni keeper of the holy sites. Manama might sometime turn to Washington for protection if anything were to upset the quali-ty of its relations with Riyadh. It has already sought military assistance on special terms, and a number of programs are under development. The U.S. has granted Bahrain status as an authorized recipient of excess American lethal equipment under the 1994 Congressional Defense Authorization Act which would permit Bahrain to acquire additional F-16 air-craft; command, control and logistics support equipment; and a HAWK air defense battery. Bahrain has also requested the loan of a Patriot air defense system from U.S. stocks.[49] The F-16s may be delivered in exchange for F-5 aircraft which the U.S. Navy requires for training purposes.

Bahrain has also requested AIM-120 Advanced medium Range Air-to-Air Missiles and Low-Altitude Navigation and Targeting Infrared (LANTRIN) systems to improve the lethality and flexibility of its F-16 fighter aircraft. For similar improvements of its ground force Multiple Launch Rocket Systems (MLRS), it has requested provision of the U.S. Army Tactical Missile System (ATACMS). In addition, it has requested, and the U.S. Government has agreed to deliver, a HAWK air defense battery and 60 additional M60A3 tanks.[50]

For its navy, Bahrain is expected to receive a U.S. FFG-7 frigate equipped with Standard air defense missiles and the Phalanx shipboard close-in self-defense system.[51] This will be the largest vessel in the country's fleet.

Qatar has border disputes with both Bahrain and Saudi Arabia. Relations with the latter deteriorated in 1994 to the point of local shooting incidents. During the October crisis on the Iraqi-Kuwaiti border that year, in spite of Doha's agreement with the U.S. for basing fighter aircraft and armor in the country, Qatar officials were accused of blocking the dispatch of GCC "Peninsular Shield" forces to Kuwait to help deter Iraqi aggression because of their displeasure with Riyadh. And the following month, Qatar boycotted a meeting of the GCC to again underscore its unhappiness. Some observers suspect that Qatar actually places its primary security reliance on its bilateral relationship with the United States, and that it is not very serious about its membership in the GCC.[52] It may be significant that in March 1995, during a visit by U.S. Defense Secretary William Perry, Doha agreed to permit the prepositioning of a set of equipment for a U.S. heavy brigade.[53]

Other observers detect two cliques within the GCC — a northern group, composed of Saudi Arabia, Kuwait and Bahrain, somewhat better coordinated for defense from the north, and a southern group composed of Qatar, UAE and Oman with less concern for the Iraqi threat.[54] The Qatar-Saudi and UAE-Saudi border disputes lend a degree of credence to the concept. It should not be overlooked, however, that in an informal, unscientific poll conducted by the author, Western observers gave Qatari and Omani troops "better than average" ratings among all those indigenous to the region.[55]

Oman, curiously independent-minded, has pursued a unique, arguably sensible, course in international affairs, especially during the rein of the current Sultan. Unlike many of its Arab neighbors, Oman has avoided the great Sunni- Shiia schism, the Arab-Israeli wars, and the isolation of Egypt in the wake of Cairo's peace accord with Jerusalem. While strongly supportive of the GCC, Oman refuses to identify Iran as an enemy, expanding, where possible, cultural exchanges with Tehran. Muscat has made peace with its former internal insurgents, bringing some of the leaders into the government. It has also settled old territorial disputes with Yemen and Saudi Arabia. Further, it has played prominent roles in settling the North-South conflict in Yemen and offered its good offices for reducing tensions between India and Pakistan. In short, Oman's security is based first on its efforts to dampen disputes and to foster accord.

This is not to imply that Oman is a dreamland in a snake pit. The ruler, Sultan Qaboos Bin Said al Said, has proposed a stronger armed force for the GCC than any of his partners are prepared to accept; and in October 1994 when Iraq was again threatening aggression against Kuwait, he agreed to the basing of U.S. fighter aircraft and armor in the country.[56] The forces of Oman, while modest, are considered competent, loyal and well led. The Sultan, himself is a graduate of the British Royal Military College at Sandhurst.

Oman has had close relations with the U.S. since 1980 when it first signed agreements granting U.S. forces access to Omani ports and airfields, and space for prepositioning military equipment. These accords proved particularly valuable during the 1990-1991 Gulf War. Unfortunately, a separate agreement for U.S. development aid to Oman of $20 million per year, which many looked upon as a quid-pro-quo for the security agreement, was cancelled by Washington, to the great disappointment of Muscat, resulting in the erosion of much good will.[57] Some observers believe that the strategic (and economic) importance of Kuwait has supplanted that of Oman in the U.S. view.

Anticipated enhancements of Omani forces include orders for British Challenger main battle tanks, 155mm long-range self-propelled artillery, tank transporters, Piranha armored personnel carriers, and naval 83 meter ASW corvettes. (Friendship with Iran clearly does not extend to Omani blindness at sea.) Two such vessels are expected to be in commission by 1997. Omani defense spending from 1996 to 2000 is expected to total $8.75 billion.[58]

TABLE 13

ANTICIPATED ARMS ACQUISITIONS OF THE SMALL GCC STATES[44]

Kuwait
6 Patriot batteries with 450 missiles
6 Hawk batteries with 342 missiles
75 FA-18 fighter aircraft
236 M1-A2 main battle tanks*
644 armored personnel carriers
254 Desert Warrior light armored vehicles
16 AH-64 Apache attack helicopters
16 UH-60A Blackhawk dual purpose helicopters
8 coastal patrol boats

* Some reports indicate a Kuwaiti interest in acquiring 760 M1A2 tanks[45]

Bahrain
? F-16 fighter aircraft
8 AH-64 Apache attack helicopters
60 M-60 tanks
1 HAWK SAM battery
? Patriot SAM batteries (on loan?)
1 FFG-7 Perry class frigate

Qatar
? Patriot SAM batteries
Upgrade of air defense system
4 Vita class fast attack boats with Exocet missiles

(Continued Next Page)

**Anticipated Arms Acquisitions of the Small GCC States
(Continued)**

UAE

390 Leclerc tanks
500 BMP infantry fighting vehicles
85 M109A3 howitzers
20 AH-64 Apache attack helicopters
24-40 F-15F fighter intercepters
? S-300 or S-300V air defense system
1,000-2,000 trucks
8 frigates
7 Panther ASW Helicopters
AS15TT and Exocet anti-ship missiles
Maritime patrol aircraft

Oman

40 M60-A3 tanks
36 Challenger 2 tanks
24 G6 SP 155 mm guns
119 V-300 armored cars (or 500 BTR-80 APCs)
? Pirana armored troop carriers
16 Hawk fighter aircraft
4 Corvettes

YEMEN

Yemen reportedly has the distinction of standing first among
all of the nations of the world in the number of small arms per
capita.[59] It has been the scene of much strife in the last twenty years, but for the most part, the action has been little more
than a sideshow to the more prominent conflicts involving bet-

ter known — and better reported — actors on the regional stage. Isolated at the foot of the Arabian Peninsula, most hostilities in Yemen have been internal — civil conflict with North against South, and religious tribalist against secular socialist.[60]

In 1990 North and South Yemen were brought together in what some observers described as a surprising and uneasy union. The national capital was established at San'a, in the North. The people had different histories; the North was dominated by an elite, skilled in balancing power between Shiia and Sunni Islamic tribal groups. The South was Sunni, organized as a "peoples' republic," and until the fall of the Soviet Union, looked to Moscow for support. Each side feared the influences of the other. Legislation to form a constitutional democracy floundered on differences in the political systems.

In 1990 and '91, true to its close ties with Baghdad, San'a refused to support U.N. Security Council action against Iraq. Instead, it called for mediation of the issue with Kuwait. This infuriated both the Kuwaiti government in exile and Saudi Arabia, which hosted some 500,000 to 800,000 Yemeni workers. Riyadh expelled the workers, while at the same time the U.S., which had been supplying about $700 million per year in aid, halted all assistance. Without the Soviet Union to fall back on, the Yemeni economy collapsed.

After the Gulf War, observers suspect, Riyadh took to meddling among Yemeni tribes, first to crack the unified government in San'a, and second to inhibit Yemeni exploration for oil in disputed border areas. This tended to erode the national unity and further depress the economy. In the meanwhile, the difficulties of the forced coexistence of Northern Islamic fundamentalism and Southern socialism were finding their way to the surface on the domestic front. Assassinations and attempted assassinations, both North and South were rife. The South resolved to secede, with Aden, again as its capital.

Open warfare broke out in April 1994. While not necessarily sympathetic to the South, Saudi Arabia sent funds and sponsored Southern purchases of arms, but to little avail. In three months the weight of Northern power overcame the rebels, and the unified state was reestablished.

From San'a's perspective, Saudi Arabia and most of the other GCC states remain basically hostile, still nursing suspicions of Yemeni collusion with Iraq in the Gulf War. As Kuwait's information minister, Sheikh Saud Nasser al Sabah, remarked in late 1994, "[Yemeni President] Ali Abdullah Saleh is an ally of Saddam Hussein, and we have no feeling of liking for him."[61] But the animosity goes two ways. The Yemeni Government believes that it has a legitimate grievance with Riyadh for supporting the Southern secessionists during the civil war.[62] And there are long-standing disputes over the location of the borders.

But it is not only history that poisons the well. Many of the Gulf states are uncomfortable with Yemen's functioning democracy. The precedent is unwelcome among governments opposed to the principle of decision by popular vote. And the discomfort may extend further. Many suspect that the strong fundamentalist group, Al Islah, led by Sheikh Abdullah Hussein al Ahmar, the second most powerful man after President Saleh, will develop along the lines of similar groups in Iran and Sudan. Especially, Saudi leaders are believed to harbor fears of a reunited, hostile Yemen with a larger population than the kingdom on their southern border — and with considerable military experience. The discovery of oil in poorly demarcated border regions has intensified concerns, and resulted in a series of troop demonstrations and frontier clashes, some entailing fatalities.

Syria has attempted to mediate a number of incidents, but observers point out that there are strong third party interests for escalating the problems rather than suppressing them. Saddam Hussein, they believe, may wish to support Yemen against Saudi Arabia as a way of deflecting attention from his problems. Similarly, Iran or Sudan may back Yemen as a way of undermining Saudi power and influence.[63]

For their part, Yemeni officials do not impress all analysts as being particularly adamant about all of their territorial claims. However, it may be that they seek to make enough of the issues that Riyadh will be deterred from making further claims of its own.[64]

According to Yemeni Vice President Abdel Rabuh Hadi, the Yemen Defense Ministry plans to reduce the size of the armed forces by 50 percent over a five year period. At the same time, interior forces will be doubled to improve internal and border security. By the first of January 1995, Northern and Southern units of the various military branches had been merged, and equipment reallocated and standardized. Most units have former Soviet equipment; a few have Western weapons. Special training programs have been instituted for former Southern troops being reequipped with Western materiel, especially F-5 fighters, M60 tanks and 105mm artillery.[65]

Vice President Hadi went on to say that some important materiel, paid for by Saudi Arabia, and smuggled into South Yemen, was captured by Northern forces and will be put into use by the unified armed forces. This includes 7 MiG-29 "Fulcrum" jet fighters and 12 Multiple Launch Rocket Systems. It also includes 56 T-62 tanks which were delivered shortly before the fighting began.[66]

Then U.S. Director of Central Intelligence James Woolsey accused Yemen of playing host to Iraqi technicians and advisers in connection with the Soviet equipment. In September 1994 Woolsey pointed out that, "During this last spring's civil war in Yemen the Iraqi regime repeatedly called for an Iraqi-Yemeni axis to encircle Saudi Arabia. Iraq followed up with offers of free military expertise to help rebuild the Yemeni armed forces."[67]

Hadi admitted that there had been Iraqi experts in Yemen in connection with the delivery of the MiG-29s, but insisted that they had simply helped to transfer the aircraft to San'a airfield and had then departed. He dismissed notions that Yemen would require much in the way of spare parts for U.S. equipment (presumably because of plans to reduce the forces), but said that he would welcome American technical experts and military advisers.[68]

Hadi also said that Yemen recognizes that it must find ways to get along with Saudi Arabia, but admitted the difficulties. The Saudis, he said, bribe Yemeni border tribesmen to accept Saudi identification cards to strengthen Riyadh's case for sovereignty. "Yemenis are really hungry," he said. The wealthy Saudis can cause much trouble, he argued, expressing the hope that the United States would bring pressure to bear on the Saudis to leave Yemen alone.

THE POWDER KEG

CHAPTER IV
Force Calculations

As noted in Chapter 1, the calculation of military power is complex. Occasionally analysts will sense a need to take into consideration certain factors which may not be in strict accord with their normal methodology. The inclusion of such factors is usually a judgment call. This is not to say that clearly extraneous considerations, such as domestic political matters, are appropriate, but rather that military studies are undertaken for a purpose, and each study, or analysis, should be properly cast to assist in decision making.

Both objective and subjective methods of analysis have utility. While most decision makers prefer a high proportion of objectivity, there is seldom a way that subjective matters can be completely removed from the calculus. And it may not necessarily be desirable to do so in every case. Sometimes the analyst's "gut hunch" regarding the quality of a force is more valuable that the most pristine, clinical judgment.

Nevertheless, the professional analyst should seek and apply whatever reasonable objective or subjective techniques may be available, within the parameters of time and expense, to provide measures of force quality and effectiveness. There need be no presumption of greater reliability of one means of comparison of over any other. However, analysts should maintain a continuing quest for the development of additional and better techniques for the illumination of significant differences between competing forces and for the development of insights useful in the reaching well considered conclusions.

SOURCES AND METHODS

This chapter deals with the derivation of combat potential indices for air and ground forces of selected Middle East countries based primarily on measurement of observable military assets — tanks, guns, aircraft, etc. Order of battle data is adapted from the International Institute of Strategic Studies Military Balance for the years from 1990 to 1995, modified where other information is persuasive.[1] A qualitative dimension is added through the application of "adjusted weapon systems performance" (AWSP) coefficients provided in The Analytic Sciences Corporation model, TASCFORM.[2] As with the order of battle data, some coefficients in the model have been amended by the author where in his judgment the model required up-dating or other adjustment.

The AWSP are numerical expressions of the anticipated value of each type of equipment on an average battlefield under average conditions. An American M1A2 tank, for instance, has an AWSP of 6.5. An F-4B Phantom II fighter aircraft has one of 13.3. This does not mean that the F-4 would necessarily defeat the tank in a one-on-one battle. On the contrary, the F-4B is optimized for engaging other aircraft — not ground targets. Nor does it mean that aircraft are twice as useful as tanks. The tank and the plane each have roles to play in the battle milieu, and at times the function of one may be more important than that of the other.

What the adjusted weapon systems performance index does reflect is the notion that over time, in a large number of engagements, the fighter would be likely to play an important role more often than the tank. The aircraft can clearly move further and faster, deliver heavier ordnance, and attack a wider range of targets than the earth-bound vehicle. These types of considerations, together with others, such as survivability and maintenance factors, are employed by knowledgeable analysts in arriving at the weapons systems AWSP. When aggregated, the products of the individual AWSP and the numbers of the various systems provide total "designated force performance" (DFP) indices. National DFPs provide a measurement of total force potential for comparison with the forces of other states. (The tables of AWSP scores used in this study are not included in the text in order to protect proprietary information.)

An important objective of this chapter is the development of estimates of future, as well as "snap-shot" current strengths of forces. Two methods are employed for the estimates. In the first, current growth rates are determined from retrospective calculations from the beginning of the decade. The growth rates are then projected ahead, assuming simple linear extension into the future. In the second, changes to the DFP, based upon reported equipment acquisitions and retirements, are determined and aggregated. Another set of projections are then made, with the adoption of certain assumptions regarding ordering practices and delivery dates. The result is the portrayal of a likely range of future DFP for each country. While it is difficult to assess the accuracy of such projections because of the many imponderables, previous experience with the technique has yielded useful insights in most cases.[3]

In any event, it should be borne in mind that DFP have limits. In particular, they do not reflect qualitative aspects of a force which are not inherent in the materiel being counted. Leadership skills, integrative and coordinative factors, doctrine, training and organizational matters are all neutral. Further, the process makes no provision for weapons of mass destruction. Analysts' concerns for conventional armaments, which have been the tools of choice for most conflicts in the Middle East (and are the principal focus of this analysis), should not obscure the realities and impact of other technology. Differences in capabilities in higher forms of conflict and weapons production, of course, tend to place countries in different classes. Most prominent here is Israel, with its stockpile of nuclear weapons, its access to advanced American research and development, and its high technology base and industrial capacity. It clearly belongs in a entirely different category from its neighbors. It is the only state in the region which can look beyond its admittedly impressive conventional capabilities to other means of guaranteeing its national security. While in the past the Arab confrontation states posed an existential threat to Israel, today it is the other way around. Israel now possess the wherewithal to pose just such threats to its neighbors.

SOURCE DATA AND OBSERVATIONS
Tables 14 through 25 contain the basic order of battle and principal equipment inventories of the major countries in this analysis.[4] Tables 26 and 27 provide similar data for the smaller countries. Figure 3 indicates the historical growth in overall air-ground designated force potential (DFP) for the countries from 1990 to 1995, and projects this information to the year 2000. Future DFP are portrayed as likely lying along the path of historic force development or as loci in an expanding fan of possible levels (shaded areas), bounded by projections of the historical patterns, on the one hand, and those indicated by anticipated arms acquisitions (from Chapter II) on the other.

TABLE 14

ISRAELI GROUND FORCES

Personnel

Active Strength:	134,000
Reserves:	365,000
Paramilitary	
Border Police:	6,000
Nahal:	7,500
Total:	512,500

Units

Divisions:		Separate Brigades:	
12	Armored (9R)	4	Mechanized
3	Infantry		(incl 1 abn)
1	Mechanized (R)	10	Territorial (R)
	(Airmobile)	5	Airborne (R)

Equipment

Major Item	Inventory
Main Battle Tanks	4,095
Recon Vehicles	400
Armored Personnel Carriers	10,000
Towed Artillery	400
Self-Propelled Artillery	1,150
Multiple Rocket Launchers	100
Mortars	2,740
Surface-to-Surface Missles	120
Anti-tank Guided Missiles	1,005
Air Defense Guns	1,045 +
Surface-to-Air Missiles	945 +

R=Reserve formation

TABLE 15
ISRAELI AIR AND NAVAL FORCES

AIR FORCES

Personnel
Active Strength: 32,000

Combat Units
700 Combat Aircraft (include 250 stored)

16 Dual Ground Attack/Air Superiority Squadrons
    5 with 50 F-4E2000   7 with 205 F-16A/B/C/D
    3 with 63 F-15A/B/C/D   1 with 20 Kfir C2/C7
4 Ground Attack Squadrons
    4 with 50 A-4N
Attack Helicopters
    39 AH-1F   42 AH-64A Apaches
    35 Hughes 500MD

NAVAL FORCES

Personnel
Active Strength: 7,000
Reserves: 10,000
Marine Commandos: 300
Total: 17,300

Combat Units
3 Submarines
3 Corvettes
23 Fast Patrol Missile Craft (equipped with Harpoon and Gabriel missiles)
40 Inshore Patrol Craft
1 Amphibious ship
3 Small Amphibious Craft

TABLE 16

SYRIAN GROUND FORCES

Personnel

Active Strength: 315,000
Reserves: 550,000
Paramilitary Workers Militia: 400,000
Gendarmerie: 8,000
Total: 1,273,000

Combat Units

Divisions:	Separate Brigades:
7 Armored	3 Infantry
(1 Rep Guard)	4 Mechanized
3 Mechanized	1 Border Guard
1 Special Forces	7 Special Forces
	1 Tank
	2 Anti-Tank

Equipment

Major Item	Inventory
Main Battle Tanks	4,600
Recon Vehicles	1,000
Armored Infantry Fighting Vehicles	2,250
Armored Personnel Carriers	1,500
Towed Artillery	1,630
Self-Propelled Artillery	400
Multiple Rocket Launchers	480
Mortars	2,400
Surface-to-Surface Missile Launchers	62
Anti-tank Guided Missiles	3,000
Air Defense Guns	2,060
Surface-to-Air Missiles	4,000

TABLE 17
SYRIAN AIR, AIR DEFENSE AND NAVAL FORCES
AIR FORCES

Personnel
Active Strength: 40,000

Combat Units
579 Combat Aircraft

9 Ground Attack Squadrons
    5 with 90 Su-2   22 with 44 MiG-25
    2 with 20 Su-24
18 Fighter Squadrons
    8 with 160 MiG-21   2 with 39 MiG-25
    5 with 90 MiG-23   3 with 20 MiG-29
Attack Helicopters
    50 Mi-25
    50 SA-342L

AIR DEFENSE FORCES
Personnel
60,000

Combat Units
25 Air Defense Brigades (130 SAM batteries)
    450 SA-2/SA-3 launchers
    200 SA-6 launchers and guns
2 SAM Regiments with 48 SA-5 and 60 SA-8 missile launchers

NAVAL FORCES
Personnel
8,000

Combat Units

2 Frigates	11 Patrol Boats
18 Missile Boats	7 Mine Warfare Ships
1 Submarine	3 Landing Ships

TABLE 18

EGYPTIAN GROUND FORCES

Personnel

Active Strength:	310,000
Reserves:	150,000
Paramilitary Central Security:	100,000
National Guard:	60,000
Border Guard:	12,000
Total:	642,000

Combat Units

Divisions:
4 Armored
7 Mechanized
1 Infantry

Separate Brigades:
1 Rep Guard Armored
4 Armored
4 Mechanized
1 Air Mobile
2 Infantry
1 Airborne

Equipment

Major Item Inventory	
Main Battle Tanks	3,500
Recon Vehicles	300
Armored Infantry Fighting Vehicles	1,080
Armored Personnel Carriers	3,834
Towed Artillery	971
Self-Propelled Artillery	276
Multiple Rocket Launchers	296
Mortars	2,000 +
Surface-to-Surface Missile Launchers	21 +
Anti-tank Guided Missiles	1,400
Air Defense Guns	1,677
Surface-to-Air Missiles	2,046 +

TABLE 19
EGYPTIAN AIR, AIR DEFENSE AND NAVAL FORCES
AIR FORCES
Personnel
Active Strength: 30,000

Combat Units

7 Ground Attack Squadrons
    2 with 40 Alpha Jets   2 with 40 Ch J-6
    2 with 25 F-4E   1 with 16 Mirage 5E2
16 Fighter Squadrons
    2 with 30 F-16A   5 with 100 MiG-21
    2 with 80 F-16C   3 with 54 Mirage 5D/E
    3 with 60 Ch J-7   1 with Mirage 2000C
4 Attack Helicopter Squadrons
    65 SA-342K (HOT missiles or 20mm guns)

AIR DEFENSE FORCES

Personnel
80,000

Combat Units

5 Air Defense Divisions
    40 SA-2 Battalions   12 Improved HAWK Batteries
    53 SA-3 Battalions   12 Chaparral Batteries
    14 SA-6 Battalions   14 Crotale Batteries
                   100 AD Gun Battalions

NAVAL FORCES
Personnel
20,000

Combat Units

3 Submarines   3 Torpedo Boats
1 Destroyer   18 Patrol Boats
4 Frigates   6 Mine Warfare Ships
26 Missile Boats   3 Landing Ships

TABLE 20
SAUDI ARABIAN GROUND FORCES
Personnel

Active Strength:	70,000
Active National Guard:	57,000
Tribal Levies:	20,000
Paramilitary Frontier Force:	10,500
Special Security:	500
Total:	158,000

Combat Units
Brigades:

3 Armored	2 Nat Gd Mechanized
1 Royal Guard	6 Nat Gd Infantry
5 Mechanized	1 Airborne

Equipment

Major Item	Inventory
Army:	
Main Battle Tanks	1,055
Recon Vehicles	235
Armored Infantry Fighting Vehicles	970 +
Armored Personnel Carriers	1,700
Towed Artillery	238
Self-Propelled Artillery	200
Multiple Rocket Launchers	60
Mortars	400
Surface-to-Surface Missile Launchers	10
Anti-tank Guided Missile Launchers	290
Surface-to-Air Missile Launchers	500 +

National Guard:

Light Armored Vehicles	262
Armored Personnel Carriers	1,100
Towed Artillery	70
Anti-Tank Guided Missile Launchers	?

TABLE 21
SAUDI ARABIAN AIR, AIR DEFENSE AND NAVAL FORCES

AIR FORCES
Personnel
Active Strength: 18,000+

Combat Units
292 Combat Aircraft

5 Ground Attack Squadrons
   3 with 51 F-5E
   2 with 44 Tornado IDS
5 Fighter Squadrons
   33 with 78 F-15C and 20 F-15D
   2 with 24 Tornado ADV

AIR DEFENSE FORCES

Personnel
4,000

Combat Units
33 Surface-to-Air Missile Batteries
   16 with Improved HAWK
   17 with 68 Shahine missiles and AMC-30SA
      30mm self-propelled guns
73 Shahine/Crotale missile fire units in static defense

NAVAL FORCES

Personnel
12,000

Combat Units

8 Frigates	6 Mine Warfare Ships
9 Missile Patrol Craft	8 Landing Craft
3 Torpedo Boats	20 Armed Helicopters
17 Patrol Craft	

2 Battalions of Marines

TABLE 22

IRANIAN GROUND FORCES

Personnel

Active Strength:	345,000
Reserves:	350,000
Paramilitary Revolutionary Guards:	120,000
BASIJ Volunteers:	200,000
Gendarmerie:	45,000
Total:	1,060,00

Combat Units

Divisions: Separate Brigades:
4 Armored   1 Airborne
7 Infantry   some Armd/Inf/Condo
2 Special Forces

Equipment

Major Item	Inventory
Main Battle Tanks	1,440
Light Tanks	80
Recon Vehicles	35
Armored Infantry Fighting Vehicles	300
Armored Personnel Carriers	550
Towed Artillery	1,995
Self-Propelled Artillery	289
Multiple Rocket Launchers	664
Mortars	3,500
Surface-to-Surface Missile Launchers	35
Anti-tank Guided Missiles	?
Air Defense Guns	1,700
Surface-to-Air Missiles	35 ?
Attack Helicopters	100

TABLE 23

IRANIAN AIR AND NAVAL FORCES

AIR FORCES

Personnel
Active Strength: 30,000

Combat Units
295 Combat Aircraft

9 Ground Attack Squadrons
    4 with 60 F-4D/E   4 with 60 F-5E/F
    1 with 30 Su-24
7 Fighter Squadrons
    4 with 60 F-14   1 with 25 F-7
    2 with 30 MiG-29

NAVAL FORCES

Personnel
18,000

Combat Units

2 Submarines	10 Missile Boats
2 Destroyers	26 Patrol Boats
3 Frigates	3 Mine Warfare Ships
2 Corvettes	8 Landing Ships

3 Battalions of Marines

TABLE 24

IRAQI GROUND FORCES

Personnel

Active Strength:	350,000
Reserves:	650,000
Paramilitary Frontier Guards:	20,000
Security Troops:	4,800
Total:	1,024,000

Combat Units

Divisions:	Separate Brigades:
7 Republican Guard	10 Special Forces
(4 armd/mech)	
19 Armored/Mech/Inf	

Equipment

Major Item	Inventory
Main Battle Tanks	2,700
Recon Vehicles	1,500
Armored Infantry Fighting Vehicles	900
Armored Personnel Carriers	2,000
Towed Artillery	1,500
Self-Propelled Artillery	230
Multiple Rocket Launchers	250
Mortars	?
Surface-to-Surface Missile Launchers	200 ?
Anti-tank Guided Missiles	1,500
Air Defense Guns	5,500
Surface-to-Air Missiles	?
Attack Helicopters	120

TABLE 25

IRAQI AIR AND NAVAL FORCES

AIR FORCES

Personnel

Active Strength: 30,000
(including 15,000 Air Defense)

Combat Units

6 Bombers: (H-6D and Tu-22)
130 Ground Attack: (J-6, Mig-23BN, Mig-27, Mirage
                      F1EQ5, Su-7, Su-20, Su-25)
180 Fighters: (F-7, MiG-21, MiG-25, Mirage
                      F1EQ, Mig-29)

NAVY

Personnel
Active: 2,500

Combat Units
1 Frigate
1 Missile Boat
7 Inshore Patrol Boats
4 Mine Warfare Craft

TABLE 26
GROUND FORCES OF SMALLER ARAB STATES

	Jordan	Kuwait	Yemen	Lebanon	Oman	UAE	Bahrain	Qatar
Personnel								
Active Strength:	90,000	10,000	37,000	43,000	25,000	65,500	8,500	8,500
Reserves:	30,000	23,700	40,000	—	—	—	—	—
Combat Units								
Divisions	4				1			
Separate Bdes	2	4 (-)	32 (-)	13 (-)	5	5 (-)	2 (-)	1
Equipment								
Main Battle Tanks	1,141	220	1,125	300	75	125	80	24
Recon Vehicles	169		310	175		-160	46	6
Armored Infantry Fighting Vehicles & Pers Carrier	1,100		329	830	19	350	135	182
Towed Artillery	115		512	215	96	108	28	12
Self-Propelled Artillery	370	56	30			88	13	28
Multiple Rocket Launchers			185	30		40	9	4
Mortars	800	6	50 +	280	92	101	18	75
Surface-to-Surface Msl Launchers			?			6	1	
Anti-tank Guided Missiles	640	68	36 +	20 +	50	275	15	100
Air Defense Guns	360	12	372	10 +	28	68		
Surface-to-Air Msl Launchers	934	84	?		190	69	65	24

TABLE 27:   AIR AND NAVAL FORCES OF SMALLER ARAB STATES

AIR FORCES

	Jordan	Kuwait	Yemen	Oman	UAE	Bahrain	Qatar
Active Strength:	8,000	2,500	1,000	4,100	3,500	1,500	800
Combat Aircraft:	82	76	69	46	97	24	12
Ground Attack Squadrons	3			2	3	1	
No./Types	50 F-5		11 F-5 16 Su-22 &-20 25 MiG21 5 MiG29	15 Jag 4 T-2 12 Hwk	9 Mirg 32 Hwk	8 F-5E 4 F-5F	
Fighter Sqdrn No./Types	2 30 Mirg	1 8 Mirg	39 MiG21		1 22 Mirg	1 12 F16C/D	
Dual Prupose No./Types		1 40 F/A-18					1 6 Alpha 6 Mirg
Armed Helos	24	16	12		42	10	20

NAVAL FORCES

	Jordan	Kuwait	Yemen	Oman	UAE	Bahrain	Qatar
Personnel	600	2,500	1,500	4,200	2,000	600	800
Frigates					1	1	
Corvettes					2	2	
Missile Boats		2		4	8	4	3
Patrol Boats	5	2	10	8	19	4	6
Amphib Shps			2	2			
Amphib Craft			2	3	3		
Mine Ships			3		3		1

FIGURE 3

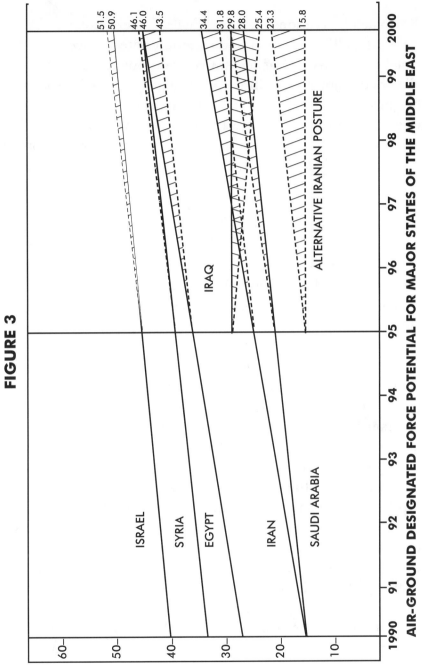

AIR-GROUND DESIGNATED FORCE POTENTIAL FOR MAJOR STATES OF THE MIDDLE EAST

Some observations regarding Figure 3 merit note:
- In addition to its class distinction noted above, Israel maintains a clear lead in conventional armaments over all other major powers in the area. Further, Israel's lead over her next closest competitor, Syria, appears to have remained essentially unchanged since the close of the 1991 Gulf War, and there is little indication of any appreciable alteration of the bilateral balance in the foreseeable future. In spite of Israel's planned acquisition of significant numbers of Multiple Launch Rocket Systems and F-15I, F-16 and F-18 jet fighters, and the prospective deployment of as many as six Arrow II anti-ballistic missile launchers by 2000, the rate of modernization of her forces appears likely to maintain its established path for the rest of the century. While strategically important, the Arrow deployments are unlikely to affect the practical balance with Syria by more than one or two percentage points in terms of designated force potential.

- Syria is the top Islamic military power in the region (Turkey aside). Its margin of superiority over Egypt, however, may narrow appreciably, primarily due to Egypt's conversion program from old Soviet materiel to modern Western equipment. For herself, Syria appears to be maintaining a respectable rate of modernization of forces along the track established over the last five years. This is reflected in Figure 3 by the coincidence of Syria's projected historic force development rate and the rate derived from new equipment acquisition calculations. Such stability may indicate a deliberate continued investment in arms without any particular attempt to challenge Israeli leadership.

- Egypt, on the other hand, may be slowing its vigorous pace of the last five years. Pursuit of the rate of modernization indicated by Egypt's weapons procurement program may actually lower its net growth to a rate closer to that established by

Syria. One of the major factors affecting Egypt's pace is its commitment to retirement of much older Soviet equipment on a one-for-one basis as new equipment deliveries occur. The portrayal of future Egyptian force posture in Figure 3 assumes that Egypt will eliminate the following equipment from its units and arsenals:[5]

890 T-54, T-55 and Ramses main battle tanks
374 Walid armored personnel carriers
 40 J-6 Chinese jet fighters
 40 Alpha jet aircraft

The scrapping or other disposal of the old equipment, of course, will tend to lower Egypt's equipment maintenance and operations costs. As beneficial as the move may be in this respect, it is counter to much experience in the Middle East. Older materiel has traditionally been used first to form additional reserve formations.

• Iraq is in a unique position among the major states. Its assessed DFP in 1995 is higher than analysts estimated at the close of the 1991 war, in spite of the U.N. imposed import restrictions. Little was known about the country's equipment loss rates during the war, so it has been difficult to track or explain changes. At this writing (1996) the IISS Military Balance does not report numbers of individual weapons types for Iraq, but only aggregate figures for broad categories, such as tanks, artillery, etc. — usually preceded by a cautionary "perhaps." Accordingly, the DFP figure for 1995 (29,800) is a rough estimate, and no earlier data is shown. The combat effectiveness of Baghdad's forces in the next five years is highly dependent upon the actions of the U.N. Security Council regarding the trade embargo. If the restrictions remain in place, the best the Iraqis may be able to do will be to hold their

forces at about their present level of effectiveness. More likely, as time goes on and replacement items and spare parts
become more scarce, the forces will deteriorate. A decrement
rate of about three percent per year, indicated by the lower dot-
ted line on Figure 3, would seem reasonable. If this occurs, it
may be possible for Iraq's closest competitors, Saudi Arabia and
Iran, to reach their avowed goals of matching Iraqi air-ground
military power.

• The Saudis and Iranians appear to be pursuing paths
close to their historic rates of growth in air-ground force potential. It should be noted that Tehran is simultaneously pressing
ahead with a vigorous naval program, which has probably
restrained its air-ground modernization to some extent. This is
reflected in the slightly lower rate of anticipated air-ground
materiel acquisitions shown in Figure 3. The Saudi rate of
arms acquisitions is expected to be substantially greater than
that shown in Figure 3, but the DFP index is intended to measure combat force potential — not simply quantities of
materiel on hand. Since Riyadh has elected for economic reasons to take deliveries of F-15S jet fighters and M1A2 main
battle tanks which it cannot immediately absorb within its
force structure, the contribution which that materiel makes to
over-all Saudi air-ground DFP has been reduced by half. This
reduces the upper limit of the Saudi DFP range in the year
2000 by over 4,300 points.

• As we have noted in Chapter II, Iran's declaratory policy regarding development of its forces is to match the threat
posed by Iraq. The present rate of growth would appear to be
adequate for that by 2000. If Iraq were to be freed from its
U.N. imposed trade restrictions, and its forces to gain access to
necessary replacement parts, and possibly new weaponry, it
would not be surprising to see the rate of Iranian air-ground
force growth accelerate to some extent in an effort to fulfill its

objective.

An alternative posture is depicted for Iran to accommodate a controversy among analysts concerning the amount of heavy equipment acquired by the country in the period 1989-1995. The alternative view credits Iran with 114 fewer artillery pieces.[6] Discounting this equipment would reduce the Iranian DFP by some 8,500 points. The alternative display indicates the range of likely outcomes in 2000 if: (a) no further equipment were to be acquired, and (b) if the full anticipated program were to be fulfilled.

Figures 4 and 5 depict the development of forces in the minor states of the region between 1990 and 1995. The historic rates of growth are extended to the year 2000 to indicate the relative levels of air-ground force potential which might be expected if there were no other factors influencing the processes. Also portrayed are the growth rates which would be required if all the weapons acquisitions programs listed in Chapter III were to be fulfilled. (The reader should note that the vertical axes of the charts in Figures 4 and 5 are substantially magnified over that in Figure 3 in order to legibly accommodate data with substantially smaller bases. Accordingly, the slopes of the lines on the first chart are not comparable with those on the latter two.)

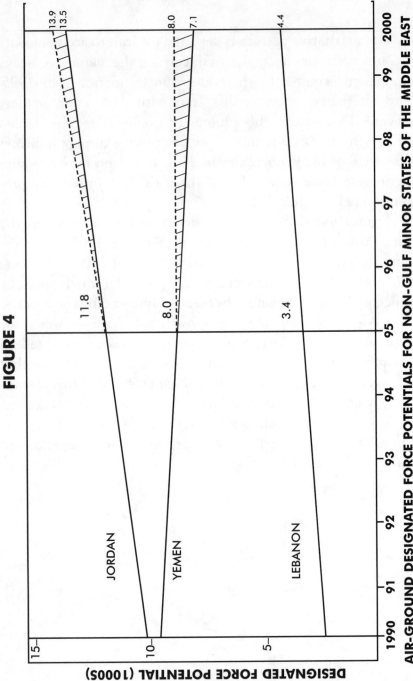

FIGURE 4

AIR-GROUND DESIGNATED FORCE POTENTIALS FOR NON-GULF MINOR STATES OF THE MIDDLE EAST

FIGURE 5

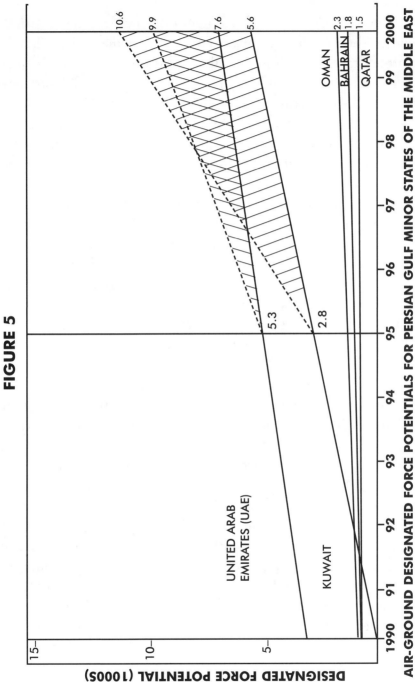

AIR-GROUND DESIGNATED FORCE POTENTIALS FOR PERSIAN GULF MINOR STATES OF THE MIDDLE EAST

• Jordan is expected to maintain its leading position among the smaller powers. This is particularly true if the United States reinstitutes a military aid program to that country as it has hinted it would in connection with Jordan's acceptance of peace terms with Israel. The upper limit of likely growth is not expected to be greatly accelerated from that of the first half of the decade inasmuch as Jordan would be expected to retire its older materiel as it receives new equipment.

• Yemen, again reunited, is unlikely to do much more than maintain its present military capabilities through the remainder of the decade. Unless Saudi Arabia were to pose a renewed challenge to Yemen security before the turn of the century, San'a might carry through with its announced intention of reducing its forces, with the possibility of a further diminution in the forces' total DFP — perhaps to about the 7,000 level. This would represent a continuation of the decrease caused through losses to both sides during the civil war.

• Among the minor states, Kuwait and the United Arab Emirates are the centers of greatest force growth in the region for the remainder of the decade — albeit from very low levels. Kuwait, having come from virtually zero at the close of the Gulf War, has demonstrated the fastest rate of growth of all of the minor powers. From 1995 onward, the rate gives every indication of accelerating. By the year 2000 Kuwait could achieve second place among its peers in air-ground force potential. The UAE, too, while not beginning from such a low base, is likely to finish close on Kuwait's heels. Considering the breadth of possible outcomes for those two countries, it is fairest to describe their race as essentially a dead heat.

• Lebanon, Oman and Bahrain may be expected to maintain their respective positions, but we can have greater confi-

dence in the latter two than in the first. Projections of Omani
and Bahraini historic patterns yield virtually the same results
as do calculations of the value of their new materiel. Little
information is available regarding the development of
Lebanese forces. Most likely it will depend upon Syrian attitudes regarding Beirut's forces' functions and missions. Indeed,
Syria may be the principal supplier of arms to Lebanon for the
foreseeable future. No ranges of anticipated DFPs for Oman
and Bahrain are shown because both methods of projection
yield essentially the same results. No range is depicted for
Lebanon because insufficient data is available for DFP calculation based upon anticipated acquisitions.

• Between Oman and Bahrain, Oman appears to be on the
more stable path. If there is a divergence between the Bahraini
historic pattern and its DFP based upon calculation of anticipated acquisitions, it lies in a slight inclination to fall behind
the documented rate of force development.

• Qatar's rate of force development is barely discernible.
Changes to a DFP under 1,000 are possible, but hardly reliable
indications of what is actually happening. There are usually
many other factors, each with subtle influences too fine to
measure, so that few useful conclusions may be drawn.

THE POWDER KEG

CHAPTER V
Comparative Analysis
Flash Points

Inherent in any military force assessment is an assumption of potential conflict between or among the parties under consideration. Hence, the analysis is dependent upon alignments which the parties may assume in a conflict. Few regions of the earth offer as rich a variety of issues over which armed conflict might occur. Besides the Arab-Israeli dispute, as we have seen, there are the rich against the poor, Sunni Muslims against Shiites (and both against Jews and Christians), fundamentalists against secularists (and both of these against royalists). There are also variations, such as the Iranian call for an Islamic war (with Persians as well as Arabs) against Israel. There are territorial disputes, historical disputes, and disputes over tactics for settling other disputes. The atmosphere is poisonous, and many combinations of belligerents can arise to subdue others. The intersections on Figure 6 below illustrate some of the potential flash points in the region from which conflicts may spring. In this analysis we shall endeavor to identify the strengths and weaknesses of each of the principal parties which might have a bearing on their relative power in context with the particular adversaries with which they might have to deal.

Israel and Iraq appear to have more enemies than the others. Israel is still in a formal state of war with most of its neighbors, regularly conducting operations against targets in one — Lebanon.   Iraq has been at war with most of its neighbors (Turkey and Jordan excepted) within the past five years, but even Turkey provided bases for forces taking part in operations against Iraq in the 1991 Gulf War.

Baghdad appears to believe that the "mother of all battles" over Kuwait continues.   Even Iraqi opposition leaders are ambiguous about Kuwaiti sovereignty.   Iraqis appear so incorrigible on the subject that prominent Saudi and Kuwaiti figures are beginning to believe that it is not solely the leadership of Saddam Hussein that is at fault, but the entire Iraqi political system.[1]

No flash point is posited between Israel and Saudi Arabia, but distance and the traditional Saudi disinclination for military ventures, rather than good will, are the principal determinants.   The anticipated U.S. sale of F-15 jet aircraft to Saudi Arabia over the remainder of the decade is unlikely to significantly impact the Arab-Israeli balance because of Riyadh's preoccupation with the security of its frontiers and the Persian Gulf and its lack of experience in the management of power projection forces.   Riyadh possesses long-range Chinese CSS-2 missiles capable of striking targets in Israel, but the Defense Ministry in Tel Aviv is apparently satisfied that it possesses sufficient deterrent power to neutralize the threat.   It may be significant that the former Mossad (Israeli intelligence service) officer, Viktor Ostrovsky, did not identify Saudi Arabia in his disclosure of Israel's list of enemy states.[2]

FIGURE 6
POTENTIAL MIDDLE EAST FLASH POINTS 1996-2000

	IS	IN	IQ	SY	SA	EG	GCC	JN	YE	TOTAL
ISRAEL		X	X	X		X		X		5
IRAN	X		X		X		X			4
IRAQ	X	X		X	X		X			5
SYRIA	X		X					X		3
SAUDI ARABIA		X	X					X	X	4
EGYPT	X									1
SMALL GCC		X	X							2
JORDAN	X				X	X				3
YEMEN					X					1

(Note: the above chart disregards small expeditionary contributions by the states in large coalition efforts, such as in the case of the 1991 Gulf War.)

ISRAEL VS IRAN

More disturbing to Tel Aviv is the possibility of conflict with Iran. Three reasons seem most persuasive. First, there is some possibility that Tehran will acquire nuclear weapons before the end of the decade. Second, the Persian government is virulently anti-Israel. And third, Iran lies at the outer edge of the envelope of American influence. The warning by the commander of the IAF, noted above, that military action may be necessary to prevent Iran from developing nuclear weapons, suggests that a potential flash point exists.

Indeed, Israel may already be in a shadow war with Iran. Israel's operations against Iranian-backed guerrillas in Lebanon and the apparently Iranian-supported bombing of the Israeli Embassy in Buenos Aires on 17 March 1992 may have been the opening blows in a new struggle. However, for the foreseeable future the military threat may be more of a simple exchange of raids than for a large scale conflict. Maj. Gen. Uri Sagi, former chief of IDF intelligence, argued that Iran still has higher priority strategic interests which would take precedence over its quarrel with Israel.[3] General Sagi did not elaborate, but it is apparent that he was speaking of Iran's concern for the continuing threat from Iraq addressed below.

Nevertheless, the possible acquisition of "Backfire" bombers by Iran represents a disturbing prospect for change in the military balance in the region. Very likely it would lower the threshold of Israeli military action against Iran in time of tension. Pressures for preemptive action between Iran and Israel would be increased on both sides. It would not be surprising if Israel were to demand that the contract not be consummated and, failing this, to threaten attack against any bases in Iran to which the aircraft might be delivered.

ISRAEL VS IRAQ

Israeli and Iraqi forces have collided in most Arab-Israeli conflicts, with the Iraqis sharing humiliation with their kinsmen in other Arab states. Iraqi units reached within six miles of the Mediterranean Sea at one point in the War of Independence (1948), but most Israeli-Iraqi actions since have taken place on

Arab ground. As Israeli strength has grown, Iraqi performance has become increasingly marginal. In the Gulf War, Baghdad's sole capability for attacking Israel was by Scud missile.

It is over two hundred miles from western Iraq to the Israeli border, through either Syria or Jordan. If Iraq were to attempt to take part in a conventional attack on Israel it would have to anticipate heavy air attacks, both during the period of eight to ten hours necessary to move a division to the front, and thereafter on its lines of supply. It is quite unlikely that even the initial movement could be made undetected in a period of heightened tension. With virtually all Israeli combat aircraft capable of ground attack missions, the Iraqi risk of heavy losses would be high.

On the other hand, if the initial move were undertaken in conjunction with a general Arab offensive against Israel, the IAF might be occupied with higher priority missions. As we have noted, the IAF's first priority is to gain air superiority; even aircraft available for ground support missions might be obliged to devote their principal effort to assisting ground forces absorbing the initial attack on the Golan Heights.

This scenario illustrates the importance of attack helicopters to the Israelis. While organized under the IAF, attack helicopters are uniquely suitable for close ground support, and would undoubtedly play a major role in that connection. In adequate numbers they could provide the essential support to the ground and relieve high performance aircraft for use in the air battle and in interdicting the enemy's rear and isolating the battlefield.

The Iraqi Air Force is in no condition to challenge the IAF and is unlikely to develop a capability before the end of the decade. Conceivably it could cooperate with a Syrian effort, but unless substantial preparations were made, to include coordinated training, communications and command doctrine, its contribution would likely be limited.

It is in the field of long-range missile attack that Iraq might have the greatest impact on Israel. As we have noted, it might not take Iraq long to reestablish its chemical warfare capability if U.N. sanctions were to be lifted without the imposition of some form of long term safeguard. Iraq has acquired considerable expertise in the missile field, and could develop improved missiles, to include quick launch solid fuel weapons with improved accuracy.

It is not clear at this point what form an Israeli countereffort might take against another attack on its cities. Unquestionably, Israeli civil defense measures will improve as a result of the Gulf War experience. The key question pertains to active measures. The IAF and the Defense Ministry are apparently at odds over whether the emphasis should be on offensive or defensive operations. The Arrow ABM has yet to prove itself and could outrun its funding before it is ready for deployment. The Patriot system, currently deployed, may have already been stretched to the outer edge of its improvement envelope for dealing with surface-to-surface missiles (SSM).

IAF spokesmen argue that primary reliance should continue to be placed on offensive operations. The Air Force leadership has strong confidence in its ability to locate missiles and to destroy them prior to launch. One should also note Israel's space-based intelligence effort and its readiness to project long-range special forces elements into potential launch areas, in context with its concept of deep battle, employing strategic assets.

The prospects for successful conventional military action by Iraq against Israel are not good. The antagonists are too far apart. Relations between Baghdad and Damascus are showing some signs of improvement, but that is not to say that the two

Ba'athist states are likely to move sufficiently close to permit true integration of tactics and doctrine between their armed forces. While Iraq has had close relations with Jordan, and may have had training elements there in recent years, the opportunities for that relationship are limited. Jordanian force capabilities are ebbing, and Israel is ill-disposed to permit significant foreign military presence in the Kingdom. In the words of the Likud Party leader and former deputy foreign minister, Benjamin Netanyahu, "Jordan is Israel's strategic depth. The crossing of the Iraqi-Jordanian border by Iraqi forces in strength would be a *casus belli.*"[4] In such a case mobilized Israeli forces might quickly overrun western Jordan. Leading elements of the Israeli active force might meet the Iraqis east of Amman, delaying their advance. In any event, the heights of the West Bank, overlooking the Jordan Valley would pose a daunting inhibition to any force attempting to attack Israel from the east. Israel appears to have every intention of maintaining a capability for reoccupying such positions in time of emergency.

ISRAEL VS SYRIA

Like most others, Syria has taken note of the importance of high technology intelligence gathering and command and control systems in the performance of coalition — particularly American — forces during the Gulf War. The Syrian leadership can be expected to internalize its observations in this regard, and Syrian forces may become substantially more sophisticated than they have been in the past. Very likely, Syria will acquire such equipment as remotely piloted vehicles (RPV) for reconnaissance, together with appropriate data links and computers to assist in target selection and fire direction. Further, it should be expected that the Syrian air defense systems will undergo significant enhancement to improve their performance against Israeli air attack.

There is a rough numerical equivalency of Syrian and (mobilized) Israeli forces in the air, but the equivalency is deceptive. Two-thirds of Syria's tactical fighter squadrons are designed for air defense, leaving but a fraction for close support of ground forces. In contrast, virtually all Israeli fighters have a ground attack capability, and four squadrons are dedicated to that purpose.

Nevertheless, Israelis evidence concern that the IAF may be inadequate to support the ground forces for the first day or two of combat. Syrian air defenses and surface-to-surface missile launchers have high priority as targets for attack by Israeli aircraft. Operations against these systems, together with defense against hostile air incursions, are expected to heavily tax the capabilities of the IAF in the early hours of conflict. Further, as aircraft become more expensive to procure and maintain, the number of aircraft may diminish, while the number of missile sites may increase, expanding the size and types of target sets.[5]

Offsetting the drain on Israeli air assets to some extent is the Israeli capability for the maintenance of high sortie ratios in comparison with the Syrians. According to one estimate, the IAF, with superior ground technical support, can generate a maximum of 4.5 sorties per aircraft per day. The Syrians, in contrast, can achieve but 2. Under sustained operations the Israelis can maintain 2.5 sorties per aircraft per day, as opposed to only 1 for the Syrians.[6]

In the ground-based air defense area, Syrian forces exceed those of Israel by more than 3:1. While not valid for calculations of the correlation of forces because air defense missile batteries do not engage one another, the ratio is a strong indication of the importance which the Syrians attach to the Israeli air threat and of their emphasis on defensive capabilities. The Syrian air defense system is presently superior to most of those found in Warsaw Pact states in the mid-1980s.[7]

The balance of air and air defense forces between Israel and Syria indicates that both sides are comfortable with the notion of conducting the air battle primarily over Syrian territory. For the less well trained Syrian aviators it facilitates ground control of operations and maximizes chances for pilot and crew recovery in case of being shot down. For the Israelis, it minimizes chances of casualties in the homeland. However, if a third party, such as Saudi Arabia or Iraq, were to assume a major role in an Arab-Israeli conflict, the air action might take place over a substantially wider area.

The most obvious asymmetry on the ground between Israeli and Syrian forces is that of size. However, some specifics merit mention. Syria has somewhat more tanks, artillery tubes and rocket launchers than Israel. Israel, on the other hand, has almost twice as many armored infantry vehicles (albeit many of old design). Further, while the bulk of Syrian artillery is towed, almost three quarters of that of Israel is self-propelled. The Syrians are apparently attempting to correct this imbalance with the purchase of 250 self-propelled pieces from Russia, noted above.[8] Clearly, the Syrians look first to firepower as the key to battle management, while the Israelis, in accordance with their doctrine, look primarily to offensive maneuver by combined arms forces.

The impact of these differences is to suggest that while the Syrians are more defensively structured than the Israelis, they still have a respectable capability for quick strike with heavy punch. If they were to seek a resolution of the Golan Heights issue by force, they would need to mount a quick strike before the Israelis had time to mobilize or to bring their air power to bear on the ground battle. If the Syrians were successful in driving the Israelis from the Golan in less than 24 hours, they might be able to hold their gains until the United Nations, or other outside authority, could freeze the action. Neither side has the capability for sustained intensive combat on a major scale. Both are highly reliant upon foreign sources for supply.

From the Israeli point of view, the Golan Heights continue to pose problems for military operations. The density of Syrian fortifications and the constrained area for maneuver raise the specter of heavy casualties, a factor which carries particularly negative connotations for Israel with its small population base. In another conflict akin to those of 1967 and 1973, the Israelis may wish to find some alternative avenues of attack.

Lebanon provides some potential answers. While the Bekaa Valley is narrow and defended by some 20,000 Syrian troops and Syrian-backed guerrillas, it represents an attractive alternative for a highly mobile force. A concerted air-ground attack northward to the Beirut-Damascus road, perhaps assisted by airborne or airmobile assault on the highway pass over the anti-Lebanon mountain range, could place Israeli forces in a commanding position overlooking Damascus from the rear, effectively outflanking the bulk of the Syrian Army. Israeli air, once it had overcome the Syrian Air Force, could probably prevent significant Syrian ground reinforcement of the Bekaa.

Still another possibility would be Israeli use of the assault routes followed in the 1982 campaign leading to Beirut. Assisted by small amphibious landings, the Israelis could force their way forward until they were on the Damascus highway again, and follow this route eastward until they were on the high ground behind Damascus. While longer, this course might minimize confrontation with the 40,000 Syrian troops believed to be in Lebanon until the final phase of the operation.[9]

Whatever the course of the conflict, major considerations,

such as the integrative quality of forces, doctrine and topography, clearly favor Israel. Nevertheless, the Syrian capability for sudden, limited notice attack, and the rough equivalency of conventional designated force potential (DFP — see Chapter IV) which may develop by 2000 cannot be dismissed. This is particularly cogent considering Israel's concern for avoidance of casualties. The threat of Syrian missile attacks on Israeli urban areas could constrain Israeli air operations to some extent. The possibility of fighting a battle to a draw, or some sort of political stand-off, might appear sufficiently attractive to the Syrian leadership to prompt such an attempt.

This discussion does not take into consideration the possibility of a prolonged conflict between Israel and Syria. As we have noted, the Syrians have given extensive thought to the possibility of a long war based upon guerrilla tactics and raids launched throughout the length and breadth of the country against hostile occupation. They probably recognize that Israel could overrun or otherwise circumvent their principal defenses, but they demonstrate a degree of confidence in their ability to ultimately drive the enemy from their soil. They might lose Damascus and other important urban areas, and perhaps suffer a blockade of their coastline, but if they could rouse the population to hold out in the mountains, and possibly the desert, they might succeed in wearing down Israeli forces over time. They have borders with Turkey and northern Iraq which might be difficult for an occupier to police, especially if the Syrian cause were to gain sympathy in those countries. Again, Israel's limited population and its concern for potentially hostile elements closer to home could weaken its staying power in the face of such a challenge, thus limiting its options.

ISRAEL VS EGYPT

Armed conflict is not expected to occur between Israel and her southern neighbor in the remainder of the century. Both countries have strong interests in maintaining the peace — even if, as some critics characterize it, it were to remain little more than a "cold peace." Nevertheless, parties on both sides of the border recognize that circumstances could change, particularly under stimulus of a sudden change in one of the governments, such as by assassination or coup.

Military actions would likely depend heavily upon how a conflict might break out. A political surprise could find both armies ill prepared. The accession to power in Cairo of radical elements intent upon resuming the struggle against Israel would generate shock waves that could sharply escalate tensions and perhaps precipitate hostilities with little time for planning. In that case, Israel might have an advantage, considering its superior mobilization system. The Israeli Air Force would likely play a dominant role initially. It might attack Egyptian airfields and command and control centers. It would probably assign high priority to targeting any Egyptian ground forces attempting to move east of the Sinai mountain passes.

On the ground, the first indications of hostilities could prompt moves by both sides to rush into the central Sinai to seize and secure the passes as early as possible. The Israelis might hope to trap some Egyptian forces east of the passes, and to destroy them by air and ground attack. An Egyptian expedition in force across the Israeli border would be a very risky venture because of the distances to be traversed and the difficulties inherent in maintaining the force. The lines of communications (LOC) running across the canal, through the passes, and across the desert would be highly vulnerable to air attack. The Egyptians would also find that they faced a rather broad front, without much opportunity for the preparation of forward defensive positions. In all likelihood, considering superior Israeli capabilities for mobile warfare, they would be playing into the enemy's hands.

Instead, the Egyptians might choose to base a defensive line on the central mountains. However, unless they could deploy sufficient air defense units to the area before the IAF began its strikes, they might find themselves in a precarious position. Their LOC would still lie across the canal, with likely bottlenecks in that area.

If, on the other hand, the Egyptians based their principal defense line on the Suez Canal, they might realize somewhat greater chances of success. Certainly they learned the lesson of retaining a mobile reserve west of the canal from the 1973 campaign. How the battle might develop as the Israelis again closed on the canal is highly conjectural.

A less precipitous change in Cairo or determination to alter policy with respect to Israel might generate a more careful alteration in Egyptian military posture. Depending upon its interpretation of the course of events, the Egyptian high command might seek to reinforce the central Sinai secretly in anticipation of conflict at some time in the future. For its part, the Israeli leadership would probably mount its own effort, intensifying intelligence gathering activities over the area. Israeli reconnaissance aircraft, accompanied by protective air superiority fighters, might penetrate Egyptian airspace as far as the Gidi and Mitla Passes, and possibly to the Suez Canal. Any Egyptian troop concentrations detected above those permitted in the 1979 Sadat-Begin treaty would prompt loud protest from Jerusalem, and possibly trigger Israeli air strikes on some troop concentrations. (No more than 22,000 fully equipped Egyptian troops are permitted between the Suez Canal and the mountain passes in peacetime, and no more than 4,000 lightly armed border guards are permitted east of the passes.)

If the new Egyptian regime showed an inclination to persevere in its preparations, Jerusalem might feel compelled to escalate the action, at least to the level of a limited air offensive, possibly followed by a degree of national mobilization. If, however, the Israelis did not detect, or were unable to document, illegal reinforcement of the Sinai, they might choose to reinforce the border area, backing it up with a low-level partial mobilization.

Of high interest to Israel would be the threat of surface-to-surface missiles from Egypt. Egypt possesses Scud-Bs, which, if moved east of the canal, could reach communities in southern Israel. Also, Egypt was a participant, with Argentina, in the development of the 900 km range Condor II missile, and undoubtedly acquired a measure of expertise from that experience. It might be able to acquire and operate longer-range weapons from China (such as the CSS-2) or other suppliers. A change of policy in Egypt toward Israel would also likely open doors to other Arab stockpiles and technology, perhaps permitting development of an indigenous weapon with assistance from neighbors.

Israeli experience with the psychological impact of Iraqi Scud missiles in the Gulf War would place heavy pressure on Jerusalem to give high priority to the location and destruction of any weapons capable of reaching Israeli soil in a future conflict. So high might the pressure be that any extraordinary preparations detected around potential launching sites or missile storage facilities might be sufficient to precipitate preemptive counter-force strikes by the IAF.

If Israel were determined to repossess the Sinai peninsula, or even part of it, to protect itself from any future aggression, it could not count on being able to recover it at the peace table. The price in all probability would be the cost of a ground offensive carried at least to the extent of Israel's territorial desires — perhaps to the passes and to Sharm el Sheikh, or perhaps to the canal. Certainly Israel would have a strong case in international forums for an extended occupation of the area, or even annexation, if it was obliged to conquer it for a fourth time.

Once joined, the course of battle would depend in part upon the success of Israel's "befuddlement" weapon and political factors extant at the time. Overall, it would seem that Egypt's military risks would be larger than Israel's in the early phases of such a conflict, and its opportunities fewer. However, recognizing Israel's dependence upon the early defeat of an opponent and termination of the fighting, it would be unwise to venture a forecast of the final outcome.

ISRAEL VS JORDAN

Jordan is not a serious threat to Israel, either alone or in conjunction with other forces. On the contrary, its location along the length of Israel's eastern border provides Israel with a measure of early warning against attack by a third party, via Jordan. We have noted how prominent Israeli leaders refer to Jordan as Israel's "strategic depth."

It should be recognized, however, that Jordan's complexion could change. Some Israeli leaders view Jordan as "the Palestinian state," and suggest that Palestinians in the occupied territories desirous of living in a country of their own should move there.[10]

Jordan is already heavily populated with Palestinians, and additional concentrations of immigrants from the West Bank and Gaza could be destabilizing to the Hashemite throne. The result could be the transformation of a weak, inoffensive (if formally hostile) neighbor into a hot bed of revanchist, perhaps fundamentalist, hatred, bent upon the destruction of the Zionist state. Israel's security problems would doubtless multiply, with little prospect for restabilization in the foreseeable future. Not unlikely, the difficulties which Israel has found on its northern border with Lebanon would be replicated in the east, but with a much longer border to patrol. In short, pressure to force Jordan into a Palestinian mold could prove counterproductive for Israel.

ISRAEL VS AN ARAB COALITION

In the event of a reconstructed combined Arab front against Israel, it is likely that the Golan Heights would be Israel's first territorial concern. In the south the great mass of Egyptian forces are west of the Suez Canal, and most would have to travel over 150 miles to reach Israel. To the east, Jordan has been severely weakened, and whether or not the West Bank were under Israeli control it could be quickly reinforced or reoccupied. The Jordan Valley would form a formidable barrier to hostile attack from that quarter even if outside forces were employed. The Arabs might be able to mount an aerial or missile war with Israel for a short period of time, but they would be in no position to prevent the reoccupation of the West Bank or to dislodge Israeli forces once deployed. In the north, by contrast, Syrian forces are virtually in attack positions, and would have to traverse no more than 25 miles to the edge of the Golan escarpment. The Israelis faced a decision regarding priorities between their northern and southern fronts in the 1973 war, and resolved it in favor of the north (Golan Heights).

We have examined the case of conflict between Israel and Syria; we must also consider the case of Israel vs Syria and Iraq in combination. If the two Arab countries were able to develop a close cooperative relationship, the mid- to long-range implications for Israel could be dangerous. Together with Lebanon, Syria and Iraq have a potential for building a formidable military alliance, complete with mass destruction weapons and delivery systems. Moreover, they could hold a frontage of about 80 miles with Israeli-held territory and have a strategic depth of some 400 to 600 miles.

Syria's new strategy emphasizing long war and operations in depth may attach lower importance to the defense of Damascus under some circumstances. Conceivably, by falling back upon the desert space and the mountains to the north, the Arab partners could make it far more difficult for Israel to achieve decisive victory on its own. Barring major power intervention, a conflict might drag on for months, or even years, sapping Israeli strength.

Israel might avoid being dragged into protracted war in depth by foregoing major ground assaults. Raids might be staged when worthwhile targets presented themselves, but the Israelis may prefer to avoid entering Damascus and to limit their ground operations far beyond it. Principal reliance for suppressing Arab operations would likely fall to the IAF and to special operations forces for mounting combat raids on the ground. Chemical or biological weapons might or might not be employed. If they caused many casualties or came into general use, there would be heavy pressure upon the Israeli leadership to turn to its nuclear weapons.

While the United States and its allies might not be under great pressure to intervene in the early stages of a conflict of this sort, it seems likely that pressures would mount the longer it continued. As soon as it became apparent that Israel could not terminate the fighting on its own terms, or as soon as MDW came into play, there would likely be strong calls from many quarters for U.S. or Western intervention and suppression of the action.

More likely than not, the force requirement for intervention at this point in the conflict would be large — perhaps on the order that deployed for the Desert Storm operation. While it might not be intended that the intervening force fight its way in, it would have to be prepared to do so. Similarly, it might have to defend itself if it were perceived as primarily aiding the interests of one side of the conflict (Israel) against the other.

An important point in this analysis is the probable capability of Israel to hold its own against an Arab coalition. The outcome might not be substantially different if Iran were to take part with conventional forces. Iran could contribute many types of forces, but its missiles and aircraft would probably be most telling, even if they were only conventionally armed. Iran's entry could be more serious if it entailed the addition of a nuclear deterrent force to the anti-Israel coalition. Such a development might either dissuade Israel from employing its nuclear weapons or prompt her to launch preemptive strikes.

Much would depend upon the general strategic situation and the attitude of the U.S. and its Western allies. If the war were otherwise progressing well, and U.S. forces were close at hand, Israel might be persuaded to forgo its nuclear option. If, on the other hand, the war were not going well and the chances of U.S. or Western intervention remote, the likelihood of nuclear warfare would be greater.

IRAN VS IRAQ

Hostilities between Iran and Iraq are a distinct possibility within the time frame of this study. There are a many outstanding issues between the two countries, and Iran may sense its current advantage for preparing for further fighting while Iraq is under U.N. supervision and sanctions. As we have seen, there is a prospect for Iran to overtake Iraqi military strength in the next few years. Further, the Iranian leadership has specifically identified Iraq as the purpose and target of its on-going arms build-up.

As became clear in the progress of the earlier Iran-Iraq war, there are natural barriers which tend to contain military operations in the border region between the two countries. Iraqi swamps west of the Tigris River and the Zagros Mountains to the east in Iran inhibit deep penetrations by either country into its neighbor. To what extent the Iranian build-up might overcome this factor remains to be seen. It is clear that, absent third country intervention, Iran could dominate the northern end of the Gulf and perhaps the airspace overhead. It might also dominate any revisitation of the "war against the cities," with "Backfire" bomber raids as well as heavy missile attacks on central Iraq.

Tehran might also calculate that the relationship between the Shiia in southern Iraq and the Baghdad government had been so poisoned by Saddam Hussein's suppressive actions in the wake of the Gulf War that the issue could be exploited to Iranian advantage. Iran might see an opportunity in this, not only to even the score with its old antagonist, but to "liberate" permanently a sizable section of Iraqi territory. The creation of a friendly Shiia buffer state between Iran and Iraq might be an attractive enough goal to justify renewal of the conflict.

IRAN VS SAUDI ARABIA AND THE GCC

Conflict between Iran and Saudi Arabia would be quite unlikely without involvement of one or more of the other GCC states, and perhaps all in concert. Iran has territorial claims on the west side of the gulf, perhaps providing some motive for military action. If the United States were to substantially reduce or to eliminate its presence in the area for any reason, the possibility of conflict might be considerably higher than it is under present circumstances.

There are three basic routes by which an Iranian incursion onto the western littoral could occur. One stretches through southern Iraq into Kuwait and Saudi Arabia; a second crosses the gulf, aimed perhaps at Bahrain or Qatar; while a third runs across the Strait of Hormuz to Oman. Either of the latter two would require both air and sea superiority by Iran.

The first route, via Iraq, might be feasible in the aftermath of a successful campaign against Baghdad. Conceivably, a friendly Shiite buffer state could assist Iranian forces transiting the country, perhaps providing some measure of security and protection for the LOC. The advantage of this route would be the ability to move heavy armored forces in sufficient strength to engage Saudi armor.

The cross-gulf route might be useful for a limited campaign to seize isolated objectives. Iranian sealift is capable of transporting about one armored brigade in a single lift. Shore bombardment and modest air defense might be provided by Iran's 3 destroyers and 5 frigates. Newly acquired Kilo class submarines might protect the convoys or be used to close the Strait of Hormuz during the operation. A rejuvenated Iranian Air Force would bear a heavy burden, with responsibilities for air cover, close support to ground forces, and troop airlift.

Iran has one airborne and four special forces brigades which might participate in the initial assault. It also has a merchant marine of some 133 ships which could supplement its amphibious vessels. Unless, however, the Iranian Air Force could neutralize the Saudi Air Force — which does not seem particularly likely considering the sophistication of the latter — the success of the operation would be difficult to foresee.

An assault operation across the strait would be simpler because of the shorter distances involved. It might, however, ultimately prove more difficult. The UAE and Oman have much more powerful forces than the other small GCC states, and the landing areas could not be isolated as easily as beach-heads on either Bahrain or Qatar. If Iran could seize a lodgment in Oman and hold it long enough to introduce sufficient force to overcome the resistance, it might ultimately prevail, but the operation would be one of high risk. Saudi air forces could be brought to bear on the landing sites in short order, and Saudi armor might arrive before the local forces could be subdued. And none of this says anything about likely U.S. intervention.

In sum, a major surface attack by Iran on its GCC neighbors does not seem to be a particularly easy matter, nor does it appear to offer an opportunity for quick seizure of a digestible objective (e.g.: Bahrain). If one were attempted, it might be in the wake of a successful campaign against Iraq, perhaps simultaneously with a diversionary effort by land against Kuwait while the main effort was mounted across the gulf.

None of this, of course, considers the possibility of brief raids by sea or air, of attacks on ships at sea, or of major power intervention. As long as the U.S. and its major allies are not engaged in conflict elsewhere in the world, and as long as access to oil is deemed critical to Western security, the likelihood of overt Iranian aggression against the GCC states with the objective of seizing and holding territory is low.

IRAQ VS SYRIA

Bad blood between the Damascus and Baghdad dictatorships set the nations at opposite poles in the Iran-Iraq dispute, and again in the Gulf War of 1991. The sour relationship between two of Israel's most powerful adversaries has been a boon to Jerusalem, minimizing chances of a well coordinated action against Israel's defenses in the Golan area. While there are some signs of rapprochement between Syria and Iraq, the possibility of conflict at some time before the turn of the century cannot be ruled out. If it were to occur, it could, indeed, be the "mother of all battles" so close to Saddam Hussein's heart.

As we have noted, Syria's conventional force power presently exceeds that of Iraq by a substantial margin, and the gap is likely to widen as long as Iraq remains under U.N. sanctions. Nevertheless, Syria could have difficulty bringing forces to bear on its eastern frontier without dangerously depleting its position on the Damascus plain and possibly compromising its position in Lebanon. A realization of its precarious position between Iraq and Israel may be a principal motivation now for Hafez Al-Assad to seek some accommodation with Baghdad.

Barring such accommodation, Syria might seek cooperation from Iran to at least pin down sufficient Iraqi forces to permit Syria to execute an offensive against western Iraq. Baghdad is about 200 miles from the Syrian border, offering a feasible military objective. As long as Syria was able to maintain control of the air, its supply lines, including possible barge traffic on the Euphrates River, should be reasonably secure. It would not, however, have a rail line in its LOC unless it chose the Tigris valley as an attack route.

Topographically, one should note the location of the large lakes west of Baghdad which might tend to inhibit east-west ground movement. The lakes could play an important part in either a defense of Baghdad or in protection of an invading force frustrated in its initial assault of the capital and seeking a fall-back position for recuperation. In any event, the lakes would make a useful objective area in their own right. A penetration to that depth toward Baghdad would likely render advanced Iraqi positions to the south untenable, prompting large withdrawals from the westernmost extreme of the country. In this case, Iraq would be denied Scud missile launching sites within range of Damascus.

The attitude of third parties toward such a conflict is uncertain. Depending upon the circumstances surrounding the origins of the dispute, and the political objectives of the participants, other parties, such as Israel or Saudi Arabia, might elect to stand aloof. On the other hand, they might desire to lend support to one side or the other, or even succumb to temptations to take advantage of perceived opportunities. Israel, for example, might wish to clear Lebanon of hostile guerrilla (Hezbullah) forces, or even to press Syrian forces to withdraw. Intervention might well carry more negatives than positives for either Israel or Saudi Arabia in an Syrian-Iraqi conflict, but that is not a question likely to be resolved in the near future.

IRAQ VS SAUDI ARABIA AND THE GCC

Clearly this is the contingency of greatest Saudi concern. Riyadh is aware that the day is approaching when U.N. controls over Iraq will be lifted, and unless they are replaced by some other regime for peninsular security, the future could resemble the past — especially if Saddam Hussein remains in power. The Iraqi-Kuwaiti border flash point was given fresh prominence when Baghdad rejected the boundary established by the U.N. between the two countries in May 1992.[11]

The most dangerous aspect of the conflict might be the lessons which Baghdad learned from the 1991 Gulf War. As we have noted, the Iraqis have apparently gained an understanding of the importance of quality forces. Presumably, they have also learned the importance of the classic principle of the offensive. Iraq may be far less disposed in the future to limiting the scope of its operations once it is committed to action. Unlike 1990, a second Iraqi offensive could entail an effort to mount high speed penetrations along the coast as far south as Qatar, or southwestward toward Riyadh in expectation of destroying the Saudi armed forces.

The distances, however, are daunting: approximately 400 miles along either axis — twice the distance covered by the Desert Storm "left hook" maneuver. Further, Iraq would have to deal with substantially stronger and more sophisticated Saudi forces, and, in the case of a coastal drive, would have little or no support from the sea.

Most damaging from the Iraqi point of view would be its inability to control the gulf or to prevent outside intervention by a major power or a reconstructed U.N. coalition. Rapid seizure of the entire eastern littoral of the Arabian Peninsula would seem beyond Iraq's capability before the year 2000. Unless Saudi Arabia and its GCC allies were to suffer severe internal disruptions impinging on their ability to defend themselves, they should be able to slow the Iraqi advance sufficiently to permit Western expeditionary forces to arrive in force before the Iraqis reached their principal objectives.

The situation would not be substantially different if Jordan and Yemen were involved — as some observers apparently believed might have occurred in the Gulf War had Iraq been more successful. The interests of those countries are in rather more limited objectives, and their forces are unlikely to be capable of much more than local operations.

SYRIA VS JORDAN

Syrian-Jordanian relations have traced an uneven course. At their worst, in the 1960s, attempts were made on King Hussein's life — on one occasion by Syrian assassins with explosives (which killed the prime minister) and on another by Syrian fighter aircraft when the monarch attempted to pilot his plane over Syrian territory. In 1970 Syrian armored units invaded northern Jordan under the guise of the PLO. An inspired Jordanian defense and some Soviet pressure on Damascus resulted in their withdrawal.

The greatest deterrent to a renewed Syrian invasion is probably the Israeli policy, previously noted, of treating such an event as a cause for Israeli military action. The Yarmuk River bed is a natural defensive barrier between Jordan and Syria in the vicinity of Irbid, overlooking the juncture of the Yarmuk with the Jordan River. To the east, however, the terrain is quite open and has numerous north-south arteries which would support invasion forces. Jordan, itself, has modest forces, but might be able to delay an invader, if it were so inclined, until a third party could intervene and resolve the matter.

SAUDI ARABIA VS JORDAN

Riyadh gave sufficient credence to rumors of Jordanian attack during the Gulf War to poison relations between the kingdoms for the foreseeable future. In addition, competition has been keen between Amman and Riyadh over the legitimacy of claims of responsibility for the maintenance of Moslem holy sites in Jerusalem. Mutual distrust is strong. If there were no desert between the principal populated areas of the two countries, border skirmishes might have become a post-Desert Storm staple.

Nevertheless, the likelihood of general warfare between the two countries is remote. There are no significant, militarily attainable objectives for either side acting alone. The rumors of attack from the west alive in Riyadh in 1990 arose in context of Saddam Hussein's call for pan-Arab action, and are not likely to be repeated within the time frame of this analysis. While we should take note of the existence of a possible flash point on the Saudi-Jordanian border, the likelihood of its ignition seems negligible.

SAUDI ARABIA VS YEMEN

Somewhat more worrisome is the possibility of a clash between Saudi Arabia and its more populous (estimated 11.5 to 13 million persons) neighbor, Yemen. As with Jordan, the Saudis harbor strong suspicions of Yemeni collusion with Iraq during the Gulf War to settle the long-simmering border dispute between Riyadh and San'a.

The Saudi Government warned Western oil companies to desist from exploration efforts in the disputed border area with Yemen. The warning was believed to include a threat of military action if it was not heeded. Further, the Yemeni press reported actions by Saudi agents to destabilize the regime of Lieutenant General Ali Abdullah Saleh by promising Saudi citizenship to border-area residents if they support Saudi territorial claims.[12] These developments came in the wake of the Saudi expulsion of an estimated 700,000 to a million Yemeni workers in the kingdom for their alleged support of Saddam Hussein. The economic impact on Yemen was severe.

The stage has been set for a low-level, possibly guerrilla, conflict between the two countries. While there is no indication of such intent on the part of either side at this writing, the potential flash point merits particularly close observation.

The Yemeni ground forces have certain advantages. While they are smaller than those of Saudi Arabia and were divided for a number of years, they are composed of seasoned veterans. More importantly, they are concentrated in the area of potential conflict, while Saudi forces are deployed largely to deal with threats from the north and east and to deal with internal disturbances. The Saudis have undertaken construction of a new military city at Jizan, north of San'a, to include naval and air facilities on the Red Sea, but it may be several years before the work is complete.[13] By 2000 it could become militarily significant, depending upon what types of forces may be deployed there. In the meanwhile, it would be difficult for the Saudis to concentrate sufficient force in the southwestern corner of the country to match the Yemenis.

On the other hand, the Saudi Air Force is substantially larger than its Yemeni counterpart. If the issue could be settled in the air, the odds would clearly favor Riyadh, but that seems highly unlikely. The Saudis lack the ground capability for bringing a ground conflict to a successful conclusion if the Yemenis are willing to sustain the casualties which an air campaign might entail. Hence, the prospect for settlement of the territorial dispute by either party by force of arms is not good.

It may have been an understanding of this that led in June 1992 to an agreement by the Saudis and the Yemenis to negotiate their differences. Considering the poisonous relationship which has prevailed between the two powers, an armed conflict on the border, should it come to that, could drag on for as long as the parties wished. Negotiations appear the wiser course for both.

INTERNAL CONFLICTS

In addition to the flash points discussed above, there is some concern among regional observers over possibilities of internal conflicts in a few countries which could spread across national borders or serve as catalysts to international hostilities. Root causes in most potential areas include poverty, perceived government corruption and militant Islamic fundamentalism. Worthy of special note is the case of Iran. There, attempts by a few to liberalize the economy failed, while oil revenues dropped by half. The government is reported to be up to $10 billion behind on debt payments. In 1994 a knowledgeable analyst argued, "At no point since the early days of the revolution has the political, economic and social condition of Iran been so fragile."[14] The following year another remarked that the Iranian regime was edging closer to collapse.[15]

Those who agree contemplate a civil war between the "liberal" supporters of President Rafsanjani and the forces of Iran's spiritual leader, Ayatollah Ali Khamenei. The latter demonstrated his strength in 1993 when he ordered 200,000 radical militia, the *Basij*, into the streets to enforce orthodox Islamic behavior, especially by women. A victory by the Ayatollah could solidify the current anti-Western path of the country, and perhaps further inflame Iran's relations with its neighbors.

The bombing of U.S. facilities in Saudi Arabia in 1995 and 1996 have illustrated the endemic dissident problem in that country. Young radical Islamic fundamentalists, many of them veterans of the Afghan War, continue to threaten the stability of the regime through embarrassing acts of terrorism against its Western partners. The course of an open campaign of opposition to the government is impossible to foresee, but one may anticipate that the loyalty of the armed forces, and more especially of the National Guard, could be determining factors in the outcome.

THE POWDER KEG

CHAPTER VI
Conclusions

The foregoing chapters of this study have reviewed the perceptions of indigenous leaders and Western analysts regarding the security regime in the Middle East. They have also presented estimates as to how the various states may develop their military components in the closing years of the century. Finally, they have identified potential flash points between countries known to harbor grievances toward one another, and sketched out possible military scenarios following from ignition of those points. This chapter draws conclusions from the preceding review regarding the relative military power of the principle states.

ISRAEL

Israel stands alone in the Middle East as a regional superpower. While its geographic and demographic bases are small, it has a skilled, educated and militarized population and a close working relationship in security matters with the United States. There is little doubt that Israel possesses a large number of nuclear weapons and the means for delivering them on all potential adversaries. Israel's nuclear stockpile may have been built upon an expectation of possible need for deterring Soviet aggression in the Middle East. Considering the demise of the Soviet Union, the stockpile may now exceed reasonable requirements.

While the possibility exists that other states in the region could also acquire nuclear weapons before the millennium, Israel has active programs for both offensive and defensive measures to counter their use. Further, it is likely that Israel's intelligence and defensive programs will employ layered elements, to include early detection of launch and tracking, and multiple interceptors, for high assurance of destruction of incoming missiles.

In the area of conventional arms, Israel appears adequately structured and armed to engage and defeat virtually any combination of hostile neighbors bent on attacking her defensive perimeter. Israel maintains a large proportion of its population under arms and has a mobilization system which has proven itself in past conflicts. The IAF, which garners 70 percent of the military procurement budget, is maintained in a particularly high state of readiness, and is unlikely to be found unresponsive to warning.[1] Further, the long distances between most of the main concentrations of Arab ground forces, such as in Iraq and Egypt, and the Israeli frontier, and the sparsity of road and rail nets would impose high risks upon those forces should they attempt to move closer. Only Syrian forces appear deployed and postured for launching a short warning attack.

While the greatest military threat to Israel lies in current trends towards proliferation of weapons of mass destruction and long-range delivery systems among potential enemies, there is another, less obvious danger. A combination of opponents prepared for a lengthy campaign could draw Israel into a prolonged conflict for which neither the IDF nor the Israeli economy would be prepared. An alliance between Syria and Iraq would appear to pose the most serious prospect in this regard. Barring intervention by the U.S. or other outside powers, Israeli forces could be drawn deep into hostile territory, beyond the capabilities of IDF logistical systems or the national infrastructure to support. The Jerusalem leadership should be wary of temptations in such circumstances to push the ground forces of the IDF beyond the reach of their logistical tether.

Besides its principal missions, discussed above, the IAF suits Israel well for executing retaliatory raids against hostile military and guerrilla units attacking or harassing Israeli settlements or security forces. However, there has been a weakness in Israeli strategy in this regard. Until the accession of the Rabin government in Jerusalem there was a notable lack of any "carrot" to match Israel's military "stick." With the exception of monetary inducements to members of the South Lebanon Army, incentives to neighboring peoples and states to cooperate in promoting stability in the area were overwhelmingly of a negative nature.

In early July 1992, shortly after his election to office, Prime Minister Rabin signaled a sharp change in policy. He argued publicly that Israel could do much to combat anti-Semitism worldwide through fair treatment of Israel's Arab minority and of Palestinians in the occupied territories. Clearly the remarks also conveyed an incentive to the Palestinians and the populations of neighboring states to adopt more cooperative attitudes toward Israel in the future. Mr. Rabin's initiative began to bear fruit in secret discussions with the PLO in Norway, and later at the meeting between Mssrs. Rabin and Arafat at the White House in Washington DC. The first concrete manifestation of progress was the creation of PLO administered territories in Jericho and Gaza. The succeeding accords in the autumn of 1995 granting expanded rule to the PLO added impetus to the movement.

Some encouragement was given to observers concerned about the dangers of reversal of Israeli policy if the Rabin government were to be defeated in the 1996 elections. An unidentified "very senior Israeli military official," (very likely a former chief of staff) was quoted in the Jewish Institute for National Security Affairs' publication, *Security Affairs*, to the effect that "Israel cannot sustain both its large standing forces and continue its economic growth." In the general's opinion, according to the report, that fact would guarantee continuation of the peace process and the reforms in the structure of the Israeli military.[2]

There is no question that much remains to be done. And it is probably true that the process could slip into reverse under a number of circumstances, but the Rabin attitude and policies pointed the way and substantially increased the chances for a lasting peace in the Middle East.[3] It remains to be seen whether the policies will survive the assassination of the prime minister and the defeat of his party in national elections, but one may hope that the implication of the "very senior Israeli military official" that further progress is assured under virtually any Israeli government is correct.

IRAQ

Iraq has slipped in its standing in the Middle East region, both as a result of its defeat in the Gulf War and of the U.N. mandated destruction of facilities for manufacture of mass destruction weapons and long-range missiles. Whereas Iraq may arguably have had the preeminent ground force in early 1991, its army has deteriorated to a point of rough parity with that of Egypt, and substantially below that of Syria. Depending upon the duration of U.N. controls, and the concentration with which neighboring countries pursue their current arms programs, Iraqi forces could slip further behind as the decade advances. Possibilities exist for Saudi Arabia and Iran to match Iraq in overall military strength by the year 2000.

Iraq has retained adequate forces for maintenance of internal control and for protection of the regime. It probably also has the capability to again overrun Kuwait and to mount large raiding expeditions into either Iran or Saudi Arabia. It is deficient in air and naval forces, however, and would be severely strained to support ground operations far from its borders for any length of time. Operations in Saudi Arabia would be particularly difficult to sustain under a well orchestrated air counteroffensive by Riyadh.

Iraqi forces are poorly postured or prepared for participation in an attack on Israel, and may remain so for some years after U.N. sanctions are removed, or possibly almost permanently if an effective arms control regime can be devised to limit its acquisition of mass destruction weapons and long-range delivery systems.

It is unlikely that Iraq will recover its former stature as a military power of influence before the year 2000. It could, however, regain a measure of strength if it were to find a kindred state with which to coordinate its policies and actions. Of its four major neighboring states, Syria would seem to offer the greatest opportunity for partnership. Baghdad's recognition of the possibility may lie behind some recurring indications of detente between the traditionally hostile Ba'athist powers. Should an alliance develop, it would probably raise concerns for the security of royalist regimes in the region. It could also have an impact of the Arab-Israeli balance by stiffening Syria's hand, and heightening concerns in Israel.

It is not clear that the military balance would be immediately affected. It would take time for Iraq to rebuild its forces and for the new allies to structure a common or coordinated defense. Communications would be a significant problem, especially where time critical information had to be passed to multiple subscribers in standard format with high fidelity, such as with air defense nets. Over time, of course, the threat to Israel could grow. For its part, Israel might establish specific thresholds (such as "red lines") beyond which it would not permit the cooperation to develop without incurring risk of Israeli attack.

However the military balance might be affected, the psychological effect would be serious, both in Jerusalem and in the streets of cities where a yearning for Arab nationalism survives. Public excitement on both sides might be high, and internal political pressures could drive the parties to blows.

Even more important might be the attitude of Moscow. Resurgent extremist factions have pressured the Yeltsin regime to slow its reformist programs and to return to more traditional patterns. A rise to power of a nationalist government intent upon restoring much of the former Soviet influence in the world could be devastating to the Middle East peace process. It could encourage extremist elements in Arab states and offer to back their maximalist demands with the sort of military assistance which has been so pernicious in the past.

SYRIA

Syria's military strengths lie principally in its strong national leadership and its large armed forces. The forces are deployed in positions from which they could shortly undertake combat operations and are adequately equipped for short-range missions. Further, they are being up-graded with new equipment, primarily of Soviet design, and may narrow the gap in combat effectiveness with Israel in some dimensions before the end of the decade. Moreover, Syria's efforts to improve its missile and chemical arsenals may significantly strengthen Damascus' hand vis-à-vis Jerusalem as the years progress.

There is little likelihood, however, that Syria can attain its previously announced goal of equivalency with Israel in a broad military sense without substantial foreign assistance. Indeed, as noted above, Syria may have changed its strategy. Its principal objective now may be the more modest one of deterrence against Israeli attack. Syria has lost its superpower patron, and it continues to be plagued by a necessity to place politically reliable, if professionally dubious, military figures in key leadership positions rather than the most competent contenders. Also, the forces continue to lack integrative ("post-conventional") sophistication. However advanced Syria's air defenses, for example, its limited industrial and training bases require that the defenses be installed on a "turn-key" basis, with minimal adjustment for local circumstances. There is little opportunity for either hard or software adaptation to special problems. As a consequence, barring a return of Russian, or possibly some other powerful foreign (e.g. Chinese), patronage, Syria is likely to remain vulnerable for the remainder of the decade to Israeli "befuddlement weapons," designed to severely degrade deployed systems with known characteristics.

EGYPT

Like Syria, Egypt possesses large armed forces, but most tend to be less well equipped. Egypt's territorial security probably rests as much upon its desert expanses as upon its army. The Sinai to the east and the Western Desert provide a measure of insulation from potentially troublesome neighbors.

As noted in this study, prominent concerns include an unstable Sudan to the south, which has shown some proclivity for meddling with the Nile waters, and internal threats from radical Islamic fundamentalist factions. While Cairo has experienced some success in dealing with the fundamentalist threat, neither problem is likely to be resolved soon. While Egypt's military and security forces may be used to counter either threat, forceful moves against internal enemies enjoy substantially less support, and from a narrower segment of the populace, than one directed abroad. At worst, the internal threat could immobilize the economy, and potentially the government. Such a development could pose the threat of a radical change in governmental policies, and hence of destabilization of the entire Arab-Israeli balance.

Egypt's current concern with Israel is less one of border incursion than one of simple strategic imbalance. Cairo deplores what it considers Israeli supremacy in military matters, fearing that its strength will continue to encourage Jerusalem to seek military solutions to political problems.

From its own perspective, Cairo fears that it, like others, could be driven down a path toward the acquisition of mass destruction weaponry, whether it would like it or not.

Failing this, Egypt's military potential is unlikely to shift significantly with respect to other powers in the region during the period of this study. As long as it remains dependent upon the United States for the bulk of its arms procurement, and oriented toward modernizing its forces with American equipment (e.g.: M1A1 tanks), it can expect to keep abreast of regional developments, but the likelihood of a change in its relative position with respect to other Middle Eastern powers — Iraq excepted — will not be great.

IRAN

Iran is believed by most analysts to have engaged in a large military build-up, apparently seeking parity with Iraq and a dominant position in the Gulf. It may also seek an influential position among the newly independent Islamic republics in the former Soviet Union. While there is speculation that it may moderate its fundamentalist fervor and perhaps restrain its agents overseas, most observers believe it to be pursuing a path toward rapid modernization and expansion of its armed forces.

Iranian rearmament of its ground and air forces is matched by efforts to rebuild its navy. Leading figures make no secret of ambitions to build a capability to control the Strait of Hormuz. Iran probably interpreted the reflagging of Kuwaiti tankers during the Iran-Iraq War as highly provocative, and is resolved to insure that such circumstances do not occur unchallenged again.

Iran is clearly disappointed in the evolution of the post-hostilities security regime in the Gulf area. Tehran believes that it should be a member of the GCC — and the most powerful member, at that. It probably blames Saudi Arabia primarily for its exclusion. As long as it is excluded it probably will make some effort to shape its forces for cross-gulf operations in the long run. Iran has territorial claims on the western shore, and the day could come when it would feel obliged to press the issue. An amphibious capability would strengthen its argument. The acquisition of Tu-22M "Backfire" bombers could contribute by providing Iran a capability for mounting disarming strikes against Saudi CSS-2 missile sites prior to an invasion attempt.

Iran appears to also harbor ideas about conflict with Israel. The "Backfires" would provide substance to its inflammatory rhetoric. Clearly Tehran is uncomfortable with the current imbalance of strike capabilities vis-á-vis Israel and may not be satisfied with waiting for the development or market availability of longer-range missile systems with sufficient accuracy to provide real military utility. It seems to seek at least a workable offensive deterrent to Israeli attack by 2000.

SAUDI ARABIA
Like its gulf neighbor, Iran, Saudi Arabia has undertaken an

ambitious rearmament program. Unlike Iran, however, the effort seems more clearly defensively oriented. There is no apparent determination to build a capability for interdicting traffic in the Gulf. Riyadh's model is the defensive posture assumed by the Gulf War coalition prior to the U.N. decision to liberate Kuwait.

This represents a major strategic change for the Saudis. The former reliance on payoffs of friends and enemies has been shifted to a reliance on armed force. Further, the orientation of the effort is virtually a full circle. While the principle concern is northward, Yemen, Jordan, Iraq and Iran are all perceived as potential adversaries.

Riyadh values its GCC partnership, but is loath to invest much capital in the organization as a military alliance. Saudi conservatism shies away from committing Saudi forces to supranational control, even if the kingdom is the dominant power. Further, it is suspicious of Iranian intentions and is not anxious to create a security regime which might come under heavy pressure from Tehran for membership and possible competition for leadership. Riyadh is more comfortable with the perpetuation of a loose association of minor states in which each develops its forces essentially as it sees fit.

Saudi Arabia is sympathetic to the Palestinian cause, but was incensed by the PLO's pro-Iraq attitude during the Gulf War. The Jordanian and Yemeni attitudes were similarly unsettling, and have poisoned relations between the capitals of these countries and Riyadh — possibly for the remainder of the decade (some say a generation).

Fulfillment of the Saudi arms program is not likely to prove as simple as it might be under different government policies. Like a number of other states in the region, Saudi Arabia tends to select its leaders primarily from among the royal family and its close supporters. Political reliability is deemed of first importance, even though it may result in less than first class leadership. The expansion of the armed forces will create additional command positions for which there may not be sufficient interested talent among trustworthy groups. If certain entrenched practices are not changed, the quality of leadership may erode further.

The possibility of Iranian acquisition of "Backfire" bombers must be unsettling for Saudi Arabia. The speed and other attack capabilities of the aircraft pose a threat of potential disarming strike against the kingdom's principal deterrent force, its Chinese CSS-2 ballistic missiles. The development is likely to increase Riyadh's determination to acquire additional F-15 or other high performance interceptor aircraft and air defense systems.

However it develops, the Saudi arms program is not likely to lift the kingdom to the front ranks of military powers in the region. Nevertheless, the increase may be dramatic. There is now a distinct possibility that, with careful planning and judicious selection of weapons and leaders, Saudi Arabia could elevate itself to rough parity with a diminished Iraq. Coupled with enhanced forces among its GCC allies, by 2000 Riyadh could find itself with a substantial deterrent force against either Iraqi or Iranian aggression.

JORDAN

Jordan remains in a period of military retrenchment, driven by both political and economic pressures. It appears to have lost its capacity, if not its will, to play a prominent role in regional affairs. It sees itself emerging, somewhat the worse for wear, from an era of simple survival, having recently nearly floundered in a veritable ocean of unsympathetic neighbors.

If there is a strength in Jordan's military establishment it is more in its traditions and culture than in the observables.

Under extended economic stringencies the combat effectiveness of its forces has eroded, and the process may continue if there is not an effort from abroad to mount a rescue. For the present, the nation's security probably lies as much in the hands of Jerusalem as it does in Amman. Certainly any Arab neighbor contemplating action against, or through, Jordan would give first attention to the likely Israeli reaction.

Whatever the truth of allegations of Jordanian-Iraqi conspiracy during and after the Gulf War, the effects on the regional military balance were marginal. Whatever covert cooperation occurred, it is unlikely to have contributed materially to either the initial advance or the post-war rebuilding of Iraqi armed forces. In mid-June 1992 Iraq suspended all domestic air flights for lack of spare parts for the aircraft. The Iraqi Airways director general, Noureddin Safi, announced at that time that the airline had lost $200 million and idled 4,000 employees as a result of the U.N. sanctions.[4] It seems unlikely that such a matter would have been permitted to happen if Iraqi-Jordanian cooperation had been extensive.

In any event, the defection of two of Saddam Hussein's sons-in-law, with his daughters, to Jordan in the summer of 1995, and King Hussein's extension of protection to them, appears to have stifled any residual cordiality between Amman and Baghdad. Clearly, the king hopes that the chilling of relations with Iraq, as well as its recognition of Israel, will open Jordan's opportunities with her other neighbors — and more importantly with the United States. No other country would seem either as inclined or as well prepared to assist Jordan in rebuilding its forces.

THE SMALLER STATES

Of the five smaller gulf states, Kuwait and the UAE are clearly mounting the greatest efforts to enhance their defense capabilities. Kuwait, unhappily situated in close proximity to two of the most powerful and most fearsome states in the area, faces the most daunting challenge. The others have better opportunities to match their forces to the magnitude and acuity of the threat. All five depend to some extent upon the United States for their security. As Saudi defenses improve, Riyadh will improve its capacity for assuming greater responsibility for regional security, but given her partners' residual skepticism of Saudi motives and intentions, it seems unlikely that the U.S. will be able to curtail its involvement.

Yemen and Lebanon are special cases — the one a client of Damascus and a potential battle ground between Syria and Israel — the other more remote, but with a sizable population and a serious border dispute with a powerful neighbor. Lebanon is unlikely to be able to insure its own security in the remainder of the decade, but the combination of location and population provide Yemen with significant advantages against foreign aggression before 2000. If San'a can manage its differences with Riyadh and focus its attention on the long neglected economic development of the country, Yemen could emerge in the new century as an important player in the region.

THE BOTTOM LINE

In sum, a net assessment of the military balance in the Middle East places Israel at the pinnacle of power, followed by a turbulent group of states, many of which harbor grievances with each other only marginally less serious than that which they nurture against Israel. Trailing Israel, but in a different class, considering the real differences between the two, comes Syria, hungry for recovery of the Golan Heights. Next are Egypt, with its large but largely obsolescent army, and Iraq, in decline under U.N. sanctions. Then comes Saudi Arabia, awakened from its years of naiveté beginning the process of building a credible military posture, and Iran, scrambling ahead with ambitions for leadership in the Gulf.

Among the smaller states, Jordan, Kuwait and the United Arab Emirates stand out. The Hashemite Kingdom is at a turning point. While rich in its history with the fabled Arab Legion, Jordan is looking for a savior to help it back on a path to relevancy after its terrible walk in the wilderness. Meanwhile, Kuwait and the UAE are exploiting their oil wealth to leap-frog ahead with ambitious arms programs. Yemen is a question mark, with few external signals of what it may become. The others, Oman, Bahrain and Qatar, soldier ahead, trying to avoid being swallowed by larger neighbors.

The likelihood of peace in the region for the remainder of the decade may be greater than for conflict at any specific potential flash point identified in this study, but probabilities diverge beyond that. Events in capitals such as Damascus, Baghdad and Tehran tend to influence history more than they should. Tranquillity is not endemic to this part of the world.

THE POWDER KEG

CHAPTER VII
Implications for U.S. Policy

The foregoing conclusions have important implications for U.S. policy in the Middle East. These may be grouped into four major areas as follows.

ARMS CONTROL

The Middle East is continuing its dangerous path in the accumulation of weapons, and the pace is quickening. Most dangerous is the trend toward proliferation of mass destruction weapons and the means for their delivery over long distances. Efforts to restrain the growth are not likely to be effective unless they are perceived to be fair to all parties. No country or group of countries can be expected to forego security programs or measures considered vital to its survival.

It is important to bear in mind that many aspects of U.S. experience in arms control negotiations in Europe do not transfer well to the Middle East. In Europe there were two major blocs, and, for most practical purposes, but two major parties to reach agreement. The Middle East, as we have noted, is multipolar, and the polarities are constantly undergoing change. The U.S., in its negotiations with the USSR, found that both sides had expectations of mutual good. Both sought stability and security at lower levels of armament and expense. Moreover, as retired Israeli Major General Yehoshafat Harkabi has pointed out, the negotiations were conducted between states that recognized each other and maintained diplomatic relations.[1]

The situation is quite different in the Middle East, particularly between Arabs and Israelis. Israel seeks security and peace essentially on the basis of the status quo. The Arabs, on the other hand, fear that peace and stability under current conditions would freeze Israel in a position from which it would have no incentive to make more than partial withdrawals from the occupied territories. Instability and tenuous peace is a basic tool for the aggrieved party to insure that the current division of territory does not become permanent. Consequently, the Arabs do not generally share the Western perception of arms control as an objective good. On the contrary, to many of them it smacks of a deceitful means for foreign (Zionist and "imperialist") interests to disarm the Arabs and to perpetuate perceived injustices.

Clearly, a number of the states, or factions within the states, have mutually exclusive agenda, particularly with regard to the order in which peace negotiations and arms controls (for both conventional and mass destruction weapons) should be addressed. There is no single order acceptable to all parties. And yet all of the issues must be addressed and contained. The community of nations cannot acquiesce to the continuation of dangerous trends while it searches for an overarching solution to difficult problems.

Some promise may lie in a simultaneity of problem addressal. Arms control can neither await political settlement, nor can it precede it. There is no fair way to order the issues. They must be undertaken together. As Egypt's foreign minister, Esmat Abdel Meguid, stated with regard to the chemical-nuclear chicken-or-egg question, "Any progress on banning chemical weapons is tied to the conclusion of a parallel ban on nuclear arms." And as Geoffrey Kemp pointed out with respect to high technology weapons, "...high technology items cannot in the last resort be decoupled from the peace process."[2]

If the U.S. is to play a useful role in the stabilization and pacification of the region, it must emphasize that no party can expect to be made completely secure unless all parties are secure. This does not mean that all combinations of belligerents must strive to become mirror images of one another — an absurd concept. What it does mean is that the U.S., and possibly other major powers, must be prepared to play a balancing role where imbalances cannot otherwise be eliminated. Most prominent in this area is the matter of nuclear weapons. If nuclear balance is to be achieved, either Israel must surrender its lead, or some formula must be devised guaranteeing the other parties in the region a measure of protection against nuclear blackmail.

A potentially fruitful path for investigation in this case may lie in the direction of a substantial reduction in the Israeli nuclear weapons inventory. If the quantity of weapons now held was based to any extent on deterrence of Soviet aggression, there should be an identifiable package which could be disposed of with minimal risk. If Jerusalem wished to temporarily retain a number of these weapons for bargaining purposes with other parties, it could probably still make a significant unilateral cut as a gesture of goodwill and for the good of the entire region.

Another path would be the application of Missile Technology Control Regime (MTCR) parameters to the missile balance in the region. This approach would place a throw-weight limit of 500 kg. on missile systems of greater than 300 km. range. An agreement along these lines would impose restrictions on Israeli Jericho missiles, but it would also bar deployment of nuclear-tipped missiles in Iran capable of reaching Israel. The MTCR has already been proposed to apply to North Korea, a principal supplier of long-range weaponry to Iran.[3]

A balance in conventional weaponry is highly important, but it is less cogent than with mass destruction weapons because the ramifications of failure are less drastic. Like the nuclear issue, however, the conventional balance question does not have to be solved through quantitative or qualitative equivalencies. Guarantees by outside powers may be applied to even the scales. And U.S. guarantees are likely to enjoy greater respect than those of most other powers or supranational organizations (unless accompanied by assurance from the United States).

There is a third area of arms control concern. As we have noted in our examination of Iraqi strength above, certain non-observables in the "post-conventional" realm are of great importance in determining the true relative military power between states. These include advanced computer technologies and their applications, particularly to command, control, communications and intelligence. As the former director of U.S. defense research and engineering, Donald Hicks, has pointed out, data-sharing networks, intelligence fusion centers, and advanced navigation and guidance systems can greatly enhance the accuracy of older weapons. They can also serve as force multipliers, critically affecting the balance of power between states of nominal equivalency. The matter is of special importance to the security of Israel which depends heavily upon such systems for maintaining a margin of military superiority over its neighbors.

The U.S. needs to develop a thorough understanding of the impact of the new technologies for shaping future arms control regimes. Certain types of reconnaissance, targeting and weapons control systems may be substantially more important than the numbers of conventional (or even of mass destruction) weapons which they support or control.

No less of concern is the increasing availability of advanced weapons systems themselves. The new Russian T-80 tank is a case in point. Experts believe that the T-80, and even some upgraded models of the T-72, may have features superior to those on the basic U.S. M-1 tank. A major effort should be directed toward limiting the distribution of advanced models of weapons and upgrade "packages" which can materially improve the basic systems.   [4]

Geoffrey Kemp has pointed out other types of arms controls and confidence building measures for dealing with limited (tactical) issues. These may be applied when two or more parties desire a temporary arrangement until the more important questions can be addressed. These he refers to as "pre-negotiations" initiatives. They include such familiar practices as "red lines," deployment restraints, and restraints on external supply. They may be unilateral, bilateral or multilateral; explicit or implicit, but to operate properly they must be understood by all concerned. As important as these have proven in the Middle East, they should not be confused with real negotiations or settlement of the grievances.[5]

SECURITY ASSISTANCE

We have noted how arms sales in the Middle East have been affected by both demand "pull" within the region and by supply "push" from major suppliers. If there is to be an effective arms control regime, all parties, on both the demand and supply sides, must play responsible roles. Arms sales are not necessarily antithetical to arms control. On the contrary, they can play a definite role in sustaining a balance conducive to peace. In the words of the U.S. Department of State:

> The United States offers security assistance to strengthen the national security of friendly nations. ...Security assistance provides vital continuity in American foreign policy and helps to build secure and stable relationships.[6]

The key lies in the proper allocation of weapons acquisition authorizations for the development of an overall regime for the region. This is most usefully determined through multilateral negotiations, possibly coupled with the extension of specific security guarantees where imbalances persist.

American security assistance may stem from any or all of: (1) recognition of need or merit on the part of the recipient, (2) the internal American political process, or (3) the foreign policy interests of the United States. The first two factors are less amenable to policy planning than the third, but all play important parts. Security assistance is best understood and most effective when it is firmly supported by all three factors.

The large military and economic assistance programs to Egypt and Israel have constituted cornerstones of American policy in the Middle East for two decades. However, as we have noted in earlier chapters, the nature of threats in the region have changed over the years, and it is not apparent that the traditional aid distribution patterns continue to serve their original purposes.

The security of Israel, a prime U.S. policy objective, is closely related to the security of the Egyptian Government, besieged, as it is, by militant extremists from within. Yet the lion's share of U.S. foreign assistance to the two countries continues to flow into traditional military programs designed to help the two deal with threats from abroad. The practice appears wasteful and poorly targeted for the circumstances of the closing 1990s.

While a definitive recommendation for change in the aid programs would depend upon a comprehensive examination of the precise security situation in Egypt, it would appear that such an examination is now in order. We have noted a growing sense among Israeli intelligentsia that U.S. economic aid to that country is no longer necessary. At the same time, we have substantial U.S. military assistance to Egypt flowing into programs which have only marginal relationship with the growing internal security problem. It may be that a far more effective internal security effort and a stronger program for economic assistance could be developed for Egypt by redirecting resources currently aimed at the Israeli economy and the Egyptian conventional forces. The security of both countries would be enhanced through such a move.

As for the remainder of the region, the U.S. is not a dispenser of much largesse. The other 12 countries under examination in this study together receive less than two percent of all U.S. foreign security assistance. The wealthy countries of the region are important recipients of American armaments, and have the means to provide their own funding.

One program which would seem to merit enhancement is that for Jordan. The kingdom has paid for its identification with Baghdad during the Gulf War, but the price has been extraordinarily high. National revenues fell drastically in connection with the U.N. sanctions against Iraq. Virtually all support from the oil producers ceased, and Jordanian workers were expelled from their former jobs in the Gulf area. The U.S. has resumed a very modest support program for the Jordanian Armed Forces, but it is hardly enough to be influential, and funds have been delivered in a spotty and disjointed fashion.[7]

The U.S. Department of State and Defense Security Assistance Agency view Jordan in these terms:

Maintenance of a stable Jordan remains a key facet of U.S. interest in the region, particularly now that we have reached a critical phase in the peace process. Since the Gulf War hostilities ended, King Hussein has adopted a helpful position on the peace process....[8]

The king has, in fact, done much more than that. He has made peace with Israel himself.

Jordan lies in a unique strategic position for the long-term security of the region. It borders on two of Israel's most powerful opponents, and, in time, is likely to form the principal Arab associate with whatever indigenous administration may emerge on the West Bank. Our review of the military balance in the Middle East reveals little cause for alarm over Jordanian arms. Riyadh's concerns appear to have sprung from a sense of imminent danger in 1990 under circumstances unlikely to reoccur in the foreseeable future. Saudi Arabia's new military programs and Jordan's retrenchment are bound to reduce those concerns.

If there is danger in the situation today, it would appear to stem from the possibility of a radicalization of Jordanian society (in the event of abortion of the Palestinian peace process) or of renewed dependence upon Iraq (if Jordan's initiatives toward the West go unanswered). Accordingly, it would seem wise for the U.S. to play a larger role in stabilizing the position of the Hashemite House in Amman through a reinvigorated security assistance program.

An important problem in the security assistance and arms sales programs in the Middle East appears to lie in a lack of a coherent, overarching policy for guidance of the program managers. A former chief of the U.S. security assistance program in Riyadh, for example, protested that he did not have sufficient guidance to assist the host country in its arms acquisition efforts. On one occasion he recommended that the Saudis be sold a number of aircraft of a particular design. Only a quarter of the recommended number was forthcoming — with no explanation of why the program should be cut by 75 percent.[9]

Ideally, the U.S. Government, including the legislative branch, would have an internally coordinated "objectives" concept for discussions among the principal weapon supplier and recipient nations. While complete closure of the document, with universal agreement among all parties would be unrealistic, the process might help to identify areas of principal difference and to improve understanding of others' concerns. It would also help the U.S. Government to develop its own plan for arms allocations, either through the security assistance program or private sale. Perfect conformance with the plan would not be as important as a narrowing of the problem for reasonable management.

TECHNOLOGY TRANSFER

The U.S. has agreements with many countries in the region related to sales of military equipment of advanced design. The closest association is with Israel, which amounts to a substantial, if unmeasured, pillar of Israel's security structure. Unfortunately, questions have arisen regarding allegations of Israeli abuse of its privileged position, casting some doubt as to whether the relationship can continue to be as close as it has been in the past. Most recently, in January 1996, the CIA produced photographs of an Israeli Lavi aircraft on a Chinese airfield. The United States provided $1.5 billion in funding and much in the way of high technology equipment and parts for the machine, and spokesmen expressed considerable concern for the apparent carelessness with which U.S. interests had

been handled.[10] Investigations of such matters have thus far
been inconclusive.

It may be less important whether the allegations are true
than whether the U.S. has placed some Israeli government officials and industrialists in an untenable position. Israel is a
manufacturer and world-wide exporter of quality military
equipment. It is heavily dependent upon the approximately
two billion dollars it earns through foreign sales of its arms to
underpin its own weapons acquisitions and to support its industrial base. With a close and many-faceted relationship with
U.S. research and development activities — governmental,
industrial, academic and independent — the country is in an
awkward position of conflict of interest. It must be expected
that some Israeli researchers and officials will from time to
time encounter significant temptations or pressures to adapt
U.S. technology to Israeli equipment intended for foreign sale.

There is a clear need for continuing low-profile, comprehensive review of U.S.-Israeli technology connections, in all
their many forms. The partnership is too important to permit
a cloud to dwell over the process, perhaps endangering benefits
currently being realized by both sides. Ideally, standing review
machinery would be chartered and maintained on a bilateral
basis to ensure that the investigations themselves would not
become causes for further suspicion or distrust. It is one thing
for the U.S. Intelligence Community to report its suspicions
from time to time. It would be quite another matter for the
two governments to address the matter as a team on a continuing and in an organized manner.

It might also be useful to make an effort to assess the value
of Israel's technical association with the U.S.. Such an assessment might prove valuable in connection with future efforts to
reach regional balance among the various parties. While a dollar figure may or may not be useful (or even possible), the prin-

190 THE POWDER KEG

cipal objective would be to illuminate the connections of greatest importance, and to identify any which might be particularly sensitive. Possibly some with greater risks than value should be terminated, or trade-offs might be found. Such assessment should contribute to a better understanding of the need for specific levels of cooperation in particular fields and, perhaps, a sense for options which might be undertaken in other fields with other countries in the region to balance the relationship with Israel.

U.S. FORCE PRESENCE

The U.S. also has agreements with a number of Middle East states pertaining to military exercises and base rights. U.S. equipment storage facilities are to be found in Israel and several of the Gulf sheikdoms, and a "floating armored brigade" with 100 M1A1 tanks and 58 Bradley infantry fighting vehicles has been deployed on Navy cargo ships in the Indian Ocean. In late 1995, these and other cargo ships, previously based as far away as the island of Diego Garcia in the South Indian Ocean, were transferred to Bahrain. The shift, together with troops ready to be flown in, provided American planners with a capability for landing a full Marine division and an Army heavy brigade — a total force of some 20,000 troops — in the Gulf area in a matter of a few days.[11] Other storage sites may be established elsewhere. The stocks in Israel may be expanded to include sufficient equipment for an entire division.[12] U.S. ground force presence is evident on a regular, if limited, basis in Kuwait, Bahrain and Egypt, primarily in connection with international exercises.

As we noted at the outset of this study, the U.S. has become a player in the Middle Eastern arena. It has committed a significant measure of its prestige to the quest for peace and has raised the expectations of all parties in the region of its determination to insure the success of its efforts. Indeed, the U.S. can take considerable credit for the low level of violence currently prevailing in the region.

But it cannot be expected that a lasting peace can be established exclusively by diplomatic and political means. There are still too many disparate interests which might be tempted to take advantage of opportunities for short-range gain by illegal means. The peace process will require time to develop, and must be undergirded by substantial strength and staying power. A modest U.S. ground force presence in the region would provide a visible statement of U.S. interest and commitment to the achievement of its goals and lend credibility to the overall effort for peace. It would seem that former Secretary of State James Baker, III had these points in mind in August 1992 when he reportedly queried Israel and Syria regarding the stationing of U.S. troops on the Golan Heights.[13]

In addition, a U.S. force presence on the ground in the Middle East might be used to off-set other types of commitments which have not proven useful in settling disputes. Prior to the 1996 Israeli elections it appeared that the country might have been prepared to sacrifice some of its territorial holdings in order to gain peace agreements with neighbors. Maj. Gen. Harkabi made this point in roundtable discussions with U.S. analysts.[14]

Under that concept the U.S. forces might have played a useful role between historic anatagonists. There was a sense that Arabs and Israelis alike would appreciate U.S. assurances that neither side would be permitted to take tactical advantage of concessions made by the other. While the circumstances under which U.S. forces might be welcome varied somewhat, according to the interests of the various players, only Saudi Arabia appeared to have strong objections as a matter of principle to the presence of foreign forces. The Golan Heights, the Jordan Valley and the Sinai Peninsula were all suggested as logical sites for U.S. troop deployments by various parties. Indigenous analysts expressed different levels of enthusiasm, but many professed to see distinct advantages to such an arrangement. Some would have insisted upon U.N. sponsorship; others considered such association irrelevant.

However, the Israeli elections changed the calculus for such initiatives insofar as the Israeli occupied territories are concerned. Whereas the former government had fostered the principle of "land for peace," the new leadership voided that policy in favor of "peace for peace." As a result, the concept of U.S. participation in a peacekeeping arrangement no longer seems apt.

Both President Assad, and the new Israeli prime minister, Benjamin Netanyahu, have invested a great deal of capital in mutually exclusive positions regarding the Golan Heights. Accordingly, that frontier must again be considered a venue of high potential for conflict. If there was a window of opportunity during the first half of the decade for employment of U.S. troops for dampening tensions, that window has closed for the foreseeable future. It would be a high risk undertaking for the U.S. Government to deploy troops in such an unstable environment.

The Saudi objections, it should be noted, have less to do with strategic concerns than with the legitimacy of the ruling family. The royal house rests largely on its claim to guardianship of the holy sites of Medina and Mecca and to its maintenance of Islamic law within the kingdom. The presence of large numbers of non-Islamic troops, however necessary they may be at times, undermines the core legitimacy of the regime. The bombing of the American housing at Dhahran in June 1996 was as much a protest against the government's toleration of "infidels" in the country as it was a blow against the United States. Any U.S. forces stationed in Arab territories should maintain as low and "temporary" a profile as possible.

In any event, the U.S. would not wish to station troops in significant numbers in the region on a permanent basis. As U.S. forces have diminished in size, the pool of troops available for extended commitment has been greatly reduced. More manageable would be the rotation of brigade size organizations for extended exercise periods — perhaps for two to three months at a time. The units might be drawn from Europe or from the United States, or both. Smaller formations, perhaps of battalion size might be detached for shorter periods for training with different host country forces. Base areas for the support of such deployments could be designated in a number of different countries — the more choices the better. Ideally, the bases would be operated by host government forces to minimize implications of a U.S. "occupation" of the area.

However done, certain principles should be established to minimize the pitfalls which may be encountered. Some of these might be:

1. U.S. forces should not be employed in locales where there is recognizable risk that they might be caught up in international hostilities. They should be considered only for areas between other national forces when all commanders agree to the allocation of space. Further, they should be deployed in sufficient strength that they are capable of defending themselves from partisan groups which do not identify with the peace process, and adequate immediate close air support should be assured.

2. In view of cultural differences, contacts between U.S. troops and Arab communities should be held to a minimum.

3. U.S. troops should not be employed to interdict terrorist

activities. Israeli troops are better trained and better psychologically attuned for this type of duty.

4. Sufficient air or sea transport should be maintained in the vicinity of the troops so that they can be quickly relocated to deal with developing threats.

5. U.S. forces should be deployed only where they have sufficient space to exercise their operational capabilities and maintain skills, and adequate provision should be made for rest and recuperation for the troops during their deployment.

NOTES

CHAPTER I

1   William J. Clinton, "A National Security Strategy of Engagement and Enlargement," July 1994 (released by Press Secretary of the White House, 21 July 1994). p, 43.

2   *Ibid.*, p. 9.

3   *Defense Daily*, 27 January 1994, p. 133.

4   U.S. Arms Control and Disarmament Agency, *World Military Expenditures and Arms Transfers 1989*, Table 1, pp. 31-72.

5   While not identified with one of the sub-regions of the Middle East, Yemen plays an important role in Saudi Arabia's security calculations and must be treated in this study.

6   "Tajik Leader Flees; Foes Announce Takeover," *New York Times*, 8 May 1992, p. A11.

7   Nicholas Bonsor, "World Lurches Toward War." *Defense News*, 21-27 February 1994, p. 36.

8   Anoushiravan Enteshami, *Nuclearisation of the Middle East* (London: Brassey's, 1989), p. 57. Some of the conflicts listed by Enteshami are not within the region of focus of this study. Accordingly, they are not counted.

9   All data is taken from the International Institute for Strategic Studies *Military Balance 1995/96*, (London: Brassey's, 1995).

10   The designated index of militarization is a combination of the order in which the countries under consideration appear on the militarization of citizenry and militarization of public wealth lists. The standings are added together and subtracted from a constant (20) to provide the index.

11   Fred Kaplan, "Hard Pressed Russia Seeks to Revive Global Arms Sales," *Boston Globe*, 29 July 1992, p. 14.

12   "Population Projections by Region and for Selected Countries: 1990 to 2025," *The World Almanac and Book of Facts 1987*, p. 635.

[13] Jackson Diehl, "Israel's Immigration Slips," Washington Post, 29 December 1991, p. A1. The rise of right wing extremist elements in Russia is likely to increase Jewish emigration. See Steven Erlanger, "In Russia, Jews Find New Fears," New York Times International, 6 February 1994, p. 4.

[14] "Settlers Issue Hots Up," Riyadh Daily, 23 January 1992, p. 3.

[15] "U.S. Reports 25% Increase in Settlements by Israelis in the Occupied Territories," Washington Post, 9 May 1992, p. A17.

[16] Comments to the author by Mr. Netanyahu, Jerusalem, 27 April 1991.

[17] "No Let Up in Construction at Settlement in West Bank," Washington Post, 23 July 1992, p. A27.

[18] Dr. Reuven Gal, Director, Israeli Institute for Military Studies, in discussions with the author, February 1992.

[19] Aharon Klieman and Reuven Pedatzur, Rearming Israel: Defense Procurement Through the 1990s, Jaffe Center for Strategic Studies, Tel Aviv University (Tel Aviv: Jerusalem Post Press, 1991), p. 82.

[20] Andrew Boroweic, "Tunisia May be Targeted Anew, Officials Fear," Washington Times, 5 May 1992, p. A9.

[21]

"Military Intelligence Analysts at Odds With State Department Over Iran War Scenario," Inside the Air Force, 28 February 1992, p. 1.

[22] In April 1992 Syrian forces withdrew from the Beirut Airport, turning responsibility for security of the installation over to the Lebanese Army. (See: FBIS-NES-92-080, 24 April 1992, p. 22.)

[23] Ariel Sharon in remarks to the author, Jerusalem, 24 April 1991.

CHAPTER II
Israel

1 Marvin Feuerwerger, "The Arrow Next Time? Israel's Missile Defense Program for the 1990s," Washington Institute Policy Paper No. 28, pp. 22-23.

2 Barbara Opall, "Unable to Stop U.S.A. Missile Sale, Israel Seeks Payback," *Defense News*, 8-14 May 1995, p. 26.

3 Robert Mahoney, "Israel Warns Agains Nuclear Arms," *Washington Times*, 16 June 1992, p. A9.

4 Michael Parks, "Israel Looks Past Borders, Arms for Long-Range War," *Los Angeles Times*, 5 February 1995, p. 1.

5 Maj. Gen. Ahron Yariv, Director, Jaffe Center, in remarks to the author, Tel Aviv, 3 February 1992; and Maj. Gen. Uri Sagi, chief of IDF Intelligence Branch in interview with Yed'iot Aharonot, translated and published in Foreign Broadcast Information Service (FBIS) NES-97-078, 22 April 1992, p. 34.

6 Moshe Arens, Israeli Minister of Defense, in remarks to the author, Tel Aviv, 23 April 1991.

7 Joris Janssen Lok interview with Maj. Gen. Bani Yatom, "Israel Looks to Export Growth," *Jane's Defense Weekly*, 10 June 1989, p. 1142.

8 Commentary by U.S. military attache to the author, Tel Aviv, 3 February 1992. Also, with regard to high technology weaponry and the window of opportunity, see Klieman and Pedatzur, p. 27.

9 Robert Rudney, "GPALS Tempts Israel to Abandon Offensive Stance," *Armed Forces Journal International*, February 1992, p. 43.

10 Ariel Levite, *Offense and Defense in Israeli Military Doctrine* (Tel Aviv: Jerusalem Post Press, 1989), p. 7.

11 U.S. military attache, Tel Aviv.

12 Yariv remarks to the author; and Shlomo Gazit and Zeev Eytan, *The Middle East Military Balance 1993-1994*, Jaffe Center for Strategic Studies (Boulder, CO: Westview Press, 1994), p. 323.

13 Estimates of Israeli 1990 defense expenditures range from 27.2

to 40 percent of the budget. See Klieman and Pedatzur, p. 61.

[14] "Rabin Meeting the Missile Threat," *Jane's Defense Weekly*, 10 June 1989, p. 1141.

[15] Yarliv interview, *Jane's Defense Weekly*, 14 December 1991, p. 1188; and "Mid East Asian FMS Orders," *Jane's*, 4 December 1993, p. 9.

[16] Yossi Melman, "Israel's Race Into Space," *Washington Post*, 17 May 1992, p. C4; Peter de Selding, "Israel Follows Slow Path Toward Early Warning Satellites," *Defense News*, 17-23 October 1994, p. 38; and Clyde Haberman, "Israel Finally Orbits its Own Spy Satellite," *New York Times*, 6 April 1995, p. A12.

[17] "Israeli Radar Ready for Arrow," *Jane's Defense Weekly*, 10 December 1994, p. 4.

[18] "Israel Set to Test Arrow-2 ABM," *Jane's Defense Weekly*, 6 May 1995, p. 15.

[19] Opall, "U.S. Agrees to Arrow Fund," *Defense News*, 8-14 May 1995, p.3.

[20] Rowan Scarborough, "Israel Missile Defense Sparks U.S. Debate," *Washington Times*, 9 March 1996, p. 1.

[21] Opall, "Israel Eyes 40 Percent Aid Hike," *Defense News*, 9 September 1991, p. 4; Scotty Fisher, "F-16, F/A-18 Dogfight for Fighter Contract Spells Good News for Israeli Industries," *Armed Forces Journal International*, June 1992, p. 19; and Opall, "Israel Seeks U.S. Supplier for Early Warning Radars," *Defense News*, 22-28 June 1992, p. 8.

[22] Scarborough, "Pentagon Said to Stall Arms for Israel," *Washington Times*, 27 May 1992, p. A4.

[23] *Defense Daily*, 2 May 1995, p. 150.

[24] International Institute for Strategic Studies, *The Military Balance 1995-1996*, p. 150.

[25] Opall, "Lockheed Offers Israel Longer-Range F-16," *Defense News*, 10-16 January 1994, p. 6. Subsequently, it was announced by CNN Television that the Israelis had decided upon the F-15I,

evening news, 27 January 1994.

26 "Israel May Buy More F-15s," (World Scene), *Washington Times*, 26 June 1995, p. A13.

27 Opall and Sharone Parnes, "Israel's Choice of F-15Is Delays Other Programs," *Defense News*, 31 January-6 February 1995, p. 3.

28 Peter Allen-Frost, "Israel Revives Submarine Plans," *Jane's Defense Weekly*, 17 June 1989, p. 1209.

29 FIBIS-NES-92-085; and Robert Holzer and Parnes, "Budget Woes Stall Development of Israel's New Barak System," *Defense News*, 11-17 June 1993, p. 21.

30 Opall, "Israel Designs Secret Missile to Hunt, Kill Airdefenses," *Defense News*, 11-17 May 1992, p.1.

31 Holzer and Neil Munro, "Microwave Weapon Stuns Iraqis," *Defense News*, 13-19 April 1992, p. 1.

32 Barbara Starr, "Israel Will Get Early Warning Downlink," *Jane's Defense Weekly*, 13 February 1993, p. 5.

33 *Congressional Quarterly*, 20 March 1993, p. 5.

34 Remarks to the author by Israeli reserve brigadier general, Tel Aviv, April 1991.

35 Clyde Haberman, "An Israeli Anxiety: Should Charity Stay at Home?," *New York Times International*, 1 February 1994, p. A3.

36 Edith M. Lederer, "Photos Detect Israel's Nukes," *Washington Times*, 19 November 1994, p. A6.

37 "Israel Under Pressure Over Nuclear Policy," *London Financial Times*, 24 October 1991, p. 4.

38 Seymour M. Hersh, *The Samson Option* (New York: Random House, 1991), p. 276f.

39 Yitzhak Rabin, in remarks to the author, Tel Aviv, 24 April, 1991.

40 Ehteshami, p. 57,

41 Michael A. Ottenberg, "Israel and the Atom," *American Sentinel*, 16 August 1992, p. 13.

42 Comments of U.S. Embassy officers to the author, Tel Aviv,

February 1992.

[43] Lederer.

[44] Klieman and Pedatzur, pp. 80-86.

[45] Parnes, "Israeli Firm Eyes Super Consortium," *Defense News*, 27 March-2 April 1995, p. 4.

[46] Ambassador Tahseen Basheer, Egyptian National Center for Middle East Studies, in remarks to the author, Cairo, 2 February 1992.

[47] Parnes, "Diplomatic Success Opens Door for Israeli Exports," *Defense News*, 26 June-2 July 1995, p. 16.

[48] See above references; and Opall, "Israel Ponders More Apache Buys," *Defense News*, 14-20 September 1992, p. 42.

Egypt

[49] Maj. Gen. Ahmed Fakiher, Egyptian Army (ret.) director of the National Center for Middle East Studies, Cairo, 2 February 1992.

[50] Fakiher.

[51] Jonathan Wright, "Tension Rises Between Egypt and Sudan," *Washington Times*, 29 June 1995, p. A17.

[52] U.S. Embassy officer comment to the author, Cairo, 2 February 1992.

[53] Caryle Murphy, "Egypt Seeks Solutions to Militants' Challenge," *New York Times*, 29 November 1992, p. A39; Chris Hedges, "Militants Plan to Increase Violence, Egyptians Say," *New York Times International*, 19 December 1993, p. 15; and Siona Jenkins, "Egypt's Internal Struggle Hurts Innocents," *Washington Times*, 3 May 1995, p. A9.

[54] Hedges, "Foreigners' Bus Shot Up in Egypt," *New York Times International*, 15 February 1994, p. A3.

[55] IISS, *Strategic Survey 1994/95* (London: Oxford University Press, 1995), pp. 142-143.

[56] Mona Eltahawy, "Islamic Group Admits Attacking Tourists,"

Washington Times, 21 April 1996, p. A5.

57 Philip Finnegan, "Egypt Seeks Surplus Gear," *Defense News,* 9 March 1992, p. 1

58 One on One (interview) "Field Marshal Hussein Tantawi," *Defense News,* 20-26 June 1994, p. 54; and Finnegan, "Egyptians make TOWs Top Priority for Modernization," *Defense News,* 10-16 April, 1995, p. 24.

59 Finnegan, "Egypt Slowly Deploys 700 M60A1 Tanks," *Defense News,* 30 March-5 April 1992, p, 3.

60 "Egypt Seeks U.S. M60s to Boost its Tank Fleet," *Jane's Defense Weekly,* 17 July 1993.

61 Christopher F. Foss, "Egypt's Winning Formula," *Jane's Defense Weekly,* 14 December 1991, p. 1181.

62 Sharon Denny and Finnegan, "Egypt Ponders Extra M1 Work," *Defense News,* 3-9 April 1995, p. 3.

63 Finnegan, "Egyptians Make TOWs Top Priority for Modernization;" U.S. Department of Defense, "Memorandum for Correspondents," No. 98-M, 7 April 1992; and "Saudi Arabia Receives $1.35b in Contractor Services," (FMS), *Jane's Defense Weekly,* 16 September 1995, p. 4.

64 "Kaman Corp. to Support SH-2G in Sale to Egypt," *Defense News,* 27 March-2 April 1995, p. 23; Finnegan, "Egyptians Make TOWs Top Priority for Modernization;" and U.S. DOD, "Memorand[a] for Correspondents," Nos. 74- and 75-M, 11 April 1994, and No. 153-M, 23 June 1994.

65 Finnegan, "Egypt Closes in On U.S. Frigate Deal," *Defense News,* 25-31 January 1993, pp. 4 and 37; and Finnegan, "Egypt Makes TOWs Top Priority for Modernization,"

66 Aharon Levran.

67 U.S. DOD notifications to Congress of Egyptian Government purchases, Nos. 335-M 19 July 1991, and 98-M 7 April 1992. Also: "Dutch Will Sell Surplus AIFVs in Middle East," *Jane's Defense Weekly,* 5 March 1994, p. 15; "Egyptian Apache Sale

Posted," *Jane's Defense Weekly*, 17 December 1994, p. 6; "TAI Delivers First F-16 Aircraft in Egypt Order," *Kuwait Times*, 19 May 1994, p. 12; "Egypt Firms Up Orders for Apache AH-64As," *Jane's Defense Weekly*, 25 March 1995, p. 6; U.S. DOD "Memorand[a] to Correspondents," 100-M 1 April 1993, 349-M 23 November 1993, 74- and 75-M 11 April 1994, 117-M 12 May 1994, 153-M 23 June 1994, 267-M 17 October 1994, 299-M 30 November 1994, and 81-M 27 March 1995; and "Saudi Arabia Receives $1.35b in Contractor Services."

Syria

68   General Mustafa T'lass, Syrian defense minister, in remarks to the author, Damascus, 20 January 1992.

69   Clyder Haberman, "Peace Pact With Syria Needed to Prevent War, Rabin Says," *Washington Post*, 25 June 1994, p. 4.

70   Amos Perlmutter, "A Problematical Package for Israeli-Syrian Peace," *Washington Times*, 19 May 1994, p. 18.

71   Strategy Report, Syria-Israel, "The Strategic Dimensions of a Syrian-Israeli Peace Pact," *Middle East Reporter*, 27 November 1993, p. 12.

72   T'lass.

73   T'lass.

74   T'lass.

75   Martin Sieff, "Assad's Commitment to Peace with Israel Questioned," *Washington Times*, 30 January 1996, p. A15.

76   U.S. military attache, in remarks to the author, Damascus, 19 January 1992.

77   Yassin Rafaiya, Ash Sharq Al Awsat (London), cited in *The Middle East Reporter*, 30 May 1992, p. 8.

78   U.S. Embassy officers to the author, Damascus, 19 January 1992.

79   Haberman, "Peace Pact With Syria Needed to Prevent War, Rabin Says."

80 Peter W. Rodman, "Assad's Game: Strongman Plays a Weak Hand," *Washington Post*, 21 April 1996, p. C2.

81 Steven Greenhouse, "U.S. Says it is Pleased Syrians Are Acting to Limit Terrorism," *New York Times*, 1 May 1994, p. A18; and Martin Sieff, "Syria Weighs Shipping Hezbollah New Missiles to Use on Israeli Jets," *Washington Times*, 21 June 1994, p. 11.

82 "Russia/Syria Sign to Smooth Arms Trade," *Jane's Defense Weekly*, 14 May 1994, p. 3; and Newsbriefs, "Syria-Russia Cooperation," Jewish Institute for National Security Affairs, *Security Affairs*, July-August 1994, p. 7.

83 Regional Briefs, "Syria Nixes Slovak T-72s," *Armed Forces Journal International*, September 1994, p. 65.

84 "Paper — Syria Buys Slovak Tanks," *Early Bird* Pentagon news summary (News Highlights), 1 July 1994.

85 David E. Sanger, "North Korea Buying Old Russian Subs," *New York Times*, 20 January 1994, p. A5.

86 Associated Press Wire News, 2 October 1991.

87 Elaine Sciolino and Eric Schmitt, "China Said to Sell Parts for Missiles," *New York Times*, 31 January 1992, p. 1.

88 Geoffrey Kemp, "'Solving' the Proliferation Problem in the Middle East," in Aspin Strategy Group, *New Threats* (Lanham, MD: University Press of America, Inc., 1990), p. 219.

89 Uri Sagi.

90 For example, see Aharon Levan, "Declawing the Nuclear Beast," *Jerusalem Post*, 23 May 1992, p. 7.

91 Tom Diaz, Syrian Said to Have Offered Chemical Weapons to Iran," *Washington Times*, 9 December 1985, p. 4A.

92 James Bruce, "Purge May Ease Path to Middle East Peace," *Jane's Defense Weekly*, 3 September 1994, p. 1.

93 "Reported $2 Billion Syrian/Soviet Arms Deal Sparks Concern," *Inside the Army*, 8 April 1991; Bill Gertz, "N. Korean Ship Unloaded Missiles," *Washington Times*, 10 December 1991, p. 6; Anthony H. Cordesman, "Current Trends in Arms Sales and

Proliferation in the Middle East," Office of Senator John McCain, U.S. Senate, Washington D.C., January 1992; FBIS-NES-177, 11 September 1992, p. 34 (*Yedi'ot Aharonot*, 10 September 1992, pp. 2,17); and "$2 Billion Arms Contracts Seen Hinging on Resolving Old Dbts," *The Middle East Reporter*, 19 December 1992.

Saudi Arabia

94 "Saudis and Yemenis Bolster Border Forces" (Regional briefing), *Washington Times*, 21 December 1994, p. A16.

95 Sciolino and Schmitt, "Saudi Arabia, its Purse Thinner, Learns How to Say 'No' to U.S.," *New York Times International*, 4 November 1994, p. A6.

96 Bruce et al., "Saudis at a Turning Point," *Jane's Defense Weekly*, 6 May 1995, p. 22.

97 U.S. ambassador's comments to the author, Riyadh, 27 January 1992.

98 Barbara Starr, "USA, Saudi Arabia Plan 'Crisis' Cooperation," *Jane's Defense Weekly*, 13 November 1993, p. 16.

99 Cited in U.S. Naval War College study, "Southwest Asia 2000: Force Structures for a New Century" (Strategy and Campaign Department, Center for Naval Warfare Studies), undated, pp. 21-23.

100 *The Military Balance 1994-1995*, p. 137.

101 Youssef M. Ibrahim, "Gulf Nations Said to be Committed to U.S. Alliance," *New York Times*, 25 October 1991, p. A9

102 Comments by U.S. security assistance officer to the author, Riyadh, 29 January 1992.

103 J.A.C. Lewis, "Saudis Order French Frigates in $3.5 Billion Deal," *Jane's Defense Weekly*, 3 December 1994, p. 4.

104 Bruce, "Saudis Taking 'Serious' Look at Canadian Ships," *Jane's Defense Weekly*, 8 October 1994, p. 1.

105 Carol Reed, "Saudi Arabia Looks at Merlin Purchase," *Jane's Defense Weekly*, 27 August 1994, p. 1.

106 Bill Gertz, "Iranian Threat Has Saudis Mulling Big Buy of U.S. Ships," *Washington Times*, 27 May 1995, p. A11; and Ronald T. Pretty (ed.), *Jane's Weapons Systems 1983-1984* (London: Jane's Publishing Co., Ltd., 1983), p. 143.

107 Interview with Lt. Gen. Thomas Rhame, *Jane's Defense Weekly*, 11 December 1993, p. 32; "Saudis Said to Seek Arms Payments Delay," *New York Times*, 8 January 1994, p. A4; and Eric Schmitt, "Saudis Near Accord to Slow Arms Payments," *New York Times*, 18 January 1994, p. A4.

108 "The Rock Beneath the Sand," Country Briefing: Saudi Arabia, *Jane's Defense Weekly*, 6 May 1995, p. 27.

109 Philip Finnegan, "F-15S Eludes Saudi Cash Crunch," *Defense News*, 23-29 January 1995, pp. 1 and 36.

110 Lt. Gen. Thomas G. Rhame, director of the Defense Security Assistance Agency, reported in Association of the U.S. Army *AUSA News*, April 1996, p. 7.

111 Bruce et al., "Saudis at a Turning Point," and "Muslim Pilgrims Gathering for Hajj."

112 Don Oberdorfer, "U.S., Saudis Agree to Use Old Military pact for Expanding Cooperation," *Washington Post*, 31 May 1992, p.10.

113 Charles Aldinger, "Saudis Agree to Increased Readiness," *Washington Times*, 20 March 1995, p. A11.

114 "Saudis Hint Easing of Stand on Iraq," (World Scene) *Washington Times*, 16 December 1995, p. A23.

115 "Saudis Paying for U.S. Troop Moves," (World Scene) *Washington Times*, 7 November 1995, p. A16.

116 "MEED Special Report Defense," *Middle East Economic Digest*, 26 April 1991, pp. 9-16; Stephen Pearlstein, "Patriot Missile Deal Expected with Saudis," *Washington Post*, 12 November 1991, p. C1; Paul Betts and David White, "Saudi Bid for F-15s Shows U.S. Hold Over Arms Orders," *London Financial Times*, 6 November 1991, p. 1; "Pentagon: No 'Cap' on F-15s for Saudis, But 98 is Enough," *Aerospace Daily*, 8 November 1991, p. 221; Opall, "Saudis Explore

Additional Buys of AWACS Planes," *Defense News*, 7-13 September 1992, p. 1; "USA Calls in Saudi $4b Unpaid Obligation," *Jane's Defense Weekly*, 20 May 1995, p. 5; and Bruce, "The Rock Beneath the Sand," *Jane's Defense Weekly*, 6 May 1995, pp. 27-31.

Iran

[117] See, for example, Anoushiravan Ehteshami, "Iran's National Strategy, *International Defense Review*, April 1994, p. 29.

[118] Andrew Borowiec, "Iran's Islamic Radicals Take Firmer Hold After Riots," *Washington Times*, 19 February 1994, p. A8.

[119] Bruce, "Civilian is Appointed as Iran's Top Soldier," *Jane's Defense Weekly*, 20 May 1995, p. 3.

[120] Borowiec, "Iranian Defends Arms Buildup, Cites Iraq Threat," *Washington Times*, 20 February 1992, p. 9.

[121] Patrick Cockburn, "Russia Helps Iran Equip its Warplanes from Iraq," *The Independent* (UK), 13 January 1992, p. 1; and Bruce, "Aircraft to Stay as Iran and Iraq Remain Hostile," *Jane's Defense Weekly*, 18 November 1995, p. 16.

[122] David Dolan, *Holy War for the Promised Land* (London: Hodder & Stoughton, 1991), p. 219.

[123] R. Jeffrey Smith, "Gates Warns of Iranian Arms Drive," *Washington Post*, 28 March 1992, p. 1A.

[124] Tim Weiner, "CIA Head Surveys World's Hot Spots for Senate," *New York Times International*, 26 January 1994, p. A6.

[125] Starr, "USA Considers Iran is 'a Major Concern,'" *Jane's Defense Weekly*, 18 March 1995, p. 28.

[126] "Iran's Late Declaration," *Jane's Defense Weekly*, 3 December 1994, p. 5.

[127] "Iran Says its Air Force Rebuilt Since Iraq War," *Baltimore Sun*, 3 February 1994, p. 5.

[128] "Iran Mounts Large-Scale Live Fire Exercises," *Jane's Defense Weekly*, 24 June 1995, p. 5.

[129]U.S., CIA, *The World Fact Book 1994*, pp. 189-190.

[130]IISS, *The Military Balance 1993-1994*, p. 108.

[131]IISS, *The Military Balance 1995-1996*, p. 133.

[132]Bizhan Torabi, "Muslim Countries Eye Silk Road Venture," *Washington Times*, 17 May 1992, p. A8.

[133]James Kynge, "Battle for Influence Back in Central Asia," *Washington Times*, 24 December 1994, p. A8.

[134]*Ibid*.

[135]Rasit Gurdilek, "Outsiders' Motives Vary for Helping Train Azeri Troops," *Washington Times*, 1 February 1994, p. A13.

[136]Bill Gertz, "Iranians Move into Bosnia to Terrorize Serbs," *Washington Times*, 2 June 1994, p. 1.

[137]Paul Beaver, "Yeltsin Announces the Halt of Exports to Iran," *Jane's Defense Weekly*, 20 May 1995, p. 6.

[138]"Iran's Submarine Fleet Increases by the 'Kilo,'" Headline News, *Jane's Defense Weekly*, 7 May 1994, p. 1. Barbara Starr ("USA Considers Iran is 'A Major Concern,'") reports that Iran may be seeking some 22 submarines. The Author considers this unlikely.

[139] Finnegan, Robert Holzer and Neil Munro, "Iran Pursues Chinese Mine to Bolster Gulf Clout," *Defense News*, 17-23 January 1994, pp. 1 and 29.

[140] John Mintz, "Sweating out the 'Sunburn'," *Washington Post*, 13 June 1993, p. H1. Steven J. Zaloga, senior analyst with the Teal Group Corporation, is reported to doubt the deployment of "Sunburns" since a land-based version has not been fielded by Russia, the originator of the weapons. Zaloga believes that the Iranian missiles may actually be less capable SS-N-2 "Styx." See "Iran Watch," *JINSA Security Affairs*, February-March 1996, p.5.

[141] Bruce, "A New Arms Race in the Gulf," *Jane's Intelligence Review*, Vol 7., No. 1, January 1995, p. 39.

[142] Bruce, "Iran Puts its 'Kilos' Through Their Paces," *Jane's Jane's Defense Weekly* 18 March 1995, p. 5.

[143]Starr, "Iran Adds New Threat With Cruise Missile Test," *Jane's*

Defense Weekly, 7 February 1996, p. 14.

144 Ibraham, "Iran is Said to Expel Arabs from Gulf Island," *New York Times*, 16 Aprtil 1992, p. A7; and FBIS-NES-92-085.

145 Bruce, "Iranian Exercises to Include SSM Firings, *Jane's Defense Weekly*, 30 April 1994, p. 1.

146 Bruce, "Iran Puts its 'Kilos' Through Their Paces."

147 Scarborough, "Navies of Iran, China, Russia Worry U.S.," *Washington Times*, 8 March 1995, p. 5.

148 "Iran Urges Gulf States to Oppose U.S. Build-Up," *News Brief*, *Early Bird*, 30 May 1995, p. 20.

149 Weiner, "Cruise Missile is Test Fired From a Ship by Iran's Navy," *New York Times*, 31 January 1996, p. A5.

150 Gertz, "Iran Obtains Patrol Boats from China," *Washington Times*, 27 March 1996, p. 1.

151 Deutsche Press Agency, "Sudan Gives Iranian Port Rights," *Washington Times*, 17 April 1995, p. A13.

152 "Iran Cultivates Ties With India in Military, Business Ventures," *Washington Times*, 21 April 1995, p. A17.

153 The higher figures were quoted by Tony Banks and Bruce, "Iran Builds its Strength," *Jane's Defense Weekly*, 1 February 1992, p. 158. Egyptian Gazette, 29 January 1992, provides "Western analysts" as its source for the $5 billion figure. Total defense budget figures for 1994 and 1995 appear in IISS, *The Military Balance 1993-1994*, p. 115, and 1995-1996, p. 133.

154 Smith, "Projected Iranian Buildup Scaled Back, Analysts Say," *Washington Post*, 18 November 1995, p. 16.

155 Bruce, "Russia in Billion Dollar Arms Sales to Iran," *Jane's Defense Weekly*, 27 March 1996, p. 14.

156 John WR Taylor, "Gallery of Soviet Aerospace Weapons," *Air Force Magazine*, March 1991, p. 65.

157 "Iran Extends 'Fulcrums' with Airborne Refueling," *Jane's Defense Weekly*, 26 August 1995, p. 16.

158 Some analysts refer to the 1,300 km range Nodong 1 as

"Nodong 2". Others believe the Nodong 2 is a later North Korean development, with a range between 1,500 and 2,000 km. The 1,300 km range Nodong 1 is then called the "Nodong 1 Mod-B." See David Wright and Timur Kadyshev, "The North Korean Missile Program: How Advanced is It?" *Arms Control Today*, April 1994, pp. 10-11; and Duncan Lennox, "Ballistic Missiles Hit New Heights," *Jane's Defense Weekly*, 30 April 1994, p. 27.

[159]Sciolino, "CIA Report Says Chinese Sent Iran Arms Components, *New York Times*, 22 June 1995, p. A1.

[160]Bruce, "Iran Claims to Have Built its Own MBT," *Jane's Defense Weekly*, 23 April 1994, p. 5.

[161]"Iranian Armor Claim Deepens Arms Puzzle," *Washington Times*, 8 February 1995, p. A14.

[162]Bruce, "Iran Claims it Has Rebuilt and Upgraded Iraqi MBTs," *Jane's Defense Weekly*, 31 January 1996, p. 18.

[163]"Iran Arming Aging F-14 With HAWK Missiles," *Washington Times*, 10 February 1995, p. A19.

[164]"Iran Boasts of EW Production," *Jane's Defense Weekly*, 28 October 1995, p. 19.

[165]Ehteshami, p. 34.

[166]Banks and Bruce, p. 158; "Iran Has Largest Display of Military Hardware," Egyptian Gazette, 29 January 1992, p. 1; and Journal of Defense and Diplomacy, October 1987, p. 51.

[167] Banks and Bruce, "Iran Builds its Strength," *Jane's Defense Weekly*, 1 February 1992, p. 158; Knut Royce, "Iran Buying 150 'Terror' Missiles," *Long Island Newsday*, 11 April 1992, p. 6; Douglas Jehl, "Iran is Reported Acquiring Missiles," *New York Times*, 8 April 1993, p. A9; and "Iran's Ballistic Missile Programs," *Mednews*, 21 December 1992, p. 4.

[168]"Iran's Reach for a Nuclear Sword," *Boston Globe*, 13 November 1991, p. 18.

[169] Starr, "C.W. Stockpile a Threat to the Straits of Hormuz," *Jane's Defense Weekly*, 1 April 1995, p. 3.

170 Ehteshami, p. 34.

171"Iran Deals for Nuclear Fuel," *JINSA Security Affairs*, February 1992.

172Reuters, "Russia Might Build Four Reactors for Iran," *Washington Times*, 21 February 1995, p. A13; and Beaver, "Yeltsin Announces Halt to Exports to Iran."

173 Con Coughlin, "Chinese Help Iran Join the Nuclear Club," *Washington Times*, 25 September 1995, p. 1.

174 Sciolino, "China Cancels Deal for Selling Iran 2 Reactors," *New York Times*, 28 September 1995, p. 1; and "China Denies Canceling Arms Sales to Iran," (World Scene), *Washington Times*, 30 September 1995, p. A8.

175 *The European*, 3 May 1992, cited in "Iran Got Soviet Nukes," *Washington Inquirer*, 15 March [sic] 1992, p.1; "A Threat to All," *Jerusalem Post*, 1 January 1992, p. 8; FBIS-NES-085, 1 May 1992, p. 41; and Martin Sieff, "Kazakh Chief May Not Control Nuclear Arms," *Washington Times*, 24 May 1992, p. A13.

176 Charles W Holmes, "Iran Nuclear Plant Gets Russian Boost," *Washington Times*, 12 February 1995, p. 1.

177 Smith; Banks and Bruce, "Iran Builds Its Strength," *Jane's Defense Weekly*, 1 February 1992, p. 159; Knut Royce, "Iran Buying 150 'Terror' Missiles," *Long Island Newsday*, 11 April 1992, p. 6; *Inside the Air Force*, 28 February 1992, p. 1; Rowland Evans and Robert Novak, "Russian Tanks in Tehran," *Washington Post*, 5 February 1992, p. 19; "New Muscle in Iran," *Washington Post*, 27 May 1992, p. A19; "Iran/RussiaWrap Up $2 Billion Arms Deal," Flight International, 21 July 1992, p. 13; and Ibrahim, "Iran Said to Commit $7 Billion to Secret Arms Plan," *New York Times*, 8 August 1992, p. 2.

Iraq

178 Shireen T. Hunter, "What is Saddam Hussein Up To?" *Los Angeles Times*, 25 September 1991, p. B5.

[179] 167. Starr, "Iraq Planned to Stage Kuwait 'Incident'." *Jane's Defense Weekly*, 17 December 1994, p. 7.)

[180] 168. Jamal Halaby, "Iraq Defector Says He Spoiled Invasion Plan," *Washington Times*, 21 August 1995, p. 1.

[181] "Jordan Storing Iraqi Nuclear Material," *JINSA Security Affairs*, March 1992, p. 8; and Paul Reid, "Finishing Saddam," *Boston Globe*, 18 February 1992, p. 13.

[182] Robert Gates interview, *Time*, 20 April 1992, p. 61.

[183] "Iraq Has Scuds, Nuke Equipment, CIA's Gates Says," *Washington Times*, 28 March 1992, p. A-6.

[184] Finnegan, Theresa Hitchens and Barbara Opall, "Nuclear Bomb is Within Iraq's Reach," *Defense News*, 12-18 September 1994, p. 3.

[185] Starr, "Iraq 'Able to Expand Military Capability'," *Jane's Defense Weekly*, 10 July 1993, p. 9; and "Headline News — In Brief," *Jane's Defense Weekly*, 29 January 1994, p. 5.

[186] Reuters "Iraq: War-ravaged Airports Completely Rebuilt," *Chicago Tribune*, 20 June 1994, p. 6; and Bruce and Starr, "U.S. Exploits Images of Military Rebirth as Iraq Rejects UN Resolution on Oil Sales, *Jane's Defense Weekly*, 6 May 1995.

[187] Alan George, "Iraq Has Blueprints to Enrich Uranium," *Washington Times*, 29 January 1996, p. 15.

[188] Sean D. Naylor, "Experts: Iraqi's Pose Less of a Threat," *Defense News*, 17-23 October 1994, p. 76.

[189] Finnegan, "Fractured Cooperation May Dash Gulf Security."

[190] "Saudis Hint at Easing of Stand on Iraq" (World Scene), *Washington Times*, 16 December 1994, p. A23.

[191] David C. Isby, "The Residual Iraqi 'Scud' Force," *Jane's Intelligence Review*, Vol. 7, No. 3, March 1995, p. 116; and R. Jeffrey Smith, "Iraq Buying Missile Parts Covertly," *Washington Post*, 14 October 1995, p. 1.

[192] "UN Envoy Details Iraq's Admission of Germ Arsenal," *Washington Times*, 24 August 1995, p. A13.

[193] Stewart Stogel, "Missile Plans May Aim at Europe," *Washington Times*, February 1996, p.1.

[194] Sciolino, "U.S. Says it's Won Votes to Maintain Sanctions on Iraq," *New York Times*, 5 March 1995, p. 9.

[195] Julia Preston, "U.S. Says Iraq Still Has Kuwaiti Arms," *Washington Post*, 11 January 1995, p. 12; Michael Gordon, "As Iraqis Scrimp, Their President Lives Lavishly, U.S. Says," *New York Times International*, 14 November 1994, p. A3; and Bruce and Starr, "U.S. Exploits Images of Military Rebirth as Iraq Rejects UN Resolution on Oil Sales."

[196] Bruce, "How Saddam is Picking Up the Pieces a Year After 'Storm,'" *Jane's Defense Weekly*, 22 February 1992, p. 284.

[197] Adel Darwish, "Saddam Executes Top Army Officers," *Independent*, 15 June 1994, p. 11.

[198] "Iraqi Officers Executed," *Arab Times* (Kuwait), 25 October 1994, p. 2.

[199] Peter Sisler, "Iraq Branding, Cutting Off Ears of Army Deserters," *Washington Times*, 5 June 1995, p. A11.

[200] John Lancaster, "Story of Iraqi Coup Bit Clouded by Uncertainty," *Washington Post*, 18 March 1995, p. 20.

[201] "Saddam Sacks CoS in Shake-Up," *Jane's Defense Weekly*, 22 April 1995, p. 4.

[202] Sisler, "Iraq Branding, Cutting Off Ears of Army Deserters."

[203] Andrew Rathmell, "Iraq — The Endgame," *Jane's Intelligence Review*, May 1995, p. 228.

CHAPTER III

[1]   International Institute of Strategic Studies, *Strategic Survey 1994/95* (London: Oxford University Press, 1995), p.131.

[2]   General Ehsan Shrdom, Chief of Staff, Royal Jordanian Air Force, Amman, in remarks to the author, 19 January 1992.

[3]   Comments by Jordanian officials to the author in Amman, 18 January 1992.

4   Jeffrey Smith, "Jordan Diverted Arms to Iraq, Obey Charges," *Washington Post*, 3 October 1992, p. A14.

5   IISS, *Strategic Survey 1994/95*, p. 130.

6   "One on One," interview with Abdel Salam Majali, *Defense News*, 7-13 February 1994, p. 46.

7   IISS, *Strategic Survey 1994/95*, p. 130.

8   "Jordan's Military Chief Eager to Resume Ties With US, Defends Role During War," *Inside the Army*, 17 February 1992, p. 3; and "Jordan MSSA Interest," *Jane's Defense Weekly*, 22 April 1995, p. 5.

9   IISS, *The Military Balance 1995-1996*, p. 137.

10 Rowland Evans and Robert D. Novak, "Good-bye Good-Conduct Check," *Washington Post*, 10 April 1995 p. A21.

11 Finnegan and Opall, "U.S. May Give Jordan Billions in Military Aid," *Defense News*, 7-13 November 1994, p. 1.

12 "Jordan Plans Spending Rise," *Jane's Defense Weekly*, 31 January 1996, p. 3.

13 Caroline Faraj, "Modernization Tops Hussein's US Agenda," *Defense News*, 27 March - 2 April 1995, p. 38.

14 Finnegan, "Jordan Pursues Sharp US Aid Hike," *Defense News*, 29 November - 5 December 1993, p. 27.

15 *Ibid.*

16 Finnegan, "Jordan Cuts Armed Forces; Plans the Sell Off Aircraft," *Defense News*, 25 November 1991, p. 1; "Jordan's Military Chief...;" Finnegan, "Jordan Pursues Military Mobility;" and Caroline Faraj, "Jordan Pledges Military Upgrade," *Defense News*, 16-22 January 1995, p. 12.

17 Author's estimate.

18 Author's estimate.

Lebanon

19 "Turkey: Trucks From Iran Were Smuggling Arms," *Jane's Defense Weekly*, 31 January 1996, p. 4.

20 Nora Boustany, "Syrian-Backed Armed Factions Hamper Lebanon's Attempt to Govern," *Washington Post,* 20 December 1994, p. A30; and IISS, *Strategic Survey 1994/95,* p. 132; Bruce, "Lebanon Gets Latest US Materiel Shipment," *Jane's Defense Weekly,* 30 September 1995, p. 19; and "Lebanon: U.S. Military Vehicles to Aid Armed Forces," *Jane's Defense Weekly,* 10 January 1996, p. 17.

21 Barton Gellman, "Lebanon: the Last Arab-Israeli Battlefront," *Washington Post,* 10 March 1995, p. 1.

22 IISS, *Strategic Survey 1994/95,* p. 132; and John Lancaster, "Israel Expands Retaliation on Lebanon," *Washington Post,* 14 April 1996, p.1.

23 Gellman.

Gulf Cooperation Council

24 GCC membership consists of Saudi Arabia, Oman, Kuwait, Bahrain, Qatar and the United Arab Emirates.

25 Finnegan, "Fractured Cooperation May Dash Gulf Security," *Defense News,* 16 March 1992, p. 6.

26 24. "Gulf Leaders Move to Bolster Joint Security," *Jane's Defense Weekly,* 8 January 1994, p. 3.

27 Bruce, "Qatari Exercises Opt-Out Deepens Rift With GCC, *Jane's Defense Weekly,* 13 March 1996, p. 14.

28 Sheik Ali Sabah Al Sabah, Defense Minister, "One on One" interview, *Defense News,* 10 February 1992, p. 38.

29 "Russia, Kuwait Plan Exercise," *Jane's Defense Weekly,* 18 December 1993, p. 9.

30 Finnegan, "Kuwait to Continue Diversification of Arms Buys," *Defense News,* 28 November-4 December 1994, p. 3; and *Washington Times,* 4 February 1993, p. A9.

31 Finnegan, "Cash Crunch May Stall Kuwaiti Arms," *Defense News,* 28 November-4 December 1994, p. 1; and *London Financial Times,* "Kuwaiti Military Waste," 20 April 1995, p. 6.

32 William J. Broad, "3 Nations Seek to Buy Spy Satellites, Causing Policy Rift in US." *New York Times International,* 23 November 1992, p. A7.

33 U.S. CIA, *The World Factbook 1994,* p. 413.

34 Regional Briefing, "UAE Plans to Buy Advanced Gunboats," *Washington Times,* 21 September 1994, p. A11.

35 Finnegan and Opall, "UAE Fighter Fuels Design Contest, U.S. Policy Worry," *Defense News,* 22-28 August 1994, p. 1.

36 Jacques de Lestapis, "Gulf Powers Procure to Protect," *Jane's Defense Weekly,* 18 March 1995, p. 38.

37 "Patriot Enters UAE Air Defense System Battle," *Jane's Defense Weekly,* 1 April 1995, p. 10.

38 Lestapis; "Sonar Offered to Oman and UAE," *Jane's Defense Weekly,* 15 October 1994, p. 17; and Finnegan, "Mideast Provides Newly Fertile Naval Market," *Defense News,* 27 March-2 April 1995, p. 6.

39 Brooks Tigner, "Dutch Will Sell Two Used Frigates to UAE," *Defense News,* 8-14 April 1995, p. 6.

40 Lestapis; and "UAE Contract Launches Shipbuilding Venture," *Jane's Defense Weekly,* 1 April 1995, p. 8.

41 Carol Reed, "Giat: Climbing Out of Crisis," *Jane's Defense Weekly,* 29 October 1994, p. 28; and Lestapis, p. 42.

42 Lestapis, p. 42.

43 "Abu Dhabi to Buy Upgraded M109A3s," *Jane's Defense Weekly,* 9 September 1995, p. 23.

44 Above references and the following: "Administration Seeks $2.5 Billion Sale of Top-Line Weapons to Kuwait," *Washington Post,* 12 March 1992, p. A23; *Middle East Times* (Egypt ed.), 28 Jan-4 Feb 1992, p. 11; Starr, "Middle Eastern Promise," *Jane's Defense Weekly,* 26 October 1991, p. 768; David Silverberg, "UAE Purchase Russian BMP," *Defense News,* 25-31 May 1992, p. 1; DOD notification to Congress of Oman purchase No. 337-M, 19 July 1991; Philip Finnegan, "Russia Extends Mideast Arms Sale

Hunt," *Defense News*, 15-21 June 1992, p. 1; "U.K. Firm Lands Qatari Deal," *Jane's Defense Weekly*, 13 June 1992, p, 1009; US Dept of State and Defense Security Assistance Agency, Congressional Presentation for Security Assistance, Fiscal Year 1993, "Qatar," p. 287; Christopher F. Foss, "Kuwait Receives First Warrior," *Jane's Defense Weekly*, 3 December 1994, p. 24; US DOD, "Kuwait Predicts Helicopter Contract in 1996," Pentagon Current News, *Early Bird* wire service, 27 April 1995; "Kuwaiti Patrol Craft Buy Finalized" *Jane's Defense Weekly*, 4 March 1995, p. 6; "Kuwait Predicts Helicopter Contract in 1996," Pentagon Current News, *Early Bird* wire service, 27 April 1995; "UAE Opts for Mixture of Pumas and Panthers," *Jane's Defense Weekly*, 1 April 1995, p. 5; Finnegan, "Oil Price Rebound May Revive Mideast Market," *Defense News*, 26 June-2 July 1995, p. 18; and Finnegan, "Industry Sees Fertile Ground in Oil-Rich Emirates," *Defense News*, 26 June-2 July 1995, p. 16.

[45]   Neil Munro, "Kuwait to Triple Tank Purchase to 760," *Defense News*, 28 September-4 October 1992, p. 18.

[46]   Associated Press, "Accounts Differ as to What Caused Rioting on Tiny Island State of Bahrain," *Naples* (Florida) *Daily News*, 1 January 1995, p. 16A.

[47]   Finnegan, "Bahrain Unrest Fails to Deter US Ties," *Defense News*, 10-16 April 1995, p. 4.

[48]   Roger Matthews and Mark Nicholson, "Bahrain Breaks Ranks and Urges Closer Ties With Iraq," *Financial Times*, 22 June 1992, p. 12.

[49]   Finnegan, "Economic Lull Slows Gulf Nations' Weapon Buying Spree," *Defense News*, 13-19 December 1993, p. 32.

[50]   Finnegan, "Bahrain Pursues Advanced US Arms," Defense News, 17-23 April 1995, p. 1; and Finnegan, "Bahrain Seeks to Boost Equipment Capability," *Defense News*, 26 June-2 July 1995, p. 18. The delivery of such an advanced system as ATACMS would seem unlikely, and may be illegal under the Missile Technology Control Regime.

51 *Ibid.*

52 Finnegan, "Shifting Alliances Shake Gulf Unity," *Defense News*, 12-18 December 1994, p. 1.

53 Paul Beaver, "Flash Points," Qatar, *Jane's Defense Weekly*, 1 April 1995, p. 20.

54 The author queried selected Western officials well acquainted with the Middle East about their impressions of the military forces they had observed, using forced choices with opportunity for individual comments. The identity of the respondents and the overall result is considered confidential.

55 World Watch Today, "Arms Build-Up," *Gulf Daily News* on Friday (Bahrain), 28 October 1994, p. 1.

56 Roger Fontaine and Dennis Mullin, "Oman at Crossroads Yet Independent," *Washington Times*, 4 January 1995, p. 12.

57 Finnegan, "One on One," interview with Sayyid Haitham Al-Said, Omani Secretary-General for Foreign Affairs, *Defense News*, 22-28 May 1995, p. 46.

58 Bruce, "Oman to Spend $8.75 Billion on Defense in 1996-2000," *Jane's Defense Weekly*, 7 February 1996, p. 15.

59 Roddy Scott, "In San'a: Arms and the Man," *The Middle East* (U.K.), July/August 1995, p. 7.

60 The historical sketch presented here is derived primarily from George Joffe, "Yemen — The Reasons for Conflict," *Jane's Intelligence Review*, August 1994, pp. 368-373; IISS, "Conflict in Yemen," *Strategic Survey 1994/95*, pp. 155-159; and Ahmed Hashim, Center for Strategic and International Studies, Washington DC, "Synopsis of Political- Military Situation in the Post-Civil War in Yemen," unpublished.

61 Eric Watkins, "Promise Them Anything," *The Middle East* (U.K.), September 1994, p. 8.

62 Mamoun Fandy, "Saudi-Yemen Clash: Is it Gulf War, Part 2?" *Christian Science Monitor*, 3 February 1995, p. 18.

63 *Ibid.*

64   *Ibid.*

65   Finnegan, interview, "One on One — Abdel Rabuh Hadi,Yemen Vice President," *Defense News*, 19-25 December 1994, p. 22.

66   "Moldova and Bulgaria Help S. Yemen Rearm," *Jane's Defense Weekly*, 15 October 1994, p. 15.

61. Finnegan, "Yemen's Iraqi Use Irks US," *Defense News*, 5-11 December 1994, p. 4.

67   Finnegan, interview with Hadi.

68   *Ibid.*

CHAPTER IV

1   The International Institute of Strategic Studies (IISS) *Military Balance* is published as a year-spanning document (e.g.: the 1995 issue is entitled "1995/96"). For clarity the data used in this volume is labled according to the actual date of publication.

2   The Analytical Sciences Corporation "Technique for Assessing Comparative Force Modernization."

3   The author developed and applied the technique in the publication of the Strategic Studies Institute, U.S. Army War College, *A Military Assessment of the Middle East, 1991-1996*, 7 December 1992.

4   The IISS *Military Balance 1995/96* (London: Oxford University Press, 1995), pp. 121-150; Shlomo Gazit and Zeev Eytan, The Jaffe Center for Strategic Studies, *The Middle East Military Balance 1993-1994* (Boulder, CO: Westview Press, 1994); and Anthony H. Cordesman, *Weapons of Mass Destruction in the Middle East*, Royal United Services Institute (London: Brassey's, 1991).

5   Author's estimate.

6   R. Jeffrey Smith, "Projected Iranian Buildup Scaled Back, Analysts Say," *Washington Post*, 18 November 1995, p. A22.

CHAPTER V

[1] Youssef M. Ibrahim, "Gulf Arabs Thinking of a Divided Iraq," *New York Times*, 2 August 1992, p.12.

[2] *The Middle East Reporter Weekly*, 22 August 1992, p. 11.

[3] Uri Sagi.

[4] Benjamin Netanyahu comments to the author, Jerusalem, 27 April 1991.

[5] Hirsh Goodman and W. Seth Carus, *The Future Battlefield and the Arab-Israeli Conflict* (New Brunswick: Transaction Publishers, 1990), pp. 62-63. Former U.S. Undersecretary of the Army Norman A. Augustine has noted, partially in jest, that if present trends in cost growth continue, the price of a single plane in the year 2054 will equal the entire defense budget.

[6] Goodman and Carus, p. 139.

[7] Goodman and Carus, p. 78.

[8] IISS, *The Military Balance 1990-1991*, pp. 107 and 119.

[9] The strength of Syrian forces in the Bekaa was given in Ihsan A. Hijazi, "Lebanese Army Finishes PLO Ouster," *New York Times*, July 6, 1991, p. A3. Colonel Ben Reuven, commander of the Israeli 188th Armored Brigade, in conversation with the author, commented that the Bekaa Valley would be a feasible avenue of attack for outflanking the principal Syrian defenses.

[10] Ariel Sharon, Israeli minister of housing, in remarks to the author and others, Jerusalem, 24 April 1991.

[11] "Iraq Rejects New Kuwait Border," AP Wire Service, 2 June 1992.

[12] Ibrahim, "Saudis Using Oil in Yemeni Dispute," *New York Times*, 7 June 1992, p. 7.

[13] Bruce, "Saudis Building Military City on Yemen Border," *Jane's Defense Weekly*, 15 May 1996, p. 3.

[14] James Wyllie, University of Aberdeen, U.K., reported by Edith Lederer, "Iran Watcher Says Civil War is Nearing," *Washington Times*, 19 March 1994, p. A9.

15 Uri Lubrani, Israeli Government coordinator in southern Lebanon; reported by Mouafac Harb, "U.S. Moves Against Iran in Danger of Backfiring," *Washington Times*, 10 May 1995, p. A14.

CHAPTER VI
1   Klieman and Pedatzur, p. 114.
2   "Top General Shuns Reliance on Military Balance Analysis," Jewish Institute for National Security Affairs, *JINSA Security Affairs*, August-September 1995, p. 11.
3   Ibrahim, "Can Egypt Bring Israelis and Arabs Together?" *New York Times*, 9 July 1992, international section, p. 3.
4   "Last Iraq Flights Cut," *Washington Post*, 17 June 1992, p.A28.

CHAPTER VII
1   Harkabi, "The Arab-Israeli Conflict on the Threshold of Negotiations," Center of International Studies, Monograph Series No. 3, Princeton University, 1992, p. 26.
2   Kemp, p. 203.3
3   "Jane's Interview" with Joseph Nye, former assistant secretary of defense for international security affairs, *Jane's Defense Weekly*, 17 December 1994, p. 32.
4   Jason Glashow, "Abrams Faces Lethal, Low-Cost Threat," *Defense News*, 17-23 April 1995, p. 1.
5   Kemp, p. 224.
6   U.S. Department of State and Defense Security Assistance Agency, Congressional Presentation for Security Assistance, Fiscal Year 1993, p. 5.
7   Comments by Lt. Gen. Teddy G. Allen, director, Defense Security Assistance Agency, to the author, Washington DC, 15 June 1992.
8   U.S. Dept. of State and DSSA, Congressional Presentation, p. 210.

9   Remarks of U.S. security assistance officer, Riyadh, to the author, 29 January 1992.
10   *Deutsche Press Agentur*, "U.S. Fears Israel Sold Plans for Jet to China," *Washington Times*, 4 January 1996, p. A9.
11   Douglas Jehl, "U.S. Ships Steam to Persian Gulf in Response to Iraqi," *New York Times*, 30 January 1996, p. A5.
12   "Floating Tank Brigade Planned," Association of the U.S. Army, *Washington Update*, June 1992, p. 4; and Thomas L. Friedman, "U.S. and Israel Working Out Deal to Offset Warplane Sale to Saudis," *New York Times*, 15 September 1992, p. A14.
13   *Haaretz*, 18 August 1992, cited in "Top of the News," *Washington Times*, 20 August 1992, p. 2.
14   Harkabi, Washington DC, 1 October 1991.

INDEX

A4-N attack aircraft, 116
Advanced Medium Range Air-to-Air Missiles (AIM120), 23, 102
Abu Musa Island, 66
Aegis class cruisers, 57
AH-1F attack helicopter, 116
Air Forces, 51, 55, 91, 116-126, 158, 174
Albright, Amb. Madeleine K., 79
Al Jama'at Al Islamiya radical group (Egypt), 41
Al-Hussein missile, 79
Al-Navid, Maj. Gen. Ali Hassaan, 81
al-Nida Republican Guard, 80
Al-Thawra newspaper (Iraq), 81
Alpha jet aircraft, 43, 120, 131
Amos satellite, 29
Apache helicopter (AH-64), 30, 37, 45, 60, 98, 105, 106, 116
Arab-Israeli conflict, 36, 84
Arab League, 64
Arab Organization for Industrialization (AOI), 43, 56
Arafat, Yasir, 168
Arens, Def. Min. Moshe, 29
Arms industry,
    Egypt, 39, 43
    Iran, 61
    Iraq, 75
    Israel, 35
    Saudi Arabia, 43, 53
    Syria, 46
Army Tactical Missile System (ATCMS), 102
Arrow missile, 29, 30, 37, 130, 143
Assad, Hafiz Al-, 6, 13, 46-52, 86, 159, 192

AWACS reconnaissance aircraft, 60, 74, 95
Adjusted Weapon System Perfromance (AWSP), 112

"Backfire" bomber, 68, 69, 74, 141, 156, 174, 176
Bahrain, 84, 100-103, 127, 128, 135-137, 157-158, 190
Baker, James, 191
Barak anti-ship missile, 32, 37
Barak, Ehud, 26, 47
Basij militia (Iran), 62, 123, 165
Befuddlement weapon, 26, 32, 37, 152, 172
Beilin, Yossie, 33
Bekaa Valley, 20, 21, 92, 147
Bedouin tribes, 55, 58
BMP infantry fighting vehicle, 80, 91, 100, 106
Blackhawk helicopter, 31, 37, 60, 105
Bodinger, Maj. Gen. Herzl, 24
Boorda, Adm. Jeremy M., 66
Bradley infantry fighting vehicle, 43, 60, 91, 190
Budgets, defense, 9
Budinger, Maj. Gen. Herzl, 31
Bulgaria, 53
Bush, George, 41
Bushehr, Iran, 72

C-130 aircraft, 87
C-801 anti ship missile, 66
C-802 anti ship missile, 67, 105
Canada, 56
Challenger tank (U.K.), 104, 150, 106
Chaparral, missile system, 120
China, 13, 18, 36, 49, 51, 63, 65, 69, 70, 72, 151
Clapper, Lt. Gen. James, 63
Clinton, President William J., 13, 33
Condor missile, 151

Crotale missile system, 56, 120, 122
CSS-2 missile, 36, 139, 151,174 ,176
Czechoslovakia, 50

Darkhovin, Iran, 71
Declaration of Principles, 36
Delilah unmanned airborne vehicle, 32
Desert Shield operation, 54
Dessert Storm, see Gulf War
Desert Warrior armored troop carrier, 105
Designated Force Performance (DFP), 113, 114, 129, 135
Dhahran, Saudi Arabia, 58, 192
Diego Garcio, 190
Dimona, Israel, 33
Dolphin submarine, 31, 37

Egypt, 3, 6, 7, 8,, 9, 10, 11, 15, 16, 19, 25, 34, 39-45, 56, 78, 88,
    103, 119, 120, 129, 130, 131, 140, 148-152, 169;
    conclusions, 172-173, 185, 186, 190
Ehteshami, Anoushivavan, 34
Eisenstadt, Michael, 77
Ekeus, Rolf, 79
EM52 rocket propelled mines, 65
Equipment, military, 13, 14, 15, 23, 30, 31, 42, 43, 47, 51, 57,
    58, 63, 68, 70, 72, 77-80, 87-91, 93, 95, 96, 99, 101, 103, 104,
    109, 110, 112, 113, 114, 115, 117, 118, 121, 123, 125, 130,
    131, 133, 136, 171, 173, 188, 189, 190
Exocet missile, 56, 65, 105

F-1 jet aircraft, 90
F1EQ jet aircraft, 126
F-4 jet aircraft, 116, 120, 124
F-5 jet aircraft, 87, 89, 90, 91, 102, 122, 124
F-6, F-7 jet fighter, 70, 74, 124, 126

F-14 jet fighter, 70, 124

F-15 jet fighter, 30, 31, 57, 60, 87, 98, 116, 130, 132

F-16 jet fighter, 30, 31, 37, 42, 45, 87, 88, 91, 98, 89, 101, 102, 105, 116, 120, 130

F-18 jet fighter, 30, 37, 89, 98, 130

Faisal, Saud, 59, 78

Fencer fighter aircraft, 19, 52, 69

Firouzabadi, Hassan, 61

France, 71, 96

FROG-7 missiles, 80, 243, 244

Fulcrum fighter aircraft, 52, 53, 69, 74, 98, 109, 118, 124, 126

Gabrial naval missile system, 116

Gadfly SAM system (SA-11), 52, 74

Gal, Reuven, 18

Gammon long-range air defense missile system (SA-5), 66, 74, 118

Gates, Robert, 62, 76, 77

Gaza, 18, 27, 152, 168

General Dynamics Corporation, 43

Gidi Pass (Sinai), 150

Goalkeeper short-range defense system, 99

Golan Heights, 16, 18, 20, 25, 46-48, 51, 142, 146, 147, 153, 158, 178, 191, 192

Gopher low altitude SAM system (SA-13), 52, 74

Gore, Vice President Albert, 88

Ground forces 30, 54, 89-90, 99, 112, 115, 117, 119, 121, 123, 125, 142, 145, 149, 157, 163

Grumble air defense missile system (SA-10), 52

Guerrillas ("terrorists"), 24, 48, 92, 93, 141, 147

Gulf Cooperation Council (GCC), 84, 94-98, 101-103, 105, 106, 108, 140, 156, 158, 160, 161, 174, 175, 176

Gulf of Oman, 64, 66

Gulf War, 2, 4, 8, 15, 21, 24, 32, 44, 53, 54, 61, 62, 63, 70, 75,

81, 84, 85, 86, 100, 101, 104, 107, 108, 130, 136, 139, 140, 142, 143, 144, 151, 156, 158, 160-163, 169, 175, 177, 186, 187

H-6D bomber, 126
Hadi, Abdel Rabuh, 109, 110
Haj, 6, 53, 58
Halifax class ASW frigates, 56
Hamas, 7
Harkabi, Maj. Gen. Yehoshafat, 180, 191
Harpoon naval missile system, 44 116
Hashemite Kingdom, 86
Hassan, Ali, see Najid, Al-, see Najid
Hawar Islands 101
HAWK missile system, 45, 60, 66, 70, 89, 91, 98, 101, 102, 105, 106, 120, 122
Hezbullah, 7, 19, 48, 49, 65, 92, 93, 160
Hicks, Donald, 183
High-power microwave weapon system, 42
HMMWV, 30
Hoar, Joseph, 78
Human Rights Watch, 82
Hormuz Strait, 64, 65, 66, 126, 157, 174
Hudong class boat, 67
Hussein, Saddam, 79, 81, 82, 85, 108, 109, 139, 156, 159, 160, 161, 162, 163, 177
Hussein, King, 85, 86, 87, 161, 177, 187
Hussien, Uday, 82

International Atomic Energy Agency, 78
International Institute of Strategic Studies, 22, 68, 131
Iran, 1, 3-21, 24, 36, 44, 50, 53, 54, 56, 57, 59, 61-72, 74, 75, 77, 92, 94, 97-101, 103, 104, 108, 109, 123, 124, 125, 132, 138, 140, 155-158, 159, 164, 165, 169, 170; conclusions, 173-174,

179, 183

Iran-Iraq War, 15, 53, 94

Iraq, 1, 3-21, 22-25, 32, 34, 36, 46, 49, 53, 54, 59, 61-63, 70, 71, 75-86, 90, 94, 96, 97, 100-110, 125, 126, 131, 132, 138, 139, 140, 141-146, 151, 153, 155, 158-161156, 158-161; conclusions, 167-171

Isfahan, Iran, 71

Islamic fundamentalism, 19, 40, 107, 164

Islamic Jihad, 7

Islamic Revolutionary Guards (Iran), 65, 70, 123

Israel, 1-21, 22-37, 39-41, 44, 46-49, 51, 52, 62, 69, 77, 78, 84- 88, 92, 93, 94, 97, 98, 102, 103, 114-116, 130, 138, 139, 140, 141-148, 152-153, 158-161; conclusions, 120, 126, 166, 185

Israel Aircraft Industries, 36

Israel Airforce (IAF), 27, 30

Israel Defense Force (IDF), 26, 35

Israeli Institute for Military Affairs, 18

J-6 jet fighter, 131

J-7 jet fighter, 120

Jane's Information Group, 22, 54

Jericho (city), 18, 27, 168

Jericho long-range missile system, 34, 35, 182

Jewish Aerospace, 36

Jihad, see Islamic Jihad

Joint Chiefs of Staff, U.S., 2

Jordan, 4, 6-11, 19, 21, 25, 34, 36, 53, 76, 84-85, 87-88, 90, 127, 134, 136, 139, 140, 142, 144, 152-153, 161-163, 175; conclusions, 176-177, 179, 186

Kaman class boat, 67

Karaoglanov, Sergei, 13

Karaj, Iran, 71, 72

Katz, Vice Admiral Douglas, 65
Kazakhstan, 64, 72
Kemp, Geoffrey, 182, 184
Khalifa, Sheik Hamad bin Khalifa al Thani, 235
Khamenei, Ayatollah Ali, 61, 70, 165
Kharrazi, Kumal, 62
Kilo class submarine, 56
Kitchen air-to-surface missile, 69
Kfir fighter aircraft, 116
Kharrazi, Amb. Kamal, 62
Khomeini, Ayatollah Ruhollah, 6, 19, 61
Knox class frigate, 44, 45
Kolesnikov, Army General Mikhail, 49
Kolokov, Boris, 49
Kukan, Edward, 50
Kuwait, 6, 12, 58, 59, 75, 76, 96, 80, 84-85, 103, 127, 135, 136,
     139, 157, 177, 190
Kyrgyzstan, 64

La Fayette class ship, 56
Lebanon, 16, 20, 49-50, 84, 91, 127-128, 134, 136, 137, 147, 153,
     178
Leclerc tank, 100, 106
Levi aircraft, 188
Libya, 15, 16
Likud Party, 17, 46, 86
London Sunday Telegraph, 72
Low-Altitude Navigation and Targeting Infrared (LANTIRN),
     102

M-1 tank, 87, 91
M-109 SP artillery, 80, 180
M113 armored personnel carrier, 80, 92
M577, 30, 37

M-60 tank, 42, 87, 88, 89, 91
Maghreb, 3
Mainstay reconnaissance aircraft, 74
Majali, Abdel Salam, 86, 102, 109
Marei, Gen. Abd Al-Hafez (Jordan), 88
Mass destruction weapons (MDW), 14, 15, 16, 23
McDonnell Douglas Corporation, 31
Mecca, 53, 58, 192
Medina, 58, 192
Meguid, Esmat Abdel, 181
Merkava tank, 37
Merlin helicopter, 56
Mirage jet fighter, 89, 98, 102,126
Mi-25 attack helicopter, 118
MiG-21 jet fighter, 118, 124
MiG-23 jet fighter, 118
MiG-25 jet fighter, 118, 126
MiG-27 jet fighter, 74
MiG-31 jet fighter, 74
MiG-29 jet fighter, see Fulcrum,
Missile Technology Control Regeime (MTCR), 182, 183
Mitla Pass (Sinai), 150
Mohamadi, Brig. Gen. Harmoun, 63
Mubarak, President Hosni, 40
Multiple Launch Rocket System (MLRS), 30, 42, 130
Muslim Brotherhood, 40

Najid, Maj. Gen. Ali Hassan Al-, 81
Naval forces, 12, 58
Naval forces, U.S., 180
Netanyahu, Benjamin, 17, 46, 144, 192
New World Order, 41
Nodong missile, 69, 71, 74
North Korea, 49, 50, 183

Nuclear Nonproliferation Treaty, 51
Nuclear weapons, 14, 51, 72, 114, 141, 182-183
Nye, Joseph, 76

Oberon class submarine, 45
Ofek satellite (Israel), 29
Oman, 84, 94, 97, 103-104, 127, 128, 135, 136, 137, 157
O'Neil, Lt. Gen. Malcom, 30
Order of battle, 115-128
Osirak, Iraq, 24
Ostrovsky, Viktor, 139

Palestine Liberation Organization (PLO), 18, 36, 168, 175
Palestinians, 6, 87, 152
Panther helicopter, 106
Party of God, see Hezbullah
Patriot air defense missile system, 29, 60, 143, 98, 105
Peace Shield, air defense system, 54
Peace Vector military sales program, 42
Peninsular Shield force, 95, 102
Perry class frigate, 99, 102
Perry, Secretary of Defense William, 59, 71, 102
Persian Gulf, 56, 65, 84, 88, 97, 101, 139
Phalanx close-in anti-missile system, 44
Pirana armored troop carrier, 104, 106
Portable Air Defense Systems, 80

Qaboos, Sultan bin Said Al-Said, 94, 103
Qatar, 43, 58, 84, 95, 97, 103, 127, 128, 135, 137, 157, 161

Rabin, Prime Minister Yitzak, 17, 18, 27, 33, 34, 48, 93, 168
Rafael defense industry, 36
Rafsanjani, President Ali Akbar Hashemi, 61, 62, 67, 71, 72, 165
Ramses tank, 131

Reagan, President Ronald, 87
Redd, V. Adm. Scott, 67
Remotely Piloted Vehicles (RPV), 144
Reserves, military, 115-128
Revolutionary Guards (Iraq), 12
Rezaie, Maj. Gen. Mohsen, 70
Rodman, Peter W., 48
Rom, Maj. Gen. Giora, 32
Romeo class submarine, 44

SA-2/SA-3, 118, 120
SA-6, 66, 120
SA-8, 118
SA-10/12, 98
SA-342K attack helicopter, 120
SA-342L attack helicopter, 118
Saar missile boats, 31
Sagi, Maj. Gen. Uri, 141
Safi, Noureddin, 177
Safir tank, 70
Sagger, 43
Sabah, Sheik Saud Nasser al-, 108
Saleh, Lt. Gen. Ali Abdullah, 163
"Samson Option," 34, 35
Sandhurst, Royal Military College, 104
Sattari, Mansoor, 63
Saudi Arabia, 3, 5-6, 43, 53, 76, 77, 63, 85, 94, 103, 107, 109-
    110, 139, 160, 162-165; conclusion, 174-176
Scarab surface-to-surface missile system (SS-21), 51
Scud surface-to-surface missiles, 15, 32, 50, 52, 57, 69, 74, 76, 77,
    98, 142, 151, 160
Settlements, 17
Shahine missile system, 122
Sharm el Sheikh, 152
Silkworm coast defense missile system, 65, 66
Sneh, Ephraim, 77

South Lebanon Army (SLA), 92
STAR-1 anti-radar missile, 32, 37
Stark, USS, 100
Strategy, U.S. national,
Strela air defense missile (SA-7),
Su-2 attack aircraft, 118
Su-7 attack aircraft, 126
Su-20 attack aircraft, 126
Su-25 attack aircraft, 98, 126
Su-24, see Fencer, 69, 74, 118, 124
Su-27 attack aircraft, 52, 74, 98
Su-30 attack aircraft, 98
Su-35 attack aircraft, 98
Sudan, 7, 19, 40, 67, 76
Sunburn anti-ship missile system, 65, 66
Suez Canal, 150
Syria, 3, 21, 25, 34, 46, 48, 50, 55, 86, 92, 127, 130, 137, 140,
     145-148, 153; conclusion, 171-172

T-54 tank, 43, 70, 131
T-55 tank, 67, 70, 131
T-72 tank, 50, 52, 67, 70, 74, 100, 184
T-80 tank, 100, 184
TAAS, 36
TAIF Agreement, 92
Tajikistan, 5
Taleb, Field Marshal Mustafa (Jordan), 87, 239
Tanks, main battle, 115, 17, 119, 121, 123, 125
TASCFORM analytic model, 112
Terrorism, 13
THAAD anti-ballistic missile system, 30
Tlas, Gen. Mustafa, (notes)
Tondar surface-to-surface missile (North Korea), 19, 71
Tornado fighter aircraft, 60, 122

TOW anti-tank missiles, 30, 37, 43, 45, 80, 91
Tu-22M aircraft, 69, 126, 174
Tucano aircraft, 43
Tunbs Islands, 97
Turkmenistan, 64
Turkey, 64, 130, 139

UH-1 helicopter, 92
Ukraine, 65
United Arab Emirates (UAE), 24, 84, 97, 127, 128, 135, 136,
    157, 177
United Kingdom (U.K.), 96
United Nations (U.N.), 23, 62, 75, 79, 169
United Nations Foreign Military Assistance (FMA), 87
United Nations Security Council, 79, 86, 131
United States (U.S.) , 1-4, 14, 33, 86, 87, 88, 90, 92, 96, 102,
    136, 154, 156, 166, 180-194
U.S. Central Command (USCENTCOM), 3, 78, 100
U.S. European Command (USEUCOM), 3
USSR (Soviet Union), Russia, 12, 22, 34, 61, 62, 63, 64, 65, 67,
    72, 77, 96, 146, 162, 166
Uzbekistan, 64

Vanunu, Mordechai (Israel), 33
Vita class fast attack boats, 105

Walid armored personnel carriers, 131
Warsaw Pact, 50, 146
Washington Institute for Near East Policy, 77
West Bank, 17, 18, 86, 88, 144, 152, 153
Women's International Zionist Organization, 33
Woolsey, R. James, 63, 109, 110

Yeltsin, Boris, 13

Yemen, 53, 84, 109, 127, 128, 134, 136, 140, 163, 164, 178
Yugoslavia, 65

ZTF Martin tank plant (Slovakia), 50
Zagros Mountains, 156
Zionism, 5
Zulfiqar main battle tank, 70

List of Interviewees and Members of Discussion Groups

United States
Mr. Khalid A. Alkhalifa, 2nd secretary, Bahrain Embassy
Rear Admiral Abraham Ben-Shoshan, Israeli defense attache
Lt. Gen. Ehud Barak, Israeli Defense Forces (ret.)
Dr. Anthony H. Cordesman, Center for Strategic and
    International Studies
Dr. Graham Fuller, The RAND Corp.
Brig. Gen. Raji Haddad, Jordanian defense attache
Mr. David Halevy, Israeli journalist
Dr. John Harvey, Center for International Studies and
    Arms Control, Stanford University
Dr. Charles Hill, The Hoover Institute
Dr. Joseph Kechichian, The RAND Corp.
Dr. Bruce Narduli, The RAND Corp.
Ambassador (ret.) Robert Newman, Center for Strategic
    and International Studies
Mr. Charles Waterman, Waterman Associates

United Kingdom
Dr. David Bolton, Director, Royal United Services Institute
Dr. John Chapman, Director, International Iinstitute for
    Strategic Studies
Dr. Roland Danreuther, IISS
Col. Michael Dewar, IISS
Mr. Peter Gail, Ministry of Defense
Ms. Rosemary Hollis, RUSI
Maj. Nicholas Innel, MOD
Air Vice Marshal Anthony Martin, RAF (ret.)
Dr. Martin Navias, King's College, Department of War Studies
Ms. Pamela Pohling-Brown, Jane's
Sr. Harold Walker, Ambassador (ret.)

Israel
Dr. Reuven Gal, Director, Israeli Institute for Military
    Studies
Mr. John Herbst, U.S. Embassy Political Officer
Brig. Gen. (resv.) Ephraim Sneh, MK, (assistant to
    Yitzakh Rabin)
Brig. Gen. (resv.) Aryeh Shalev, Syrian Specialist, Jaffe
    Center
Lt. Col. Frank Wyman, Asst. U.S. Army Attache
Maj. Gen. (ret.) Ahron Yariv, Director, the Jaffe Center
In conjunction with others:
    Maj. Gen Avihu Bin-Nun
    Def Min Moshe Arens
    Maj. Gen. David Ivry
    Maj. Gen. Itzak Mordechai
    Housing Min. Ariel Sharon
    Dep. Fgn. Min. Binyamin Netanyahu
    President Haim Hertzog
    Mayor Teddy Kollek
    Yitzak Rabin, MK (later Prime Min.)
    Mr. Hanan Alon, Def. Ministry

Egypt
Col. Joseph Englehardt, U.S. Def. Attache
Mr. Stanley T. Escudero, U.S. Embassy Political Counselor
Maj. Gen. William Fitzgerald, Chief, Office of Military
    Cooperation
Roundtable discussion at National Center for Middle East
    Studies:
    Amb. Tahseen Basheer (former Egyptian Amb. to Canada)
    Maj. Gen. Ahmed Fakiher (ret.), Director of the Center
    Maj. Gen. (ret.), Ahmed Abdel Halim
    Amb. Mohamed Aafez Ismail, (former foreign minister
        and national security advisor to President Sadat)

Dr. Mahir Khalifa

Mr. Aly El Din Mourad

Roundtable discussion at Al Ahram Center for Political
and Strategic Studies:

Brig. Gen. Murad El Dessouki (ret.), military analyst

Mr. Emad Gad, international affairs analyst

Dr. Ahmed Ibrahim, military analyst

Dr. Mohammed El-Sayed Said, Director of the Center

Mr. Mohamed Abdel Salaam, military analyst

Dr. Hassan Abau Taleb, Chief, International Political
Branch

Third roundtable discussion:

Mr. Nabil Fahmy, Office of Fgn. Min.

Mr. Mahdi Fath'allah, Secretary, North American
Affairs, Fgn. Min.

Mr. Harlan Lee, U.S. Embassy Dep. Political Officer

Mr. Abdel Rahman Salah, Office of Fgn. Min.

Mr. Reda Shehata, Dir., Foreign Affairs Office

Syria

Col. David Anthony, U. S. Def. Attache

Maj. Gen. Jabriel Bitar, Syrian Army (ret.)

Gen. Mustafa T'lass, Def. Min

Mr. George Mallek, U.S. Embassy political officer

Def. Attaches of France, Germany, Canada and Italy in
roundtable discussion

Saudi Arabia

Mr. Abdul Aziz bin Mohsin Al-Tuwaijiri, Dep.
Commander, Saudi Arabian National Guard

Col. Ralph Capio, Chief of Staff, U.S. Training Mission

Amb. Charles W. Freeman, Jr., U.S. Ambassador

Maj. Gen. Victor Hugo, USA (ret.), Vinnel Corp., advisor
to Saudi National Guard

Col. Gary W. Nelson, U.S. Def. Attache
Mr. William Pierce, U.S. Embassy, Counselor for Pol-Mil
    Affairs
Maj. Gen. Thomas Rhame, Chief, U.S. Training Mission
Col. James Ritchey, U.S. Def. Attache
Richard A. Smith, U.S. Counsellor for Pol-Mil Affairs
Maj. Gen. J.G. Taylor, Mgr. of Saudi Arabian National
    Guard Modernization Program

Jordan
Lt. Gen Salem Al-Turk, Chief of Staff
Maj. Gen. Nabih Ayoub, Director, Joint Staff
Prime Min./ Def. Min. Sherif Zaid Bin Shaker
Col. Donald Dubay, U.S. Def. Attache
Lt. Gen. Ehsan Shardom, Chief of Air Staff
Field Marshal Abu Taleb, Chairman JCS

Kuwait
Abdulah Y. Bishara, 1st Dep Prime Minister
Brig. Gen. Robert R. Ivany, Chief, Office of Military
    Cooperation (U.S. Embassy)
Col. John Macel, Chief, U.S. Liaison Office
Brig. Gen. James L. Noles, Chief, U.S. Defense Review
    Group
Mr. Matthew Tueller, U.S. Embassy political officer

Bahrain
Maj. Gen. Khalifa Bin Ahmed Al-Khalifa, Def Minister
    nd Deputy Commander-in-Chief Bahrain Def Force
Dr. Khalid Al-Khalifa, Asst Prof. Historu, Univ. of
    Bahrain
Dr. Abdulla M. Alsadiq, Center for Studies and Research
Dr. Hamad Ali Al-Sulayti, Act. Dir. Center for Studies
    and Research

Amb. Charles W. Hustler, U. S. Ambassador
Dr. Abdulla M. Alsadiq, Center for Studies and Research
Dr. Hamad Ali Al-Sulayti, Act. Dir. Center for Studies
    and Research
Mr. Richard Roberts, U.S. Embassy Pub Affairs Officer
Mr. Tom Williams, U.S. Embassy political officer
Roundtable discussion:
    Dr. Abdul Laif Al-Rumaihi, Univ. of Bahrain
    Mr. Ahmed Kamal, newspaper editor
    Mr. Ahmed Jassim, lawyer
    Mr. Ali Rabea, member of parliament (in suspension)

Qatar
Ahmed Abdulla Al-Mahmood, Undersec. Fgn. Affairs

Oman
Ahmed Sulaiman Saleh Al-Maimani, Sp. Advisor to
    the Sultan
Lt. Col. Walter J. Cooner, Jr., U.S. Def Attache
Amb. David J. Dunford, U.S. Ambassador
Ms. Elizabeth McKune, U.S. Dep. Chief of Mission
Mr. Roger Shafer, American Business Council of Oman

ABOUT THE AUTHOR

Maj. Gen. Edward B. Atkeson, USA (Ret.) is a senior fellow at the Institute of Land Warfare, Association of the U.S. Army, and a senior associate at the Center for Strategic and International Studies. During his military service he served as Deputy Chief of Staff Intelligence, U.S. Army Europe, and later as a member of the National Intelligence Council under the Director of Central Intelligence. He also served with the Bureau of Politico-Military Affairs, Department of State. General Atkeson holds a BS degree from the U.S. Military Academy and an MBA from Syracuse University. He is a graduate of the U.S. Army War College, and subsequently served as deputy commandant of that institution. He was a fellow at the Center for International Affairs, Harvard University, from 1973 to 1974.

General Atkeson is a frequent writer and speaker on military affairs, having contributed over 80 articles to military journals and other publications. He is the author of three other books: *The Final Argument of Kings: Reflections on the Art of War* (HERO Books, 1988), A *Military Assessment of the Middle East 1991-1996* (Strategic Studies Institute, U.S. Army War College, 1992), and a novel, *A Tale of Three Wars* (U.S. Army War College Foundation, 1996).

THE POWDER KEG

ANNEX
Deep Strike Surface-to-Surface Missile Systems in the Middle East

SYSTEM	RANGE (km)	PAYLOAD (kg)	CEP (m)
Israel			
Jericho I	650	500	1,000
Jericho II	1,500	1,000	2,000
MGM52 Lance	130	200	437
Jericho III*			
Egypt			
Scud B	300	1,000	900
Scud C	500	680	900
Sakr-80	80	200	
Vector	600	453	1,200

(Continued Next Page)

SYSTEM	RANGE (km)	PAYLOAD (kg)	CEP (m)
Iran			
Oghab	40	300	
MGM52 Lance	130	200	437
Nazeat	130		
CSS-8 (M-7/8610)	150	190	
Scud B	300	1,000	900
Scud Mod C	500	680	<Scud B
Hatf-3*	600	1,000	
Iran-700 (Scud C)*	700	500	<Scud B
Al Fatah*	950	500	
M-18 (Tondar-68)	1,000	400	
Nodong I*	1,000	1,000	
DF-25*	1,700	2,000	
Iraq			
FROG-7/Laith	70	435	600
Scud B	300	1,000	900
Al Hussein	650	500	1,000
Al Abbas	950	300	3,200
Saudi Arabia			
CSS-2/DF-3	2,700	2,500	1,000

(Continued Next Page)

SYSTEM	RANGE (km)	PAYLOAD (kg)	CEP (m)
Syria			
FROG-7	70	435	600
Scud B	300	1,000	900
Scud Mod C	500	680	<Scud B
M-9	600	300	300
SS-21	120	453	360
Yemen			
FROG-7	70	435	600
Scud B	300	1,000	900
SS-21	120	453	360
Hezbollah Guerrillas (Short-Range Missiles)			
Katyusha Rocket	20	19	132

* In Development

Sources of above data: Bill Gertz, "Scud's Bigger Brothers," *Air Force Magazine*, June 1994, pp. 52-57; Byron E. Greenwald, "Scud Alert!: The History, Development and Military Significance of Ballistic Missiles on Tactical Operations," School of Advanced Military Studies, U.S. Army Command and General Staff College, monograph, 17 December 1994, p. 37; David C. Isby, *Weapons and Tactics of the Soviet Army* (London: Jane's, 1981), p. 211; IISS *The Military*

Balance 1995/96, pp. 281 and 283;   Janne E. Nolan, *Trappings of Power: Ballistic Missiles in the Third World* (Washington DC: Brookings Institution, 1991), p. 71;   and Anthony H. Cordesman, *Weapons of Mass Destruction in the Middle East* (London: Brassey's, 1991), pp. 56-57.